The Supply Chain Imperative

DALE NEEF

AMACOM

American Management Association

New York • Atlanta • Brussels • Chicago • Mexico City •
San Francisco • Shanghai • Tokyo • Toronto • Washington, D.C.

Special discounts on bulk quantities of AMACOM books are available to corporations, professional associations, and other organizations. For details, contact Special Sales Department, AMACOM, a division of American Management Associations, 1601 Broadway, New York, NY 10019. Tel.: 212-903-8316. Fax: 212-903-8083.
Web Site: www.amacombooks.org

This publication is designed to provide accurate and authoritative information in regard to the subject matter covered. It is sold with the understanding that the publisher is not engaged in rendering legal, accounting, or other professional service. If legal advice or other expert assistance is required, the services of a competent professional person should be sought.

Library of Congress Cataloging-in-Publication Data

Neef, Dale
The supply chain imperative : how to ensure ethical behavior in your global suppliers / Dale Neef.—1st ed.
    p. cm.
    Includes index.
    ISBN 0-8144-0783-8
1. Industrial procurement. 2. Business logistics. 3. Fraud—Prevention.
4. Swindlers and swindling. 5. Business ethics. 6. Consumer protection.
I. Title.

HD39.5.N445 2004
658.7'2—dc22   2004004902

Printing number

10 9 8 7 6 5 4 3 2 1

Contents

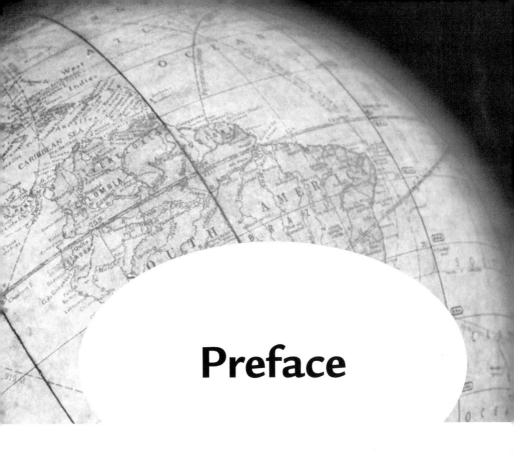

Preface

Publicity is justly commended as a remedy for social and industrial diseases. Sunlight is said to be the best of disinfectants.

—Louis Brandeis, U.S. Supreme Court Justice

On Labor Day I happened to walk by a small tour that was looking up at one of the older buildings on the corner of New York's Washington and Green streets. This was the Asch building, now part of New York University, where in 1911, on a beautiful spring Saturday, the horrific "Triangle Shirtwaist" fire consumed the top three floors of the building, killing 146 young girls working in the garment industry. Trapped inside with the doors locked, the fire had quickly swept through upper floors, fueled by the fabric, dust, and wooden girders. Mostly immigrants, newly arrived in America, many of the 500 girls trapped in the building were forced to throw themselves from the ninth storey to the pavement below in a desperate attempt to avoid the flames. No fire hoses could reach the upper

floors, the flimsy fire escape had quickly collapsed, and the firemen's nets ripped through hopelessly, time and time again, under the weight of the young girls. The bodies continued to fall for over two desperate hours.

The deaths of the 146 young women highlighted not only problems with lack of concern for worker safety, but also revealed the broader concerns of low wages, long hours, and child labor that remained largely unregulated throughout America at that time, forcing politicians, labor leaders, businessmen, and the public to reexamine basic labor and safety policies in the workplace. In fact, the appalling events of the Triangle Shirtwaist factory, and the horror that was felt by New York and the country when the unsafe and brutal working conditions under which the girls were forced to work were revealed, ushered in a new era in labor reforms in the United States. It has been said that the New Deal began with this terrible tragedy, in that within the next three years, a raft of city, state, and federal laws were enacted to regulate working conditions and worker safety. The Triangle Shirtwaist factory became a rallying cry for union activists and humanists, and during the next 20 years, legislation was passed at a federal level that finally included, in 1938, the Fair Labor Standards Act which established the basic rights of workers in America—a minimum wage, restricted child labor, safe working conditions, and premium pay for overtime.

This type of "sweatshop" labor is largely a thing of the past in the United States, of course. But during the last 15 years, as major corporations have relocated manufacturing operations to low-cost labor markets oversees—or outsourced that manufacturing altogether to factories in those markets—the same stories and scenarios, a century later but just as disturbing, have returned to haunt us.

There are hundreds of examples. In 2002, for instance, a number of well-known U.S. retailers settled a class-action lawsuit brought on behalf of 30,000 garment workers on the pacific island of Saipan for $20 million. The group of nearly 60 defendants included prominent brand name retailers such as Abercrombie & Fitch, Target, Gap, and J.C. Penney. The lawsuit, involving federal and state courts in San Francisco and Saipan, claimed that thousands of workers, including many from China and the Philippines, were effectively kept in indentured servitude in U.S. territories. The clothing being made bore the label "Proudly Made in America."

It was still the same level of exploitation as a century before, but the difference was that this time it was independent suppliers, and not the companies themselves, that were running the sweatshops. And, of course, there is a fundamental difference between the responsibility that the American Triangle Shirtwaist Company had for its New York workers and the responsibility that a large sporting goods company has for its suppliers overseas.

Or is there?

"If a customer calls our 800 number and complains that the sole got separated from the shoe," reasoned a Reebok executive recently, "We can't very well say 'Oh, that's not Reebok's responsibility, that shoe is made by an independent factory in Korea.' We have to take responsibility for the quality of the product even though we don't make it ourselves. The same applies to the working conditions. If a customer calls up about working conditions at one of our suppliers we have to take responsibility for those working conditions."[1]

That reasoning, and the fact that an executive from an important sporting goods company would use it, surely reveals how much things have changed in the past decade. The reality is, fundamental changes are occurring in the world economy that are forcing nearly every manufacturing and distribution company to begin to reassess its relationship with its suppliers in an extended, global supply chain. As a result, these companies are facing many of the same social and environmental issues that plagued domestic company operations in America or Europe only a few decades ago, today hidden behind locked doors in sweltering conditions thousands of miles away from the pastel carpets and air conditioned lobbies of the corporate head office. And as many activists, labor unions, and politicians point out, this is not a problem that is going to go away soon, nor is it going to be resolved by the governments in countries where these factories reside. After all, most of the developing world governments want and need the investment capital, and they have often been only too eager to turn a blind eye to sweatshop conditions, official corruption, or environmental exploitation in order not to scare away corporate buyers. It is for this reason that so many activists, academics, and investors contend that there is essentially no other force for good, apart from the financial muscle of the buying company itself, that can hope to curb these types of practices.

Companies should be concerned with these issues purely from a humanitarian point of view, of course. Even the most hardened businessman would concede that their company has some duty to avoid working with a supplier that purposely exploits the environment or its workers. And even if monitoring and reporting on suppliers results in an overall cost to a company, many critics and humanitarians would argue that such expenses—like providing office security, safety equipment for workers, or health care protection to employees—is all a part of doing business in the modern world. Moreover, few would advocate equivalent treatment of workers at home in the United States on the grounds that it was "more efficient" to pay meager wages, to be indifferent to workplace dangers, or to pollute the environment. After all, we are no longer living in 1911.

---

1. Creelman, David, "Interview: Alice Tepper Marlin SA8000," HR.com at *www.3.hr.com /index.cfm/WeeklyMag/47271289-A70A-47BF-BF86246888BB5E705.*

But the reasons corporations should be concerned about such social and environmental exploitation go beyond humanitarian concerns. There are also compelling business reasons for ensuring good behavior among overseas suppliers, as investors, consumers, activists, and the public at large become increasingly sensitive to double standards and indifference when companies speak of their commitment to "corporate social responsibility" and yet continue to turn a blind eye to the plight of workers or the environment in foreign economies. More and more, companies are realizing that they can't.

As leading global corporations, many of them American, are beginning to appreciate, the reality is that a company's reputation is no longer insulated from the transgressions of its overseas suppliers, even (as we will see throughout the book) if it has no legal ties to that supplier other than the production contract itself. It is therefore, now more than ever, essential that a company understands the types of risks that they now face—in terms of reputation damage, consumer boycotts, a drop in share value, or litigation—because of these suppliers, and develops a comprehensive program to eradicate that risk. At the minimum, that risk management program requires suppliers to accept higher social and environmental standards, and requires companies themselves to adopt new nonfinancial (social and environmental) reporting practices. It is only through a formal, standardized supplier monitoring and social and environmental reporting process that companies can hope to remain aware of the actions of these suppliers, satisfy the needs of investors and the demands of activists, and ultimately protect their own reputation.

So how should the modern corporation begin to monitor what is happening in its supply chain? How does a company know whether suppliers in far off lands are employing children, bribing officials, or dumping toxic wastes that might bring the company into future litigation? Equally important, how does a company know if NGOs, activists, or the press are beginning to target one of its suppliers—and therefore by association, the company itself—with charges of employee or environmental exploitation?

These are the many compelling questions that should be worrying U.S. company executives now operating in a global environment, and some of the many issues that we address in this book.

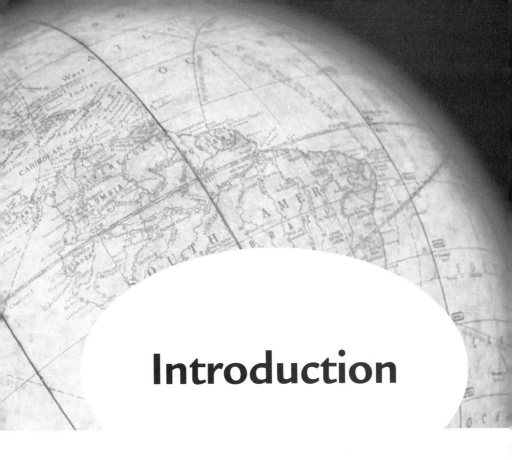

Introduction

In 1998, many will remember the huge media uproar when activists
reported that the Kathie Lee range of handbags (designed and marketed
by Kathie Lee Gifford and Wal-Mart) were being produced at the Qin Shi
factory where over 1,000 workers were forced to work 12–14 hours a day,
seven days a week, with only a single day off each month under contracts
that amounted to indentured servitude. Their average earnings were calculated at 3 cents per hour. Forty-six percent of the employees, despite often
having worked for the factory for many months, had never been paid
anything. Fed two meager meals every 24 hours, the workers were allowed out of the factory for only an hour and a half each day, and were
housed in tiny rooms shared by 16 people. When workers protested
against their conditions, some 800 were fired.[1]

Three years later, in August of 2001, one of San Francisco's largest
garment factories, Wins of California, Inc., which employed low-paid

---

1. "Wal-Mart Dungeon in China," *National Labor Committee for Worker and Human
Rights*, July 13, 2003, at *www.nlcnet.org/report00/introduction.html*.

immigrant workers and produced clothes for the U.S. Army and the U.S. Air Force as well as prominent retail leaders such as Sears, Wal-Mart, K-Mart, and J.C. Penny, was accused by state and federal labor officials of violating wage and employment laws, and owing its workforce more than $850,000 in unpaid wages.[2]

These are only two of the hundreds of examples (many of which we will look at in this book) where well-known corporations in the last several years have become embroiled in reputation—and share value damaging—disputes concerning the behavior of their suppliers. In fact, so diligent and effective has the nongovernmental organization (NGO) and investor community become that these types of disputes now appear regularly in the media, damaging individual corporate reputations and further eroding public confidence in "corporate social responsibility" and American business in general.

Concern about the exploitation of workers and the environment in factories in developing countries is not new, of course. The collective conscience of the developed world really first became aware of the ethical ties between corporations and their overseas business partners in 1984 when a catastrophic chemical leak killed some 3,800 people and left 2,700 others permanently disabled at a Union Carbide pesticide plant, owned and operated by Union Carbide India Ltd., in Bhopal, India. The effect was devastating, not only on the families and the community, but also on Union Carbide, which in 2001 merged with a subsidiary of The Dow Chemical Company after having been directed by the Indian Supreme Court to pay damages that amounted to $470 million in 1989.

During the same year as the Union Carbide settlement, the Exxon Valdez oil spill in Alaska released 11 million gallons of oil into the Valdez Narrows after the tanker left the shipping lanes and ran aground. The environmental catastrophe, played on television screens throughout the world, cost Exxon nearly $2.1 billion for cleanup, and is still being disputed in the courts—and in many ways has sullied the company's reputation for an entire generation.

Collectively, these incidents began to create a frustration and anger that was targeted against "big business" and capitalism, and during the 1990s, this coalesced in a powerful if poorly defined movement that has reshaped the modern business environment. Growing in momentum throughout the 1990s, the anticapitalism movement exploded onto the global scene at Seattle in 1999 when more than 50,000 activists gathered to protest World Trade Organization (WTO) activities. Those protests, often violent and uncoordinated, continued through Prague, Quebec, Washington, D.C., Davos, and Genoa.

2. David Lazarus, "Law Closing in on Factory S.F. Garment Maker Accused of Not Paying Workers for 3 Months," *San Francisco Chronicle,* Friday, August 17, 2001.

As disparate and sometimes competing groups have tried to address every issue from debt relief to HIV/AIDS, however, this anticapitalism, antiglobalization movement has recently become more amorphous and less effective, and most would agree that attempts to disrupt world economic forums through street protests have ultimately meant that the movement has lost much of its legitimacy in the eyes of the public. When combined with the fact that the movement has suffered from the lack of a simple, unifying message, the antiglobalization steamroller has, for now at least, lost much of its momentum and support.

Yet, as the antiglobalization movement has waned, a more focused, more prescriptive movement has emerged. A surprising collaboration of activists, NGOs, investors, lawyers, academics, politicians, and business leaders have, over the past several years, begun to espouse a new global business framework that is growing in legitimacy. Under the heading of "corporate social responsibility," this new framework has incorporated several key strategies that are proving to be surprisingly successful.

First, activists have **shifted their focus to tangible and commonplace environmental and human rights issues.** This has meant that it is no longer necessary for an NGO or pressure group to focus on a major oil spill or a devastating chemical leak in order to attract broad attention. They have emphasized more general, ongoing concerns, such as the use of lumber from rainforests, hourly wages and working conditions, or the disposal of toxic chemicals in specific factories. It isn't that the issues have changed, but activist focus has shifted to a large extent to broad ongoing questions of policy, and away from indictment of companies over single, specific incidents. This new focus on the practical day-to-day issues is much more proactive, allowing activists to search out violations and expose corporate activities to public scrutiny on an ongoing basis.

A second important characteristic of this new drive toward forcing greater corporate responsibility is a policy known as **market campaigning.** Realizing that publicity was their most effective tool, a powerful and increasingly effective combination of NGOs, pressure group activists, and international bodies has shifted its efforts specifically toward exposing— naming and shaming—large and well-known corporations. This strategy is based on the idea that if industry-leading companies such as Shell, Nike, Chiquita, McDonald's, or Home Depot are forced to change policies publicly, those improvements and reforms will also be adopted by lesser-known companies in the same industry. The larger and better-known the brand name, the more effective the campaign. This policy, however unfair, is nonetheless extraordinarily effective.

Finally, and most importantly for most companies, during this same period there has been an effective attempt by activists to **make corporations responsible for the actions of their suppliers and subcontractors,** even when the corporations themselves have no direct role in governing those third-party business partners. This dramatic shift in responsibility up the supply chain, holding large and powerful corporations responsible for the actions of their suppliers, includes naming and shaming companies, encouraging consumer and investor boycotts, and, increasingly, litigation that involves both civil and criminal prosecution. This effort to essentially create an "ethical supply chain" has proven to be the latest and most effective means for driving reform in global business.

What is important to understand is that these strategies are fundamentally different, both in focus and in effect, than the more limited activist-sponsored activities of the 1990s. Too often still portrayed as just another business "fad" (i.e., comparable to business process reengineering, activity-based costing, or total quality management), corporate leaders are now beginning to appreciate that the corporate social responsibility movement will ultimately have a much more profound and lasting effect on how companies are organized and managed than the efficiency movements of the last two decades. In this sense, the CSR movement is more accurately compared to the establishment of the generally accepted accounting principles (GAAP) in financial accounting, which had a revolutionary effect on the investment community, financial markets, and the broader economy.

One reason for this is the new emphasis on **shareholder awareness.** With the extraordinary explosion in mass public stock ownership that took place in the past decade, publicly listed companies have become very vulnerable, and very sensitive, to incidents that can adversely affect their reputation—and therefore their share value. A decade ago, most corporate leaders and board members only focused on maintaining stock price stability. But in the late 1990s, as increasing share value became the principle focus of a company's strategy, the relative power of shareholders, and the volatility that comes with broad, public stock ownership, increased significantly. With this strategic focus on share price, however, has come new vulnerabilities. Investors are acutely concerned about any event that might result in damage to a company's overall reputation, triggering a rush to sell and a precipitous collapse in the stock price. This wariness extends to investors ranging from day-trading housewives to large investment brokerages.

Moreover, the investment community increasingly has come to demand this sort of information—information concerning a company's ethical policies and risk management practices—as a matter of right. "Analysts need to start paying attention to how companies manage CSR as one element of risk assessment," says John Ruggie, Director of Harvard University's Center for Business and Government. "The investing public is entitled to know what a company is doing to manage these risks, because they can affect stock values and have even led to corporate bankruptcies."[3]

Whatever the merits of this singular focus on shareholder value, it means that U.S. companies have a particularly strong incentive to prevent any adverse publicity (deserved or not) from damaging their reputation and their stock value. Therefore, under the new realities, companies are now scrambling, often for the first time, to gain control over the unethical behavior of their own employees (not least their executives) as well as those of their suppliers, as a way of assuring investors that no ethical scandal is likely to endanger the value of their investment.

Moreover, alerted by the astonishing and outrageous scandals involving corporate executive accounting fraud over the past three years, **the media** has aggressively taken on the role of whistle blower on issues of corporate behavior to an extent that they never did in the past. As a result, corporate ethics have become a common issue in major newspapers and journals, and an increased area of interest to investigative reporters, government agencies, and state attorneys general.

"The definition of responsibility, at least here in the United States, is changing," warns Martin Ogilvie Brown, of PricewaterhouseCooper's Sustainable Business Solutions group in New York. "That seems to have been driven by the last few years of corruption scandals and ethical challenges that we have had here. Is that going to translate into this broad corporate responsibility and sustainability agenda? I don't know; but I think it is pushing in that direction."[4]

All of this has fundamentally altered the way that companies—particularly multinational companies—behave, and those changes are being more and more universally applied. It is hard to imagine, for example, a major company a decade ago even mentioning social or environmental policies in its annual report, its company statements, its burgeoning Web site, or its advertising campaigns. Yet today, nearly every company boasts—however flimsy the supporting evidence—of its commitment to "corporate social responsibility."

Angered and bruised by recent corporate scandals, however, investors and market analysts are no longer willing to accept unsubstantiated claims about corporate propriety made by a company's public relations department. As basing investment policy on financial statements alone has become more dangerous, analysts are increasingly utilizing proxy statements and company reputation scans, attempting to better gauge the nonfinancial "measures that matter." It is that same investment community that is

---

3. John Ruggie, "Managing Corporate Social Responsibility," *The Financial Times*, October 25, 2002.

4. Interview with the author, November 6, 2003.

now seeking (and in Europe, demanding) verified reporting on a company's social and environmental performance.

Nor will investors be impressed by companies simply giving money away through corporate philanthropy, something that has been touted as "corporate social responsibility" by companies for too long. After all, the average investor in the postbubble market doesn't care about philanthropy, they care about the value of their investment. And as we will see throughout this book, a powerful way of protecting share price stability is to create—and transparently report on—an effective supplier monitoring program.

Accordingly, since the late 1990s, the combined effects of pressure group activism, an attentive media, and a super-responsive investment community has meant that many companies have begun to focus greater effort under the umbrella movement of what has become known as "corporate social responsibility." Particularly in Europe, this movement is rapidly and relentlessly pushing companies toward adopting new policies and practices which will mark a fundamental evolutionary step for the modern organization that is as important as the quality improvement movement of the past two decades. In fact, for all these reasons, it is hard to imagine a top-tier company a decade from now that won't have in place an ethical supply chain program with supporting social and environmental standards and reports. These are the sorts of issues that we examine in this book, and in Chapter One, "Strategic Concerns," and Chapter Two, "The Extended Global Supply Chain: New Problems and New Responsibilities," we will be looking at the various new pressures that are inherent in the global economy that are forcing companies to accept greater responsibilities for the actions of their suppliers.

It has not only been the external pressures of globalization that have forced companies toward accepting greater responsibility for maintaining an ethical supply chain, however. Internal organizational issues associated with a decade-long "supply chain revolution"—large-scale outsourcing, greater design and materials management collaboration with suppliers, and the evolution of strategic sourcing techniques—all mean that companies today are more concerned than ever about the dependability of their suppliers. Dependability and quality, as we will see, however, do not sit easily with workers being forced to work 16-hour days for 3 cents an hour for 80 and 90 hours each week.

In short, many companies are beginning to find that along with external pressures (investors, activists, consumer boycotts, litigation), internal operational issues are driving companies toward a more efficient supplier management program. Accordingly, in Chapter Three, "Risky Business," we examine the many new risks inherent in the extended supply chain and consider what industries are finding themselves most exposed to these risks.

So how have companies reacted to these changing pressures and new risks during the last five years? In Chapter Four, "Companies Behaving Badly," we will look at the short, tortured history of corporate-supplier relations in this new order, where companies have gone from completely denying responsibility for the actions of their suppliers in the early 1990s, to a general acceptance of responsibility for their suppliers' behavior in 2003.

A New Ethical Supply Chain Framework

Leading companies have responded to these various pressures by developing a new approach to supplier management that includes four important elements:

- A corporate ethical and risk management framework
- The adoption of internationally accepted labor and environmental process and performance standards
- A supplier monitoring and audit program
- Reporting on social and environmental performance

As powerful as the arguments in favor of this type of approach may be, however, both in terms of risk and reputation management and for the humanitarian good that it brings, most U.S. companies are still a long way from adopting this sort of comprehensive ethical supply chain program. In contrast, this type of approach is quickly becoming the expected norm among European companies as the combined Corporate Social Responsibility (CSR) and Social, Environmental, Accounting, Auditing, and Reporting (SEAAR) movements converge and grow in legitimacy among the European Union companies, governments, and academic institutions. In fact, so rapid is this framework of internationally accepted codes of conduct, supplier monitoring, and social and environmental reporting being adopted in Europe and Japan, that there is a growing risk that a CSR "schism" is beginning to develop between European and Japanese companies on one hand (who see the duties of CSR as being best fulfilled by establishing an ethical supply chain, adopting standards, and completing social and environmental reporting) and U.S. companies on the other, which are more likely to interpret CSR responsibilities in light of good corporate governance and philanthropy.

Will adoption of standards and nonfinancial reporting requirements in the European Union and Japan force U.S. companies to adopt similar programs? With litigation and legislation moving in the same direction at home, will U.S. companies resist this powerful movement and risk another potential World Trade Organization (WTO) standoff? In Chapter Five, "The SEAAR Movement," we examine the rapid evolution of the nonfinancial, social, and environmental reporting movement in Europe and explore the likely repercussions of this growing gap in both perception and actions between the two major trading blocs.

Getting from Here to There

Creating and maintaining an ethical supply chain doesn't come about easily; it has to be planned, resourced, and managed. So what does a company need to do in order to put in place this type of ethical supply chain framework? In Chapter Six, "Who Is in Charge Here?: Organizational Responsibilities for an Ethical Supply Chain Program," we look at the key activities necessary to monitor and manage the ethical supply chain at an organizational level, and explore the many groups within a company who are now, or should be, involved in a company's ethical supply chain process.

Given these diverse, often competing, groups and interests within the modern company, how should company leaders set about developing an ethical supply chain program? Leading companies contend that a corporate ethics and risk management framework is at the heart of any ethical supply chain. This framework, explored in Chapter Seven, "The Corporate Ethics and Risk Management Framework," includes:

- A company value statement and a comprehensive code of conduct that governs employee behavior (including the behavior of employees in the company's tier-one suppliers)
- An ongoing business case for action
- Adoption of internationally endorsed process and performance standards
- Measurable and verifiable indicators of performance
- A program for building awareness and support both for company and supplier employees
- A comprehensive supplier program
- A nonfinancial (social and environmental) reporting program

Without this basic ethical framework, companies are often lacking the expertise, the management focus, and the necessary ground rules for dealing with questionable behavior, whether within the company's own direct operations or its extended supply chain. Accordingly, in Chapter Eight, "Choosing an Aspirational Code of Conduct," we look at how companies are combining corporate codes of conduct with new, internationally endorsed codes of labor and environmental behavior, in order to create a written "moral minimum" statement of their values. And as with any program that requires corporate resources and investment, one of the first critical steps for any organization contemplating this type of approach is to develop a credible business case that will help stakeholders—the Board, senior management, investors, and the supplier community—to understand the business and financial drivers behind the program. Accordingly, in Chapter Nine, "Creating a Case for Action," we look at the key costs and benefits associated with an ethical supply chain program.

As we will see, although codes of conduct are important as a means of espousing corporate principles, they are less helpful when trying to provide detailed guidelines for social and environmental activities within the supply chain. Accordingly, companies are increasingly turning to emerging social and environmental performance and process standards that provide a detailed and effective set of processes and policies by which companies monitor, adjust, and report on corporate social and environmental activities throughout the supply chain. For those who are following the rapid development of these standards—a hybrid of the quality movement and generally accepted accounting principles—there can be no doubt that they will become an important new feature of the modern global corporation.

Accordingly, in Chapter Ten, "Choosing Performance and Process Standards," we explore the most important tools that have emerged in this area—tools such as the SA 8000 performance standards, ISO 140001 environmental standards, the Ethical Trade Initiative, and AA 1000 process guidelines—and explore why a combination of these new tools is beginning to provide multinationals with much of the logical and process infrastructure for their ethical supply chain framework. In Chapter Eleven, "Creating Measurable and Verifiable Indicators of Performance," we look at the type of performance indicators that can help a company's organizational leaders gauge the program's progression and success.

Creating a successful ethical supply chain framework, of course, requires a strong program of communication, not only among company and supplier management and employees, but among the broad set of company stakeholders (investors, customers, unions, government agencies, NGOs) that are interested in a company's activities in this area, and can directly affect the success of the program. In Chapter Twelve, "Building Awareness and Support for Codes and Standards," we explore ways that companies can go about identifying and communicating with these various stakeholders.

One of the most important aspects of these rapidly evolving standards is that they are designed to help parent companies monitor, manage, and assess the social, ethical, and environmental performance of their suppliers. This supplier management program, a combination of emerging international standards and leading strategic sourcing techniques explained in Chapter Thirteen, "The Supplier Program," requires dedicated resources, a formal management program, and a new approach to supplier sourcing. It also requires a strong communication program and supplier training and monitoring activities that may be unfamiliar to most companies. And it will also require some form of supplier performance audit, covered in Chapter Fourteen, "The Audit Process."

As many companies are finding, even with strong direction and incentives, it is likely that many supplier factories and farms, particularly those in developing economies, will not at least initially be in "conformance" to a company's ethical codes and standards. So what does a company do when it finds its suppliers are guilty of employing children, overworking employees, or dumping toxic wastes? Withdrawing the contract is the ultimate sanction, but in the end only harms the company, the supplier and, invariably, the supplier's employees, who in most cases are desperately in need of the work. In Chapter Fifteen, "Compliance Issues," we examine the vexing issues associated with supplier noncompliance and explore some of the more innovative responses that leading companies have developed to bring suppliers into conformance.

A company's good efforts should be acknowledged and rewarded, and transparency in these efforts is essential for gaining the trust of the investment community. In Chapter Sixteen, "Reporting on Your Good Work—Moving Toward Triple-Bottom-Line Accounting," we look at the Global Reporting Initiative, and explore the types of activities that are necessary to create a strong social and environmental "sustainability" report. In order to help collect and manage this important and auditable information, and to measure compliance against various, often complex, environmental and worker safety requirements, companies are turning to enterprise-wide Environmental Management Systems (EMS), Environmental Health and Safety software, and knowledge management systems and techniques to help monitor performance and manage their document retention program. These subjects are examined in Chapter Seventeen, "Systems to Monitor and Audit Social and Environmental Performance Within the Supply Chain." And finally, in Chapter 18, "Pulling It All Together: The Switcher/Prem Carl Study," we look at how one innovative company has worked with its overseas supplier community to put many of these leading practices in place.

These are the types of activities that the modern corporation needs to put in place in order to reduce risk, protect its reputation, live up to its stated values, enhance the productivity of suppliers, and improve the lives of their employees. In short, these are the types of steps that are necessary for companies to establish an ethical supply chain.

CHAPTER ONE

Strategic Concerns

There are many reasons why companies today are being forced to make a serious effort to ensure good social and environmental behavior by suppliers and business partners in their extended global supply chain. Those new pressures, including relocation of the manufacturing base and nongovernmental organization (NGO) and shareholder scrutiny, are effectively forcing companies to reassess their relationship with overseas suppliers for which a decade ago they assumed little or no responsibility.

Taking responsibility for the management of an ethical supply chain that extends to a corporation's supplier community is an evolutionary step of great importance to companies and to the global economy, and marks an important trend in the development of the modern corporation. The reason this new level of responsibility is increasingly being accepted by corporations worldwide—which was not the case just a decade ago—is worth analyzing, because it comes as a result of new, inescapable pressures on companies that are inherent in the new global economy.

Globalization

The most obvious reason companies today need to be concerned with actively helping to manage—or at least to monitor and be aware of—the ethical, social, and environmental policies of their suppliers and subcontractors is that, as part of the process of globalization, more and more organizations are either sourcing their products directly from overseas suppliers, or have relocated large portions of their manufacturing base to operations in low-cost labor markets. It is a fact of life in the global economy: For the foreseeable future, modern multinationals will continue to pursue strategies based upon the twin policies of a) cutting costs in domestic operations through delayering, downsizing, and automation and b) relocating manufacturing and assembly operations and outsourcing labor-intensive operations to low-cost labor markets in the developing world.

This relocation of the manufacturing and production base to cheaper labor markets overseas has been one of the key features of the emerging global economy, and although by no means a new phenomenon, when combined with efficiency increases, it is likely that so much of our low-skill manufacturing will be sourced through foreign operations that by 2015, less than 10 percent of the U.S. workforce will be involved in manufacturing. Moreover, while there are many cost advantages associated with this relocation, most companies are today—or will be very soon—facing corruption and human rights and environmental issues associated with their foreign supplier network that are very different from those that they have traditionally dealt with in their domestic markets.

The extent to which this globalization of the modern enterprise is occurring is best seen by looking at any of the Fortune 200 companies. Nike, a good example of the modern western apparel company, actually owns no manufacturing facilities of its own, choosing instead to outsource all its production to more than 900 contract factories worldwide, employing around 600,000 workers in their supply chain. The company has approximately 50 contractor factories in China alone, employing more than 110,000 workers.[1] A global parcel delivery company such as DHL now operates in 229 countries; Intel has offices and manufacturing plants in over 40 nations. Dole, the largest distributor of fruit in the world, has 61,000 employees with 5,000 suppliers, 90 percent of which are based in developing nations. Walt Disney's consumer products division makes toys and garments through licenses with nearly 10,000 manufacturing facilities in 50 countries. Gap Inc. sources apparel from about 2,500 supplier facilities in 55 countries.[2] In short, most of these companies have pared down their domestic operations over the past 15 years so that they could focus on their "core competencies"—design and marketing. The remaining manufacturing and assembly services have been contracted out on a global basis. We are not at the beginning of that process of global relocation, of course, but neither are we anywhere near the end. The reality is that companies today understand that they can take advantage of inexpensive and pliant labor in developing economies, reducing their production costs, increasing profits, and making their stock more valuable to investors.

There is no doubt that this process of relocation will continue in search of both low-cost labor and ever-expanding sales. Emerging markets are expected to continue growing at over 6 percent a year for at least the next decade, almost twice the rate of growth expected for the United States, the European Union, or Japan (see Figure 1-1). Not only are labor costs much lower, but local production will increase the likelihood of local sales in the

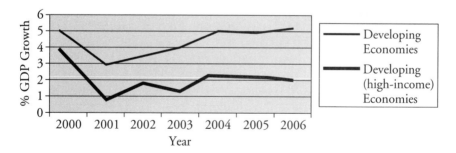

FIGURE 1-1   Global GDP Growth Rates

Source: Financial Times/World Bank: "Global Economic Prospects," *The World Bank,* at *www.worldbank.org,* as cited in De Jonquieres, Guy, and Swann, Christopher, "World Bank Sees 5% Growth for Poorer Countries," *The Financial Times,* September 4, 2003, p. 7.

---

1. "Made in China. The role of U.S. companies in denying human and worker rights," *National Labor Council,* May 25, 2000.

2. "Labor Standards Initiative," *As You Sow Foundation* Web page at *www.asyousow.org/laborstandards.htm#mcd.*

future. It simply makes sense that companies will need to reduce their presence in the 25 percent of the world that is virtually satiated with products—apparel, automobiles, televisions, refrigerators, computers—and focus on selling to the remaining 75 percent of the world's population as they continue to purchase basic items today and, as they become wealthier, luxury goods in the future.

Integral to that process of globalization for companies, however, is the expansion and increased fragmentation of their supply chain. Today, products are purchased, manufactured, assembled, and sold without regard to borders. Components are purchased from around the world, consolidated in one nation, shipped to a production facility in a second country, stored in several others for distribution, and once the product is sold and used, it may be collected and disposed of by other subcontractors in countries around the world. All of this means that most companies today are either buying products from, or actively engaged in outsourcing production or assembly from, subcontractors that are located in these low-cost labor developing markets. In fact, a quick survey of various growth industries reveals the extent of globalization already taking place.

Let's begin with the automotive industry, today on the brink of what promises to be a massive expansion in global demand for cars and trucks throughout the developing world. In 1950 there were less than 70 million automobiles in the entire world. Today there are more than 700 million and that number is estimated to jump to well over a billion by 2050, almost all of that increase produced, purchased, and driven in developing countries.

These markets are critical for the continued viability of the leading auto makers, as the glut of automobiles in the United States and the European Union contributes to price deflation and forces auto makers into desperate measures (such as 0 percent financing schemes). Add to this the pension and health care costs of massive corporations such as GM and Ford, the continued slump and price deflation in Japan, and new tolls and a greater emphasis on public transportation in Europe, and the result is a potential disaster for one of the key industries within the G7 economies. Without question, all of this means that the bulk of both manufacturing and sales is directed toward developing nations, such as Mexico, China, Thailand, Egypt, India, where growing prosperity and huge populations provide a massive new global market. As those auto manufacturers continue this relocation process, more and more of the hundreds of thousands of suppliers that today feed that massive production process (and the maintenance services that follow) will also begin to relocate, or to rise up indigenously, in these low-cost labor markets so that they will be within easy distribution routes to these new automobile factories.

To help fuel those millions of automobiles, previously unexploited areas of the globe such as western and central Africa promise to become the focus of petroleum company efforts—particularly as continued conflict in the Middle East makes dependence on traditional supplies of crude oil increasingly risky. African nations own 8 percent of the world's oil reserves, and crude oil imports from this area of Africa to the United States are forecast to jump from 15 percent of total U.S. oil imports to 25 percent over the next decade, meaning a certain expansion of western petroleum facilities in previously undeveloped areas of Africa such as Nigeria, Guinea, and Angola. In fact, U.S. and European oil executives are focusing their attention on western Africa, with estimated $200 billion in new oil revenues expected to accrue to African governments in the next 10 years, bringing the greatest inflow of capital and infrastructure in the continent's history. With U.S. government officials making sorties to the area now on a monthly basis, and President George W. Bush making an unprecedented (and previously perceived as unnecessary) visit to the African continent in 2003, observers and critics have been prompted to contend that, with the oil-savvy administration in Washington, the United States is preparing for an "historic, strategic alignment" with the area that will inevitably lead to a greater U.S. commercial and military presence on the continent. The continent that George W. Bush in his campaigning days said had no strategic importance to the United States is now, potentially, seen as an important new source of future American oil, and is being afforded the status (i.e., increased foreign aid, medical and health care support, weapons, military and security training) that was once reserved for countries in the Middle East.

This area of central and southern Africa, however, is notorious for corruption and human rights violations, and rightly or wrongly, western oil interests will be considered duplicitous unless they actively demonstrate that they maintain consistent standards for avoiding environmental and worker exploitation. Already this African emphasis is having its effect on oil companies. One of the most well-known cases, *Wiwa* v. *Royal Dutch Petroleum Co.,* involves a civil lawsuit filed against the Shell Oil company that alleges that the giant multinational was complicit in human rights violations—specifically, the persecution and execution of environmental activists—by the government security forces in Nigeria. Other prominent lawsuits and disputes have involved western petroleum companies in Africa. British Petroleum/Amoco admitted that it paid the Angolan government $111 million in 2001; a new multibillion dollar project in Chad involving a consortium of oil companies led by ExxonMobil has been plagued with corruption concerns, and Chevron is embroiled in a lawsuit, charged with serious human rights abuses in neighboring Nigeria. These cases all reflect the dangers and difficulties of the extended supply chain.[3]

---

3. Charlotte Denny, "Scramble for Africa Will Fuel Misery," *The Guardian Weekly,* July 3-1, 2003, p. 21.

Similarly, other areas that once sustained the developed world economies are shifting their focus to developing world markets. Fast food retailers and soft drink distributors continue to seek out new markets in Africa, South and Central America, and Asia. With that expansion comes new and often unanticipated responsibilities. In a continent ravaged by the AIDS/HIV epidemic (in many African nations, up to 40 percent of the adult population are infected), employee safety as well as contributions to humanitarian relief efforts have become part of a company's license to operate. Yet, as a good illustration of how a combination of good intentions, poor judgment, and a focus on public relations can backfire on a company, in the autumn of 2002, Coca-Cola found itself the object of worldwide protests and ridicule when they misguidedly announced with some fanfare that they intended to spend some $5 million a year on HIV/AIDS treatment for the employees of its African bottlers. Whatever the good intentions, $5 million was seen by many as a derisory amount, provoking indignation among its many stakeholders. The incident illustrates not only the continued higher expectations of companies working in developing markets—after all, the company had broken no laws and was offering to dedicate funds to help employees—but also the increased need for companies to be able to better understand and gauge the effects of their actions in different cultures and in an increasingly more ethically demanding global environment.

Nowhere is the dilemma of promise and peril more obvious than in China, which has already become the premier location for apparel, automobile, and electronic component producers (and many others) as the old communist regime continues to give way to market liberalization and the region's economy grows. Again, using Coca-Cola as an example, the company has invested more than $2 billion in China, India, and Indonesia in recent years, three nations that alone account for nearly 40 percent of the total global population. While growth in its traditional markets such as the United States has remained steady at 4–5 percent, Coca-Cola is anticipating growth rates in sales in the Asian markets doubling every 20 years.[4] McDonald's and Kentucky Fried Chicken have some 700 stores in China already; Proctor and Gamble is the biggest seller of shampoo in the Republic; and between them, Motorola, Ericsson, and Nokia have 90 percent of the growing mobile phone market there.[5]

---

4. Brent Chrite, "Local Knowledge Will Provide the Key," *The Financial Times,* August 26, 2002, p. 4.

5. James Kynge, "Doing Overtime in the Workshop of the World," *The Financial Times,* October 29, 2002, p. 7.

The reality is, despite the sometimes frosty relationship between the two governments, U.S. companies and American consumers are integrally involved in China's economic growth. In 2002 the United States imported more than one-third (36 percent) of China's total exports, including 1.2 billion garments, which accounted for $39 billion in U.S. retail sales in 2002. Nearly every stuffed toy in America (95 percent) comes from China, and one-third (27 percent) of all wooden furniture is assembled there. Sixty percent of all shoes sold in America are made in China, and the rapid expansion of China's electronic and computer assembly industry is growing each year by more than 75 percent. With some *150 million migrant workers* now looking for jobs in China's fast-growing coastal cities, their Pearl River Delta area alone today is pulling in nearly $1 billion in worldwide investment each month.

In fact, most economists believe that China will overtake the United States very soon as the world's most favored nation for foreign direct investment (FDI) with an estimated $55 billion capital inflow from multinationals rushing to take advantage of the newly liberalized Chinese markets.[6] This rapid economic growth promises an almost inexhaustible labor market to further fuel the continued relocation of global manufacturing. As a result, every major western apparel, small item, electronic component, and automotive manufacturer has now moved into the country.

Many of the factories that are emerging in these fast-developing regions, including Mexico and Central America, produce goods for hundreds of the industrialized world's most prominent brand labels. In the electronic component industry, for example, a typical factory such as Flextronics, located in Zhuhai, China, assembles electronic products for many of the West's most powerful companies: Microsoft, Philips, Dell, Apple, Sony, Ericsson, Motorola, Nokia, and 3-Com. Japanese firms such as Canon, Honda, and NEC have spent billions relocating their plants in China, with Japanese investment in China in 2001 exceeding $4.6 billion. In return, last year China surpassed the United States as the largest exporter to Japan.

And this relocation is not limited to just low-skill labor. Increasingly, higher-skill work—software engineering, electronic component design, Web site development—are all outsourced to these new markets. Forrester Research has predicted that this dramatic relocation of both high- and low-skill production will involve more than 3.3 million U.S. information technology jobs moving overseas in the next decade.

Whatever the pros and cons for local employment in the developing economy may be, shifting production to areas such as China, Africa, or Latin

---

6. Ibid.

America can be fraught with problems for the parent companies involved. Disney provides a good example of how even the most family-friendly brand names can be caught out by poor labor practices. During the summer of 2000, a Hong Kong-based industrial committee investigated working conditions in 12 regular and seasonal factories in the Guandong province in China that were being used to produce Disney theme toys and garments, mostly for export to the United States and Europe. Most of the factory workers were young, female workers, sometimes as young as 16.

Disney, comparatively advanced with its ethical supply chain framework, has a corporate code of conduct that clearly requires its suppliers to adhere to high employment standards and national labor codes, and the company has put in place an independent monitoring system for inspection of suppliers in order to ensure that these standards are met. But the investigations found that despite these precautions, labor violations—excessive hours, poverty-level wages, dangerous working conditions, overcrowded and dirty living accommodations—were commonplace in factories making Disney toys. In one factory, it was alleged that up to 24 workers shared a single dormitory room, receiving salaries of between $49 and $85 each month (between 13.5 and 36 cents an hour). During the peak production season, employees were required to work up to 17 hours a day, seven days a week. Their pay several months in arrears, employees at one factory went on strike, but once they had received their pay, all who had participated were fired.

Needless to say, these are the types of issues that outrage consumers and terrify investors in the developed world, where similar conditions were outlawed and eliminated decades ago. As a result, a combined movement from socially responsible investors and American religious groups, together holding more than $1 million in Disney shares, has joined with human rights activists to demand that Disney agree to independent monitoring of its factories, to create a living wage policy for its contract factory workers, and to create reliable investor reports concerning policies and workplace improvements. In their shareholder proposal, this shareholder group warned that "without reports validating progress toward implementing the Code of Conduct, lasting damage could occur to our company's reputation, brand value and its long-term profitability."[7] The situation is a good example of the yawning gap between stated goals and reality in the global supply chain.

There simply is no escaping the fact that an ever-growing portion of western manufactured goods are dependent upon the continued low wages ($100–$150 per month) and unforgiving working hours that are inherent to these developing economies. Although there are many strong humanitarian

---

7. "Working for Disney Is No Fairy Tale," at *http://members.tripod.com/~cawhk/9904/9904art02.htm.*

arguments in favor of this economic expansion, and all indications are that these types of manufacturing jobs are highly sought after in developing economies, human rights activists rightly point out that employment conditions can be brutal.

And, of course, workers in these low-wage labor markets are only at the beginning of their economic growth cycle; just beginning to have money to acquire all of the material necessities of life that are today taken for granted in the West—a TV, a car, a VCR. Today's low-wage production markets will quickly become future markets for sales of Western companies' manufactured goods. With average economic growth rates hovering around 6 percent in these developing markets (compared with an average growth rate of little more than 3 percent in most Western economies even during the explosive growth of the late 1990s), Western corporations are increasingly dependent upon these emerging markets to fuel continued global economic expansion. In short, in nearly every way, the wealthy one quarter of the global population living in the advanced economies are now dependent upon the three quarters of the population living in relative poverty for their continued prosperity. That means that the globalization of the supply chain is set to increase dramatically in the years to come.

And, unlike the several interim economies such as Singapore, Malaysia, or Taiwan that inherited and then quickly passed on low-wage production because of wage inflation and a limited labor supply during the first wave of foreign direct investment in the 1980s and 1990s, China and India, for example, have a potentially limitless supply of low-cost labor. Counting surplus farm workers hoping to migrate into such jobs, the labor supply in China alone will soon expand by 400 million. That is good for the nation's economy as a whole, but it also means that the built-in regulation of limited labor and rising wages—supply and demand pressures that are integral to most other economies—does not apply, leaving China in a position of potentially becoming a giant, inexhaustible sweat shop. And despite growing prosperity and exposure to Western company policies, in many of the countries upon which the supply chain for U.S. manufacturing is now dependent—China, Cambodia, Columbia, Mexico, Burma/Myanmar, Pakistan, Indonesia, many Middle East countries, and even South Korea—trade unions are repressed or outlawed altogether. In 2001, over 4,000 trade unionists were arrested worldwide and more than 220 union leaders "disappeared."[8]

Whatever the pros and cons of this new global arrangement in terms of economics and human rights, the situation provides considerable

---

8. "Annual Survey of Violations of Trade Union Rights," International Confederation of Free Trade Unions, June 9, 2003, at *www.icftu.org/list.asp?Type=ALL&Order=Date &Language=EN&STEXT=annual+survey+of+violations*.

ammunition for pressure groups that see blatant exploitation of the poor and the uneducated at the hands of Western multinationals.

Of all the emotional and disturbing issues that emerge from foreign labor practices, no issue is more explosive than that of child labor. There are at least 246 million children globally—one in every six children in the world between the age of 5 and 17—that are currently engaged in the types of work that the International Labour Organization contends should be abolished: work that is so hazardous as to put their wellbeing at risk. Around 8 million children fall into the nastiest forms of work, such as forced labor or conscription for serving in armed conflict. Most of those children are working in the Asia-Pacific region (127 million), but nearly a third of all children in Africa are involved in child labor.[9]

A recent BBC report reflects a typical situation for Chinese child workers. Fangang, a young girl in the southeastern Chinese city of Fuzhou, was employed by the Tebiete handicraft manufacturing company to work 12-hour days in their factory. Like many other girls, she had just graduated from primary school. Although she was supposed to be receiving 200–400 yuan each month, her room and board costs meant that after a year she had still not been paid. The situation, played out with hundreds of thousands of other children in the country, promises a life of little more than indentured servitude.[10]

Similarly, India is a targeted labor market for multinational companies creating software, electronic components, and apparel. The government, according to Human Rights Watch, continues to indulge exploitation of workers, including an estimated 60 million children involved in full-time labor, with traditional practices such as bonded labor, meaning that both children and adults are routinely required to work as part of a "loan" given by companies to their parents or families. These indentured workers, essentially modern slaves, make up a significant portion of labor for the garment and apparel industry. The practice is particularly rampant in silk manufacturing where an estimated 350,000 children, often as young as five years old, routinely work 12-hour days, sometimes seven days a week. There is too often little concern for employee health and safety. Unsanitary, unsafe working conditions are commonplace, and physical abuse is routine.

Yet, and this is an important point, national labor and safety laws are officially quite strict in India and China, demonstrating one of the key issues now facing global companies which buy products from these factories, or

---

9. "Child Labour Presentation," *International Labour Organization*, 2002, at *www.ilo. org/declaration*.

10. "China: Fujian Company Fined in Child Labour Case," *BBC Monitoring Service*, January 13, 2003.

which subcontract for manufacturing and assembly in these areas. Despite the fact that India's Supreme Court and the national Human Rights Commission have both ruled that these laws must be obeyed, these types of violations remain routine. Given that is the case, argue activists, the responsibility for ensuring that these laws are enforced must fall not only on national governments (over which the NGOs have little power), but also on corporations (over which NGOs can have considerable influence).

And as we have already seen, even U.S. domestic suppliers can be guilty of similar levels of worker exploitation. For example, during the now famous raid in El Monte, California, in 1995, police found more than 70 illegal Thai immigrants being held against their will within a barbed wire compound being forced to sew garments for 15 hours a day, seven days a week. More recently, nearly 50,000 young women and girls from China, Thailand, and the Philippines were found to be working in similar conditions on the U.S. territory of Saipan. The clothing they were sewing had labels proudly declaring that the garments were "Made in the United States." To get a good idea of how little these garment workers are paid, a recent study found that even if the salary for Mexican and U.S. apparel workers were to be doubled, it would only add 50 cents (1.6 percent) to the production costs of a man's shirt that retailed for $32 in the United States.[11]

These types of revelations, often involving illegal workers, are not as unusual as it may seem. Migrant workers picking fruit in the United States have essentially become a third-world labor supply, in terms of wages, health care, and living and working conditions, within our own borders. And despite the fact that, since an executive order in 1993, federal contractors are supposed to certify that child labor has not been used in manufacturing any of the products that they purchase, it is estimated that the government has been buying $57 million worth of products made in industries in which child labor is common.[12]

What all of this means is simply that as competition continues to force companies to compete in the global economy, corporations will continue to face potential pitfalls associated with buying low-cost goods through suppliers. "Companies protect and enhance their brand equity," warns BSR, the U.S.-based business responsibility research and consultancy group, "by ensuring their operations—and those of their business partners—are conducted in a manner consistent with human rights principles.

---

11. John Miller, "Why Economists Are Wrong About Sweatshops and the Anti-sweatshop Movement," Ford School of Business, at *www.fordschool.umich.edu/rsie/acit/ Documents/Miller-Challenge.doc.*
12. Teresa Fabian, "Supply Chain Management in an Era of Social and Environmental Accountability," at *www.sustdev.org/journals/edition.02/download/ sdi2_1_5.pdf.*

Businesses are increasingly aware that they share responsibility for their suppliers' employees who manufacture, grow, or produce their goods, and recognize that they can improve supply chain management in the process. Companies working in zones of conflict are also realizing that they built their license to operate by developing practices consistent with human rights principles."[13]

The arguments for and against globalization are complex and important, but whatever your particular position as a company or a business manager, it is important to realize that these and similar issues mean that companies are facing a new era in monitoring and reporting of the social and environmental activities within their extended supply chain that will require some fundamental rethinking of corporate strategy, and involve more than mere public relations efforts—donations to local charities and a boastful Web site—to convince activists and investors that they are on top of the situation.

The Growing Power and Influence of NGOs

But there is another fundamental force at work in the global economy that is accompanying this worldwide relocation of the manufacturing base. Even for those companies that are not directly involved with overseas markets, or thought at first that outsourcing production to low-wage foreign markets would essentially relieve them from good employment and environmental responsibilities, the last decade has brought new pressures for better behavior from the growing network of increasingly powerful and effective pressure groups.

In response to this process of globalization and these types of social and environmental exploitation issues, during the past 15 years there has been an explosive growth in the number of activists, pressure groups, and NGOs that now actively monitor both the domestic operations and extended supply chain behavior of corporations worldwide. There are approximately 30,000 NGOs operating in international markets,[14] including development agencies, single-activist groups, corporate watchdogs, labor rights advocates, and wide-ranging environmental agencies such as Greenpeace and the World Wildlife Fund. Importantly, as a group they have grown enormously in authority and sophistication over the past decade. Recently able to pay higher salaries and attract talented and dedicated workers—reporters, advocates, lobbyists, lawyers—NGOs today

---

13. "Introduction to Corporate Social Responsibility," *BSR White Papers*, May 2, 2002, at *www.bsr.org/BSRResources/WhitePaperDetail*.

14. "NGOs, Sins of the secular missionaries," *The Economist*, January 29, 2000, p. 25.

can compete with company public relations offices and corporate counsel in a way that was inconceivable a decade ago. Salaried employees of Amnesty International, Human Rights Watch, the World Wildlife Fund, or Greenpeace now form viable groups composed of a young, educated, and capable elite.

These pressure groups also have an unprecedented collection of new technologies at their disposal to quickly communicate and raise money for a particular cause. The most powerful of these, of course, is the Internet. A good example of the power of the Internet to mobilize worldwide support for an environmental cause was the 2001 attempt by Mitsubishi to develop a desalination plant in the San Ignacio Lagoon, in Baja California, Mexico. The factory itself was to be constructed in an area off the coast that served as a breeding ground to the endangered species of gray whales. Campaigners and environmental activists mobilized an online petition via the Internet and managed to collect over one million signatures, capturing media attention and eventually forcing Mitsubishi to withdraw the construction proposal.

If people are easily swayed by advertising, they are equally swayed by real or created scandals reported in the press. A quarter-page advertisement spread in a national newspaper may cost $100,000, and may have marginal effect in terms of sales or brand recognition. A single headline article on exploitation of children, a dangerous product, or an environmental catastrophe, on the other hand, can cost a company millions by ruining its reputation at a stroke.

"The journalists really hone in on any type of negative news," says Jim Kartalia, President of Entegra Corporation and a specialist in risk and reputation management. "With the Internet a lot of that type of information is spread around the globe much more quickly and a lot more people are aware that corporations are falling down on a lot of these issues. And because of the technology, the impact is that much greater and that much faster."[15]

Increasingly, at least according to polls, the public is beginning to see the rise in authority and legitimacy of NGOs as a valuable counterbalance to the uncaring corporations whose drive for profits disregard human suffering and environmental exploitation in other countries. Moreover, NGOs are much more effective in projecting a favorable image to the public because their goals and motives are seen as less self-serving than traditional trade unions, the activist power base of the past. Unlike unions, pressure groups are much less susceptible to charges that they are attempting to blackmail management out of pure self-interest. NGOs themselves are not seen as the beneficiaries of their efforts, but instead are seen as working

---

15. Interview with Jim Kartalia, January 23, 2002.

for the good of the environment, or for workers without a voice. And although there may be a legitimate argument that these NGOs depend for their existence upon being able to continually create media-worthy controversy, they are nonetheless broadly supported in their missions by the public.

Moreover, with the ascendancy of NGOs, tactics tend to be very different than those employed by unions in the past. Pressure groups uncover things that could be hidden two decades ago, and where unions worked through threats of collective strike action, pressure group strategy usually focuses on exposing and discrediting companies publicly. This threat of public shame constitutes influence on an altogether new and unprecedented scale.

It is probably because of their relative independence that NGOs seem to be so highly regarded among the public. And although many of these pressure groups are still seen as fringe activists by American business leaders, they are actually becoming a powerful force in the global economy. Europe, in particular, has seen a significant leap in recognition and trust of NGOs among the public. In a recent survey by Edelman, the top three brand names in Europe in terms of trust were Amnesty International, the World Wildlife Fund, and Greenpeace—all are NGOs and each receives public trust ratings of between 60 and 75 percent. The four highest ranked corporations in terms of trust, on the other hand, were Microsoft, Bayer, Shell, and Ford, which ranked only between 35 and 45 percent: only around half that of the trust factor associated with the NGOs.

"We believe NGOs are now the Fifth Estate in global governance," concludes Richard Edelman, CEO of Edelman Research. "The true credible source on issues related to the environment and social justice."[16]

As they have grown in popularity, NGOs have also learned to wield their power unmercifully. What every company executive dreads most is finding that their organization has become a target of a pressure group campaign. NGOs have become particularly effective at targeting high-profile companies with extensive media campaigns, hoping that improvements forced on industry leaders will then trickle down to other firms, allowing their influence to extend to small, privately owned companies with a low public profile. This approach, known as "market-campaigning," has proven to be highly effective in forcing major companies to scramble to take actions to improve supplier activity that was once thought beyond their control or responsibility. In Europe, Oxfam, Greenpeace, the World Wildlife Fund, and Amnesty International have all focused on mobilizing public outrage through media campaigns that focus almost exclusively on well-known, market

---

16. "U.S. Attitudes on CSR Move Closer to Europe's," *Holmes Report,* April 25, 2002, at *www.holmesreport.com.*

leading brands that are quickly picked up through the Internet, television, or the newspapers in the United States.

As Gary Gereffi, professor of sociology and director of the Markets and Management Studies Program at Duke University notes, "Market campaigning, which focuses protests against highly visible branded retailers, is only about 10 years old, but in the words of one Greenpeace activist, 'it was like discovering gunpowder for environmentalists.'"

The program by environmentalists to protect forests is a good example of this policy in action. "The firms that felt the pressure most keenly were not timber extractors such as Georgia-Pacific, Weyerhaeuser, and International Paper," suggests Gereffi, "But retailers, specifically the big do-it-yourself centers such as The Home Depot and Lowe's Home Improvement Warehouse stores. The Rainforest Action Network, Greenpeace, Natural Resources Defense Council, and other NGOs launched major grass-roots campaigns against these retail giants in the late 1990s. Ultimately, this type of pressure meant that both Home Depot (August 1999) and Lowe's (August 2000) declared their preference for Forest Sustainability Council-certified products."[17]

"By targeting firms such as Gap Inc. or Home Depot—firms at the retail end of the supply chain with direct links to customers—NGOs," Gereffi concludes, "are able to wield the power and vulnerability of corporate brand names to their advantage."[18]

Listing, Naming, and Shaming

Another effective tactic used by these pressure groups and NGOs that has been particularly attractive to the media is to develop rankings for companies in various ratings and benchmarks. These "Best and Worst Lists" can be influential and sometimes damaging to companies. The Multinational Monitor's "Ten Worst Corporations" is a good example, as is Corpwatch's Greenwash Awards for worst corporate environmental practices (cosponsored with Greenpeace). Calpers (The California Public Employees' Retirement System) publishes each year its influential annual "focus list" of companies that it cites as the worst examples of corporate and financial governance. It is a chief executive's worst nightmare to find that his or her company has been named and shamed on one of these types of lists.

---

17. Gary Gereffi, Ronie Garcia-Johnson, and Erika Sasser, "The NGO-Industrial Complex," *Foreign Policy,* no. 125, July/August, 2001, at *www.foreignpolicy.com.* Copyright 2001, Carnegie Endowment for International Peace.

18. Ibid.

Less showy, but effective nonetheless, online research facilities and archives also now provide activists and investors with a wealth of information concerning company behavior. In the United Kingdom, for example, Business in the Community sponsors the Corporate Responsibility Index, which now includes 122 companies, including half of the FTSE100, and provides benchmarks for measuring how these companies affect their workplace, community, and environment. Business in the Environment's Index of Corporate Environmental Engagement provides similar benchmarks, comparing companies against each other on the basis of their environmental performance and management approach. Similarly, AccountAbility International, the organization responsible for devising the AA 1000 process standards, has developed a Web-based initiative known as Gradient, which rates and then ranks companies on their supply chain labor and environmental standards. As with many of these emerging comparative indices, the concept behind the Gradient Index is that relevant industry data on supply chain leading practices needs to be established so that all companies within that industry can be compared. "Gradient's central insight," says John Sabapathy, Program Manager at AccountAbility, "is that companies' integration of labor issues into key business functions (e.g., risk management, buying, quality assurance, stock management) significantly informs their capability to deliver against supply chain labor standards."[19]

Importantly, the index is not confined only to large organizations whose brand name is well known, but extends monitoring to smaller or less well-known "stealth companies" (in the words of John Elkington of AccountAbility), that in the past have been able to avoid being held to more stringent standards of behavior. The Gradient Index applies supply chain management standards to vertical industry sectors in a way that allows for a comparison between company practices (see a fuller explanation of Gradient's criteria in Chapter Ten).

The rise in both effectiveness and public acceptance of these and other NGO tactics has been one of the least appreciated, but most important, realignments that have occurred in the global community in the past decade. As we have seen, NGOs now find strong support among the investing and the buying public, at a level that would have been unthinkable 10 years ago and should be the envy of any corporation. In short, NGOs are no longer a fringe movement in the global economy.

Few business leaders, on the other hand, have really come to appreciate the powerful and often legitimate role that these activists play in helping to shape and regulate global business behavior. Most companies interviewed

---

19. "Moving Up the Learning Curve—Corporate Management of Supply Chain Labour Standards," *Sustainability* at *www.sustainability.com/news/articles/core-team-and-network/John-Sabapathy-gradient-index-mar-02.asp*.

(and American-based executives in particular) still see NGOs as adversaries, to be avoided whenever possible, and to be crushed when necessary. Corporate executives still too often dismiss NGO complaints, assuming that obfuscation and legal delays will allow the company to outlast any pressure group campaign.

If that was the case a decade ago, it is a very risky policy today. After all, though legal cases represent a significant tool for NGOs, simply naming and shaming companies through the media constitutes a formidable strategy in itself. And a damaged reputation is much less easily rebutted by either the corporate public relations or legal departments than it was in the past.

In reality, all parties would benefit from greater cooperation between companies and NGOs, but mutual acrimony continues. A recent survey involving 133 NGOs found that in order to win over NGO support, corporations urgently needed to "reassess their global responsibilities," and to exercise "moral leadership" in the global markets where they were now active. The survey found that 62 percent of NGOs believed that corporations were "not concerned with ethical conduct" (which, interestingly, was a somewhat lower figure than in a recent Harris Interactive survey that found that 73 percent of Americans rated corporate America as below average when it came to corporate citizenship).[20] Forty-one percent of NGOs thought their present relationship with corporations was "antagonistic," and nearly half said they had no relationship at all with key companies. And this is despite the fact that nearly 80 percent of European and American opinion leaders claim to want NGOs and corporations "to partner on tough issues."[21] It is an unproductive, if not destructive, mindset, and business leaders would do well to begin to appreciate both the authority and legitimacy of these NGOs in the modern global economy.

Shareholder Scrutiny

It is not simply the rise of NGOs and media pressure, however, that has forced companies to focus on the poor labor or environmental activities of their overseas business partners. With the rapid expansion of the Internet in the late 1990s came also an expansion of share ownership, not only

---

20. Jay Culbert, "A Guide to Contemporary Sources of Information on Corporate Social Responsibility," *Washington Council on International Trade*, July 2000, p. 12.

21. "U.S. Attitudes on CSR Move Closer to Europe's," *Holmes Report*, April 25, 2002, p. 2, at *www.holmesreport.com*.

among Americans, but also among the general public in developed economies around the world. Today more than 100 million Americans have invested either directly or institutionally in shares. Many are acutely sensitive to a collapse in share price, and are among the first to react to news from an NGO, the Securities and Exchange Commission (SEC), or the media that might damage a company's reputation. Even if these investors take no particular ethical position on human rights issues or environmental violations in the supply chain, the slightest hint of a scandal can trigger a rapid sell-off. Institutional investors, too, though usually less influenced by short-term issues, have become increasingly sensitive to sudden and devastating share price declines with the announcement of an SEC investigation or an environmental spill.

Even more important, many of these investors have begun to avoid investing in companies that have a reputation for permitting unacceptable social or environmental activities in their supply chain in the first place. A simpler and more stable investment policy, of course, is not to have to monitor the activities of a risky company but instead to invest in a more dependable and stable company—one that has strict and transparent policies with regard to activities (including those of its suppliers) that could potentially damage its reputation and stock price.

Of course, the development of the Socially Responsible Investment (SRI) movement reflects these types of investment concerns. Over the past 10 years, socially responsible investing—investing in listed companies that can demonstrate that they adhere to higher standards of ethical, social, or environmental performance—has continued to provide another compelling reason for companies to demonstrate their commitment to good behavior in these areas.

Once considered a marginal set of indices in the world's major stock exchanges, socially responsible investment has expanded in the United States to $2.34 trillion in 2001. In the summer of 2002, partly no doubt as a reaction against the wave of corporate scandal, ethical funds had a net investment gain of $200 million even while equities had a net redemption of $3.4 billion.[22] Today, nearly one out of every eight dollars under professional investment is invested in companies that have been screened for these higher levels of social and environmental responsibility. Calvert, the fund managers, has estimated that by the end of the decade socially responsible investment will account for 10 percent of all investment in the United States. Similarly, Britain now has more than 60 ethical trusts, a leap of 36 percent between 1999 and 2001.

The United States has a dedicated ethical index (the Dow Jones Sustainable Asset Management Index), as does Canada (the Jantsi social

---

22. Sarah Murray, *The Financial Times*, October 2, 2002.

investment index) and Britain (FTSE4 Good), each of which monitors companies according to their policies concerning corporate governance, environmental reporting, corruption, human rights issues, and environmental product design and disposal policies. Some, such as the FTSE4 Good (which rates more than 300 major British companies, including around three quarters of the FTSE 100) now require companies to produce publicly available reports on their approach to social and environmental management.[23]

These socially responsible indices are not without teeth. In 2002 the FTSE4 Good index dropped several prominent companies including Abbot (oil and gas services group) and Heywood Williams (building materials) for failing to meet required human rights and stakeholder criteria.[24] Such an ignominious release from a major ethical index is, of course, quickly trumpeted loudly in the business and investment press.

An increasing number of fund managers also offer these types of SRI portfolios. Calvert, for example, offers 18 socially screened funds, and completes research on 1,000 domestic and international companies each year, looking at various nonfinancial criteria including ethical, social, and environmental performance. Many institutional pension fund holders, such as the State of California or the AFL/CIO, also screen companies in which they invest for superior social and environmental performance. One of the most active funds in this area, the California Public Employees Retirement System (Calpers), with $150 billion in managed assets, is the world's largest pension fund, and one of the most vociferous advocates of socially and environmentally conscious investment.[25]

And of course, as recent accounting scandals have brought into question the legitimacy of company financial reports, many asset managers have adopted broader criteria for investing in companies, focusing on the transparency of corporate activities, the ethical policies adopted by management, and often, the company's willingness to adhere to newly emerging labor and environmental standards, and to publish the company's performance against those standards.

That is why even asset managers that do not deal specifically in SRI funds are now examining proxy statements when selecting stocks. As

---

23. "2001 Report on Socially Responsible Investing Trends in the United States," *SIF Industry Research Program*, November 28, 2001, at *www.socialinvest.org;* and Rupert Jones, "Jobs & Money: Money: Ethical investment: A bad year for FTSE4Good," *The Guardian,* July 27, 2002.

24. Terry Macalister, "Abbot kicked off good-guys' index," *The Guardian,* September 17, 2002.

25. Alison Maitland, "Scandals Draw Attention to 'Superficial' Measures," *The Financial Times,* December 10, 2002, p. IV; and see also "Calvert Social Responsibility Criteria," *Calvert Asset Management.*

investors increasingly turn to these types of indices for information concerning a company's social and environmental approach and risk and reputation management framework in order to judge a company's likely stability and growth, companies are scrambling to at least show that they are aware of the importance of these issues to investors.

In fact, there are many indications that the market is moving toward integrating these types of minimum standards—corporate governance methods and strong compliance with good social and environmental standards—into the vast majority of indices, as a response to the fact that too many investors are wary of the reputation damage that indifferent corporate policies in these areas can invite.

In what some are heralding as a significant step toward forcing corporations globally to accept a uniform human rights policy, for example, the "Globalizing the Principles Network," a group of religious investors and activists with representatives from 22 countries, published in May 2003 new "Principles for Global Corporate Responsibility: Bench Marks for Measuring Business Performance," which reflects the Universal Declaration of Human Rights and the core labor rights set out by the International Labor Organization (ILO). These "Global Bench Marks" provide a variety of standards and criteria for corporations, including guidelines on issues such as workplace conditions, pollution control, contract supplier guidelines, stakeholder involvement in corporate decision making, and public reporting.

"The Bench Marks provide an economic imperative for investment managers from affluent nations," says Helga Birgden, Chair of the Christian Center for Socially Responsible Investment, "to assess the sustainability of their portfolios in terms of management of financial, environmental, social and governance risks. . . . The Bench Marks challenge the all too prevalent practice of corporate social responsibility, which does little for social change and justice, instead it calls on companies to aspire to global sustainability."[26]

Similarly, in the United Kingdom, the association of British Insurers—representing corporations that control 20 percent of the UK stock market—have now published guidelines for companies that include a requirement for reporting on their policies for managing risks in social and environmental policy. As we will see in the next chapter, the United Kingdom and other European nations are moving rapidly toward incorporating these requirements into law. Britain already requires pension fund trustees to declare in annual reports how they use social, environmental, and ethical issues when making their investment decisions. Similarly, Australia passed

---

26. "Religious Investors, Advocacy Groups Issue First Global "Bench Marks" for Corporate Behavior," *The Interfaith Center on Corporate Responsibility*, May 20, 2003, at *www.iccr.org/news/press_releases/GP_pressconf/pr_gp_release.htm.*

a requirement under their Financial Services Reform Act that took effect in March 2003, whereby all investment firms are required to disclose "the extent to which labor standards or environmental, social or ethical considerations are taken into account."[27]

What all of this reveals is that there is a growing appreciation by institutional investors that the social and environmental policies that are pursued by a company's management team—through the company's extended supply chain—represent important criteria for judging the future stability of a company's share value.

"At the end of the day," contends Hewitt Roberts of Entropy International, a UK-based social and environmental consulting and software provider, "CSR (corporate social responsibility) and good corporate governance will become the normal way of doing business—there will be no funds other than ethical funds—because they are not sustainable in the long run if they do not provide the necessary kind of investment governance and investment guarantees."[28]

Whatever its limitations, the SRI movement is another powerful reason why companies need to begin to take the activities of their suppliers more seriously, and to manage the ethical, social, and environmental aspects of their supply chain in a more coherent way.

Beyond the Pressures of Globalization

In this chapter, we have explored just a few of the important new pressures—globalization, the rise in power of NGOs, and unprecedented shareholder scrutiny—that a company confronts in a dramatically changing global environment. These are the very real pressures that are forcing companies to rethink the boundaries of their responsibility within the extended supply chain.

But not all pressure for change is coming from external forces. Apart from these formidable external pressures, there are internal structural changes to the modern manufacturing and distribution organization that also compel companies to reassess their supply chain responsibilities and to consider a closer monitoring of suppliers in developing countries. We turn now to these organizational changes; part of a broader "supply chain revolution" that demands that companies make supplier monitoring and control much more a part of their strategic management policy.

---

27. William Baue, "Australia to Require Investment Firms to Disclose How They Take SRI into Account," *Social Funds.com*, January 3, 2003, at *www. socialfunds.com/news/ print.cgi?sfArticleId=998*.

28. Interview with Hewitt Roberts, February 13, 2003.

CHAPTER TWO

The Extended Global Supply Chain: New Problems and New Responsibilities

*A*s we saw in the last chapter, there are many reasons companies now, more than ever, need to pay attention to social and environmental issues within their extended supply chain. These include a relocation of the manufacturing base, growing NGO and activist pressures, increased scrutiny by investors, and the instantaneous and ubiquitous nature of the Internet. There are also, however, organizational-level changes that have occurred during the past decade — part of the "supply chain revolution" — that have greatly affected a company's ability to *control and monitor product safety and social and environmental issues, and make it more imperative than ever that corporations manage their suppliers more effectively.*

A Decade of Shifting Responsibilities

For anyone involved in manufacturing or distribution, it is well understood that over the past 15 years there has been nothing short of a revolution in supply chain management processes and systems. Consider, for example, the plethora of quality and performance techniques such as ISO 9000, Six Sigma, Baldrige, Total Quality Management, vendor-managed inventory, and Business Process Reengineering that have been adopted by most modern companies. With a relentless focus on reducing costs, companies have streamlined production methods using new manufacturing processes and systems. Enterprise Resource Planning systems, Customer Relationship Management, advanced forecasting and planning systems, and e-procurement and online markets and auctions have all helped to revolutionize the way the modern company purchases materials and manufactures, assembles, sells, and delivers products. Although these techniques have often required changes to support tasks in human resources, accounting, or corporate governance, for the most part they all have been focused almost exclusively on improving the production and distribution process: in short, the supply chain.

It is true that not all of these processes, standards, and systems have delivered on their promises, but on the whole, the movement has been effective in reducing inventory carrying costs, shortening product development cycles, increasing product variety, and linking forecasting and planning with manufacturing and supply in a much more cogent way. Equally important, these systems are nearly all based on the premise—one that has guided supply chain management thinking for the past decade—that there is a fundamental advantage in shifting responsibility for production, inventory carrying, and holding costs as much as possible to suppliers and distributors.

This dramatic shift of responsibility toward external parties has been effective in streamlining processes, breaking down bureaucracy in the corporation, and reducing the company "footprint" considerably during the past decade. At the same time, it has resulted in two important strategic changes.

First, effective sourcing and relationship management of suppliers has become an issue of strategic importance for the modern corporation. After all, the impact of supplier performance on a company's bottom line, particularly in an ever-more collaborative and extended global supply chain, is critical. For the average manufacturing or distribution company, purchased materials account for between 40 and 60 percent of total revenues, and more than half of all quality and customer satisfaction issues arise directly from those purchased goods.

As we have seen, however, as a company's success is more dependent upon the performance of their suppliers than ever before, companies are now also more vulnerable than ever to charges of "guilt by association," when those suppliers are found to be guilty of poor environmental, product safety, or employment practices. In short, despite the effort to shift more and more responsibility for manufacturing to business partners, companies have been surprised to find that they have not been able to rid themselves of all the legal, ethical, and quality responsibilities that come with that production process—even when their suppliers are geographically very distant or organizationally and legally separate.

Equally important, despite all of these important economic and organizational changes, the procurement (vendor-relations) function for most companies has actually changed very little in the past 20 years. The supplier management function still remains, principally, with mid-level procurement officers. Criteria for supplier selection, though possibly reviewed by the chief operating officer, is usually high-level and flexible, left mainly to the discretion of the purchasing department. Strategic sourcing techniques still tend to focus almost exclusively on supplier performance in terms of quality, price, and delivery, which helps little in developing more collaborative relationships or, importantly, ensuring that suppliers are not endangering corporate reputation through illegal or unethical social and environmental practices.

The reality is that, for most manufacturing and distribution organizations, despite all these fundamental changes and growing pressures to monitor and control supplier behavior, the supplier management function has failed to keep up. In short, procurement is still completing operations in much the same way as they did 50 years ago, when suppliers were local and production operations were on-site.

In order to better understand the gap that has grown between the changing needs of the modern manufacturing or distribution organization and the current supply chain procurement practices, it is important to consider three fundamental changes to the traditional supply chain that have come about in the past decade.

- **Collaborative Planning and Integrated Materials Management.** First, as we have seen, in an effort to shorten product cycle times and to increase inventory efficiencies, during the last decade, companies have shifted responsibility for production and materials management, whenever possible, to their suppliers. With that shift in responsibility has also come the need for stronger collaborative alliances. Collaborative planning, supplier managed inventory, shared product databases, electronic procurement, Just-In-Time (JIT) supply techniques, and advanced planning and scheduling software all create greater efficiencies within the supply chain that require closer buyer–supplier relations, tying together the various organizations involved much more closely, in terms of both legal and production responsibilities. This means that although costs are shared more widely, so is responsibility and thus blame for errors or failures.

In short, greater dependency and closer collaboration with suppliers brings with it new levels of responsibility because of the closer association. "Because you're crossing enterprise boundaries to conduct collaboration," says Janet Suleski, a senior analyst at AMR Research, "there's a new, broader set of business ethics, one that takes into account the effect that your decisions have on other businesses."[1]

• **Outsourcing.** But consolidation and greater levels of collaboration constitute just one effect of the supply chain revolution that has taken place over the last decade. More important is the continuing trend toward outsourcing to external suppliers huge portions of the purchasing, holding, production, assembly, finishing, and delivery process.

This outsourcing movement began many years ago when companies first began to refocus on their core competencies and to outsource or subcontract activities that required noncore specialist knowledge or production. "Suppliers," notes the OECD, "are no longer restricted to traditional component suppliers. Suppliers have become complex (technical) solution partners ranging from large multinational companies often larger and more "global" than the manufacturers to small but nevertheless very competitive design and engineering firms."[2]

This outsourcing trend has now reached dramatic levels. Enormous portions of what was integral to a company's manufacturing process in the past is now often completed by other organizations, often in other parts of the world. As we have already seen, companies such as Nike, for example, no longer own any factories themselves, but work with 900 contract factories in more than 50 different countries. So extensive has this restructuring become that, as a result of extensive outsourcing, the very concept of the legal and operational boundaries of company responsibility are now being called into question.

• **Strategic Sourcing.** As a natural result of the combined shift toward collaborative design, materials management, and unprecedented outsourcing, one of the most important and strategic activities facing the modern

---

1. Clinton Wider and John Soat, "The Trust Imperative," *Information Week*, July 30, 2001.
2. "Supply Chains and the OECD Guidelines for Multinational Enterprises, *OECD Roundtable on Corporate Social Responsibility*, OECD Headquarters, June 19, 2002, p. 2.

company has become managing the relationship with its supplier base. More than ever before, the modern corporation depends on its ability to develop and maintain strategic partnerships with suppliers, distributors, manufacturers, and retailers—to such a level that today, managing those strategic partnerships has become a required core competency. For that reason, supplier management and strategic sourcing, areas once thought to be the exclusive domain of procurement officers, has today become a strategic concern for companies: key to maintaining a competitive operational advantage.

During the early phases of this supply chain revolution in the late 1980s, it appeared that there was little downside to this combined approach of outsourcing, collaborative product management and strong supplier sourcing techniques. After all, shifting production and inventory holding costs to specialized suppliers only made sense. Companies could shed their costly plant and local production workforce and simply contract out manufacturing at a much lower cost with specialized factories in developing nations. Corporations no longer needed to provide costly infrastructure when they could simply purchase or contract with specialist producers to complete great segments—production, assembly, transportation, disposal—of the supply chain. By the late 1990s, information technology platforms—Enterprise Resource Planning (ERP), Supply Chain Management systems, Advanced Planning and Scheduling, Materials Management systems—were all being developed to allow companies to manage a supply chain with dispersed responsibilities in a collaborative way. Vendor-managed inventory techniques were integrated with Just-in-Time (JIT) practices and collaborative planning tools. Strategic sourcing modules were created for ERP platforms. In time, this radical extension of the supply chain became so widespread that, as we have seen, many former manufacturing companies no longer engage in these production processes, limiting their efforts almost exclusively to design and marketing.

"In North America," says Nicholas Eisenberg, CEO of Ecos Technologies, "companies have outsourced more and more of their operations. The things that they used to make—what most people in the street think a company make—well, they don't make it. They may put it together, and they certainly market it, but they don't make it. And that actually puts a lot more pressure on companies from a risk standpoint, because it takes them farther away from control of the risk—and puts the risk outside the four walls."[3]

One of the most positive outcomes of this outsourcing movement has been that it has provided developing world suppliers not only with an opportunity to sell to the rest of the world, but also to learn from modern

---

3. Interview with Nicholas Eisenberg, August 25, 2003.

management policies and techniques. "Managers in these companies become familiar with the demands of advanced consumer markets and business partners as well as with management practices used for accountability and legal and regulatory compliance," explains the OECD, advocating this type of approach, in part, because of the advantages it brings to smaller, often developing-world, suppliers. "These include control of product flow and quality, inventory and facilities management, record keeping and tighter labour and environmental management."[4]

But this outsourcing model also has its obvious drawbacks. With this dramatic shift toward dependency on business partnerships has also come an unexpected downside, which is that companies have lost significant control over key issues concerning product safety, environmental, health, and employment quality issues.

For that reason, from an operations point of view, this extended supply chain, which may include hundreds of subcontractors in multiple countries, requires competent strategic sourcing to ensure that the suppliers selected can be trusted to produce the goods on time, at a high level of quality. Yet, in reality, the effect of the supply chain revolution has had almost the exact opposite effect. Levels of collaboration and scrutiny, difficult to achieve in the early years with local or regional suppliers, have proven to be even more difficult to achieve in a global supply chain strategy. Fearing interference in their management techniques and greater pricing pressures, developing-world factories have tended to keep buying companies, whenever possible, at arm's length. And despite the continued dependence on outsourced suppliers, relationships between U.S. companies and overseas suppliers tend to be more formal, and involve lower levels of collaboration, than ever before. Even large companies such as Nike or Gap Inc. may often only contract for a small percentage of a factory's output, and therefore have much less direct control over the supplier than is often supposed. Short-term contracts and low-cost bids undermine the longer-term relationships that were more typical in the past, particularly with domestic operations.

Not only has that close buyer–supplier relationship (a fundamental tenet of the supply chain revolution) been undermined, but delivery dependability and quality issues are often rife, and brutal conditions, poor management, and environmental indifference can potentially create liabilities for the buying company in terms of unsafe products, or, as we have seen, guilt through association with social and environmental exploitation. And as many companies have moved toward outsourcing other areas, such as waste management, they can also find liability extending downstream

---

4. "Managing Working Conditions in the Supply Chain," *OECD Working Paper on International Investment*, no. 2002/2, June 2002, p. 1.

beyond the production process itself. Issues such as dangerous toxic and other waste disposal, use of prohibited or dangerous ingredients such as asbestos or carcinogenic materials, and employee exposure and injuries all constitute not only a potential supply chain delay, but a potential corporate reputation disaster. Accordingly, much of this activity lies beyond a company's immediate operational control.

"At present," says Teresa Fabien of PricewaterhouseCoopers, "most attention is placed on addressing reputation risks associated with the sourcing of inputs (such as the environmental performance of a cotton farm) and at the manufacturing or conversion stage (such as use of child labour to stitch footballs)."

"These should not be the only area of concern in the supply chain," she concludes. "At each stage of the supply chain process companies are exposed to a range of different reputation risks. Often these risks are overlooked, not identified and therefore not managed."[5]

Apart from increased risk, many have begun to wonder if the very fundamentals of the supply chain revolution have been called into question by this drive toward overseas outsourcing. After all, the benefits of outsourcing were thought to be achievable only if companies developed a closer working relationship with their suppliers—collaborating in product design, sharing demand information so that they could ensure JIT inventory. The very concept of outsourcing was predicated on the idea that a company would be able to create strong, collaborative working relationships with their suppliers, ensuring performance and consistency through strategic sourcing techniques. That is what the strategic sourcing initiative has been all about. With the onset of global outsourcing, however, companies have suddenly suggested that their supplier relations are less important, and that they only have a "contractual" and distant relationship with foreign factories and farms.

Does this mean that the fundamental ground rules for the supply chain revolution need to be reconsidered? Probably not. After all, the principles of collaboration, quality, systems integration, and inventory management are all still the same, whether the supplier is down the street or on the other side of the globe. The more efficient the manufacturing process, the lower the costs (even if the baseline for wages is 31 cents rather than $24 per hour).

The reality is that just as with the evolution of supply chain efficiency that has been occurring domestically for the past 30 years, there will be

---

5. Teresa Fabien, "Supply Chain Management in an Era of Social and Environmental Accountability," *Sustainable Development International,* Edition 1, (no date) p. 29, from the Sustainable Development Commission at *www.sustdev.org/journals/edition.02/download/ sdi2_1_5.pdf.*

continued pressure on companies to work more closely with their overseas suppliers and business partners to improve productivity and to reduce costs. There is a competitive "dialectic" that drives companies continuously toward increasing efficiencies and lower costs throughout their supply chain, and that inevitably means that issues such as excess overtime, worker health and safety, product wastage, or union disputes—all of which add to costs and reduce delivery dependability and product quality—will need to be addressed. It is ultimately in the interest of the buying company to assist suppliers in these improvements, because companies are even more dependent upon their suppliers for ensuring quality products and on-time delivery than ever before. And given that the advantages of low-wage labor are now available to all (including the competition), companies are already actively seeking to help their tier-one suppliers to reduce costs by adopting modern manufacturing methods and quality controls, and implementing stronger health and safety programs.

This being the case, it will be increasingly more difficult for companies to claim to investors, customers, NGOs, or unions that they have a strict contractual relationship with their suppliers, and therefore do not share in the operational or legal responsibilities for their abuses. These arguments will be even more difficult to make in the future, as the competitive dialectic relentlessly presses companies to work more closely with their suppliers to gain the sorts of efficiencies that have been at the heart of the quality movement in developed-world operations.

CHAPTER THREE

Risky Business

*T*he complexity of a company's supply chain and the relative ownership of responsibility at each phase vary enormously between corporations and industries. Accordingly, the amount of control a buying company has over its suppliers, and the relative risk that social and environmental violations on their part poses to that company, depends on many factors, including industry focus, the number of suppliers, the complexity of its supply chain, and even the relative importance of the buying company in its marketplace.

Obviously, these supply chain risks are most acute in manufacturing and distribution companies, but many of the same principles apply to service organizations as well. Certainly, every company has a supply chain that involves some form of social or environmental impact. Obviously, if a corporation's processes, purchases, and services are so benign that they have little impact on the environment, a company needs to be much less concerned than those that are involved with manufacturing, extraction, or distribution of goods, and are obviously in the forefront of events. But even if an organization deals purely in services, it will still purchase paper that comes from forests or is recycled, serve coffee that is harvested by low-paid workers, or select computers with electronic components that are produced in Asian factories. Every company is today expected to deal fairly and legally with employees, and may still face business partner or domestic supplier issues concerning fair pay, employee rights, or ethical practices.

After all, taken to its extreme, the supply chain even in a service organization creates a responsibility bond between the company and all of the organizations worldwide with which they have a business relationship. In fact, one of the defining tenets of globalization is the interrelationship between economic entities (companies, banks, markets) worldwide. One of the most effective, if ethically questionable, approaches to stopping animal testing, for example, has been pursued against Huntingdon Life Sciences, the UK laboratory and drug-testing company that has been targeted by animal rights activists after a damning television report alleged cruelty and indifference to laboratory animals. Although HLS was forced to de-list from the London Stock Exchange and relocate to the United States under a different name, animal rights activists have now extended their harassment as far as Seattle where in 2002 they attacked the company offices of Marsh & McLennan because they had reputedly acted as HLS's insurance brokerage. Although roundly condemned for these secondary targeting tactics, the actions highlight the extent to which activists can push responsibility down the extended supply chain.

In fact, even in its more traditional sense, a modern supply chain goes well beyond just manufacturing or purchasing of a product. The modern, global supply chain extends from raw materials through to the point where a product is either discarded or recycled by the customer. This "dirt to dirt" process includes, either directly or through a network of suppliers and distributors, some aspect of extracting materials or growing produce, purchasing, transportation, production and assembly, storage, and delivery. It will also involve product safety for the lifetime of the product, and sometimes disposal when the product's use is at an end.

Risky Business

So how does a company begin to assess its level of relative risk in terms of supplier performance? There are several ways to categorize exposure. One group that often find themselves at high risk are companies that have **a fragmented supply chain,** with each phase of the supply chain operating almost entirely independent of the others. Organizations such as grocery chains that deal in fast-moving consumer goods and produce are a good example. They may purchase products through a network of suppliers who themselves buy from many thousands of small producers or farmers. Similarly, a building supply chain will usually deal through middle market consolidators that deal with hundreds of small suppliers worldwide.

The difference between forest and paper products presents a good example. With most furniture, shelving, or lumber purchased at a retail store such as Home Depot or Lowe's, the goods originate from a single source, or at least can be traced through an obvious chain from sawmill through to retail supply. For that reason, retail outlets have found it a fairly straightforward process to request a Forest Stewardship Council's (FSC) certification from their suppliers (for more on FSC certification, see Chapter Ten). Paper products such as those sold by Office Depot or Staples, on the other hand, are often purchased from hundreds of sources, making that type of certification program much more difficult.

In the early stages of the evolution toward outsourcing and supply chain fragmentation, having multiple levels of subcontractors seemed to insulate the buying company from charges of poor supplier behavior, but lately even organizations with a more fragmented supply chain are being held responsible for their relationship with various upstream, and occasionally downstream, suppliers. Sainsbury's, one of Britain's largest grocery chains, provides a good example of this new level of exposure and responsibility.

"Sainsbury's supply chain is typical of many large UK supermarkets," says Liz Fullelove, Manager for Socially Responsible Sourcing at Sainsbury's Supermarket. "We have about 2,000 suppliers providing our 'own-brand' goods and we accept responsibility for monitoring labor standards in those. Many of these suppliers also source from within their own supply chains, be these factories or farms. So, even among the suppliers providing own-brand goods, we are probably taking the produce of a million farms across the globe."

As a representative from another UK retailer admits, keeping track of this ever-changing supply chain can be difficult. "I can know my supply chain at 9 A.M. then by 10 A.M. it's all different. We deal with about 1,300 suppliers, involving maybe 5,000 factories, but if buyers can't get goods from the usual source, they'll find another. The supply base is growing all the time."[1]

Companies that deal in **low value goods,** whether as part of an assembly process or through direct sales to consumers, also remain at considerable risk from charges of exploitation, simply because an ever-increasing majority of these types of manufactured goods are produced and assembled in low-wage labor conditions. Toys and garments, kitchen utensils, plastic goods, and low-cost tools are all likely to involve some level of low-skill labor, often overseas. Moreover, unlike expensive or complex products, low-value goods offer an easy option for consumer resentment and rejection, in that outrage (i.e., switching to another, similar low-cost product) involves little personal economic sacrifice.

Similarly, any time a company becomes the **direct interface with the retail public,** the relative risk to their reputation—in the case of product safety issues, or poor supplier performance—increases. Again, large grocery store chains, home supply stores, automobile manufacturers, large retail stores—virtually any company that ultimately has responsibility for selling products directly to the public—are more vulnerable than the vast number of second- and third-tier suppliers that remain largely unknown to the public, to the media, to analysts, or to activists. With a well-recognized brand name and a potentially transparent supply chain, these companies are (often disproportionately) in the frontline of consumer, activist, and investor pressures for ensuring that ethical management policies extend throughout their supply chain.

In this same vein, companies that are dominant **market leaders or have well-known brand names** are much more likely to be targeted by activists and held to high supplier standards. As we have already seen in Chapter Two, one of the most effective NGO and activist pressure techniques is to target well-known brand name companies—Nike, Home Depot, Coca-Cola, Reebok, K-Mart—knowing that consumer and investor leverage is highest among these market leaders. Many other less well-known companies may also purchase similar goods from the same overseas factories, but will receive much less activist attention.

"Where resource-extractive firms like timber giant Georgia-Pacific may be isolated from consumers and thus insulated from negative press," explains Gary Gereffi, professor of sociology and director of the Markets and

---

1. Mick Blowfield, "Fundamentals of Ethical Trading/Sourcing in Poorer Countries," *The World Bank Group* at *http://wbln0018.worldbank.org/ESSD/essdext.nsf/26ByDocName/ FundamentalsofEthicalTradingSourcinginPoorerCountries.*

Management Studies Program at Duke University, "companies such as Staples Inc. (a current Rainforest Action Network target) are much more vulnerable. By using tactics such as boycotts, banner hangings, leafleting, and other direct action, NGOs force retailers to take proactive labor and environmental stances."[2]

"Some companies make mistakes," says Narayanan Sreenivas, general manager of Environmental Compliance Consultants (ECC) International. "But these small mistakes can cause public relations disasters. News reports don't emphasize the name of the small supplier that is not socially responsible but dwell on the big company that purchases from it."[3]

Yet even organizations that have less public exposure and operate under the radar of most NGOs and activists (known as "stealth companies" by AccountAbility's John Elkington) may soon be targeted by activists. Indices such as AccountAbility's Gradient Index begin to offer analysts, consumers, and the media direct access to comparative information on corporate performance.[4]

Equally, and this is something that companies such as Nike (see *Nike Versus Kasky* in Chapter Five) have learned the hard way, a company can find itself under increased scrutiny if it has previously **boasted of its "corporate social responsibility"** without authentication, and these claims are later questioned by activists.

All of this means that companies today are placed in an awkward position where, while still retaining ultimate responsibility (at least in the eyes of activists and many investors) for producing a safe product in a safe and employee-friendly way, direct control over those factors is actually shifting more and more toward third-party business partners over which, unless a formal program is undertaken, the buying company has little control. The combination of collaborative manufacturing and outsourcing has meant that companies are now—more than ever—vulnerable to poor supplier or subcontractor performance, both in terms of bottom line costs and in terms of protecting their reputation.

---

2. Gary Gereffi, Ronie Garcia-Johnson, and Erika Sasser, "The NGO-Industrial Complex," *Foreign Policy,* no. 125, July/August, 2001 at *www.foreignpolicy.com.* Copyright 2001, Carnegie Endowment for International Peace.

3. Marites Villamor, "Filipino Exporters Urged to Comply with Global Standards," *BusinessWorld* (Philippines), June 12, 2002; see also *www.vpac-usa.org/humanrights/vietnam/mcdonald.htm.*

4. "Moving Up the Learning Curve—Corporate Management of Supply Chain Labour Standards," *Sustainability* at *www.sustainability.com/news/articles/core-team-and-network/John-Sabapathy-gradient-index-mar-02.asp.*

The Global Supply Chain

In a global supply chain, the sourcing path is usually much less straightforward than in the past (see Figure 3-1):

Consider the various levels of company–supplier relationship that now routinely exist:

Tier-One Suppliers

These are the company's most important suppliers, critical to production or to supply. Sometimes domestic, more often foreign based, these suppliers are usually selected and managed directly by the company's procurement professionals. This strategic sourcing process—whereby procurement officers choose and monitor supplier performance—has been one of the areas of greatest emphasis for companies in the past decade. Yet, as we will see later, the very fact that supplier credentials and performance are formally reviewed by corporate officers in a strategic sourcing exercise makes it

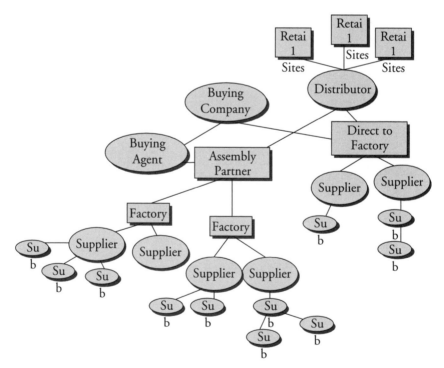

FIGURE 3-1 The Extended Supply Chain

easy for activists to point the finger of blame back to the company when these suppliers are found to be violating employment or environmental standards. There are many good examples.

• A factory owned by Mandarin International that was operating in El Salvador fired 350 workers when they formed a union to protest against harsh working conditions. Mandarin International was one of Gap Inc.'s major suppliers, and the action was in violation of Gap's freedom of association clause in its code of conduct. Under pressure from NGOs, Gap agreed to have the factory monitored independently, and to force Mandarin International to improve working conditions and permit unionization.[5]

• For nearly two years, Benetton has been trying to refute charges that one of their major Turkish suppliers was manufacturing Benetton brand label clothing using child labor. The accusations revolve around work taking place at the Bermuda textile factor in Istanbul, where a series of investigations by Italy's largest trade union, CGIL, contended that the Bermuda factory was employing minors but never registering them on the official payroll.

All of this highlights the difficulties of a company in the modern, extended supply chain, and as Neil Kearney, the general secretary of the Brussels-based International Textile, Garment and Leather Workers' Federation, points out, if the accusations prove true, given new realities, Benetton will need to take some sort of action.

"They can't wash their hands [of this], saying that it's not their responsibility," he says. "Today the power of control lies with the retailer. Nobody has goods made today through sub-contractors without checking out the premises. They send in quality-control people to ensure that the goods carrying their label are up to scratch."[6]

• In September, 2000 CNN reported that McDonald's had been accused by labor rights activists of having their Snoopy, Winnie-the-Pooh, and Hello Kitty toys made by a factory in China that employed underage workers that were paid less than $3.00 a day for a 16- to 20-hour workday. McDonald's issued a statement saying it "takes these issues very seriously. Our Code of Conduct for suppliers makes clear that we will not tolerate any substandard practices." Despite the promise by McDonald's of a full-scale inquiry, there have been calls for a boycott of the restaurants.[7]

---

5. Gary Gereffi, et al., op. cit.

6. "Benetton Fails to Halt Child-Labour Row,"Global March Against Child Labour, at *www.globalmarch.org/cl-around-the-world/italy-benetton-fails.php3.*

7. Mike Chinoy, "Activists Claim McDonald's Toys Made With Child Labor," CNN.com, September 6, 2000, at *www.cnn.com/2000/ASIANOW/east/09/05/mcdonalds.child.labor/.*

Tier-Two Suppliers and Below

Depending on the size of the buying company and the scale of its strategic sourcing exercise, tier-two and below suppliers may still be considered within a major company's supply chain span of responsibility. A lot depends on the nature of the relationship. Long-term suppliers, even if they service other major buyers as well, for example, may still be seen as falling within the parameters of a company's responsibility for review and monitoring. There seems to be a direct and fairly logical correlation based upon the extent to which a supplier contributes—or is indispensable—to the success of a company's production and the level of responsibility that activists apply. As we will see in Chapter Thirteen, ranking and prioritizing these suppliers according to their importance, relationship, and relative risk is one of the first steps in developing an ethical supply chain program.

There seems to be no formal method for drawing the line of responsibility, but generally speaking, if suppliers only provide spot-market goods, or if they are selected through tier-one suppliers, local plant staff, or another third-party, there seems to be general agreement that the original buying company is seen as less culpable when local issues arise. But franchising operations often fall into these categories, as do distribution networks.

Coca-Cola, for example, had to withdraw its products from four northern European countries in 1999, after a health scare caused by a batch of substandard carbon dioxide used by one of its bottlers/distributors resulted in a total of 115 Belgian and 80 French Coca-Cola drinkers—mostly children and students—suffering from nausea, headaches, and stomach cramps after drinking Coke. After initially dismissing the incident, explaining that "after thorough investigation, no health or safety issues were found," Coca-Cola was forced to recall 2.5 million bottles from Belgium, Holland, Germany, Spain, and Saudi Arabia when those countries' governments banned the sale of Coca-Cola–owned brands, such as Coca-Cola, Fanta, or Sprite, until the company could provide a "satisfactory and conclusive explanation." There were many lessons to be learned from the incident about risk and reputation management, but the important point is that the press did not focus its fury on the bottler which produced the defective carbon dioxide; they focused exclusively on chastising Coca-Cola.[8]

Supplier's Suppliers

Part of the problem is that many tier-one and tier-two suppliers themselves serve as an assembly or transportation clearinghouse, maintaining

---

8. "Coca-Cola 'Regrets' Contamination," *BBC News Online*, June 17, 1999, at *http: news.bbc.co.uk/2/hi/europe/371300.stm*.

relationships with hundreds of smaller suppliers from around the world. U.S. or European companies may simply send raw materials or partially assembled materials to these factories for assembly and completion. Even then, overseas suppliers may subcontract out that work. At what point does the original buying company's responsibility for these suppliers end?

"Many companies take their manufacturing, ship it overseas and it's subcontracted out three, four, or five times," says Anita Green, director of social research and corporate activity at Pax World Funds, the SRI fund managers. "So by the time you get the bottom level, to the people that are actually making the goods, you don't have any idea what the conditions are."[9]

This vast network of multiple, often single-person or family subcontractors, is frequently where many of the most egregious environmental, health, and safety violations occur. After all, developing-world suppliers have the same outsourcing pressures as any other company. Accordingly, an ever-increasing portion of the work that is done in overseas labor markets is completed not in factory settings, but in homes and small shops—essentially outside the formal economy. Completed for the most part by women (estimates are around 90 percent), these "at-home" workers constitute an invisible workforce, screened from any of the protections of company, national, or international labor or environmental protections.

These at-home workers are responsible for making an incredible variety of the everyday goods used by Americans: sewing clothing, soldering electronics, stitching together footballs, assembling automobile parts, or simply packaging goods. These workers, in countries such as India, China, Vietnam, Cambodia, Thailand, and Mexico, are seldom protected by minimum wage or hour legislation, and remain well beyond pledges to eliminate this type of "sweatshop" per piece work made by the major multinationals that ultimately pay for their services. As individuals, they have little leverage to demand higher wages or a less demanding schedule, always fearing unemployment if they fail to produce items on time. It is a recipe for low-cost consumer goods, which provides much-needed employment for developing-economy workers, but only at a price. Environmental and social violations are rampant.

Downstream Subcontractors Including Product Disposal and Recycling Partnerships

Even with these various categories, it is important to remember that it is not only product assembly services that present a potential danger to a

---

9. Sarah Murray, "GLOBAL INVESTING: Seeking the golden rules for SRI investors," *The Financial Times,* October 2, 2002.

company's reputation. Downstream contracted services for waste or used-product disposal, for example, constitutes one of the greatest subcontractor risk areas. Similarly, construction and maintenance work, even in domestic operations, are often carried out by small contractors employed on a short-term, often spot, contract. With little oversight, vague contracts, and little monitoring or record keeping, even these small service contractors can create company liabilities.

Vertical Industries Most at Risk

Most corporations, whether service or production orientated, domestic or global, vertically integrated or fragmented, will have some concerns with supplier behavior based on these types of characteristics and supplier relationships. But early pressure for supply chain monitoring has often fallen on several vertical industries, and it is companies in these areas that are being forced to pioneer some of the most innovative practices with regard to an ethical supply chain. Consider some of the industries where dependence upon suppliers tends to make companies vulnerable to potential disasters.

> ### Challenges in the Extended Supply Chain
>
> Table 3-1 is a recent attempt by the Ethical Trading Initiative in the United Kingdom to create a detailed study of the challenges that UK companies faced in their extended supply chain. It provides a summary of how corporate members purchased supplies in 2000 compared with the percentage of suppliers they were able to evaluate.

Light Goods Manufacturing

Soft and plastic toys, footballs, housewares—all constitute a massive loosely related light goods manufacturing industry that today is almost entirely dependent on labor from developing economies. India's homewares export market, for example, employs approximately six million people, and U.S. purchases alone (textiles, leather, handicrafts, carpets, cookware, etc.) account for some $3.4 billion. Most of these goods—an estimated 65–70 percent—are created by subcontractors.[10] This vast industry area, possibly more than any other, contains all of the potential criteria for social and environmental exploitation—large subcontractor networks, low skills, low wages, child labor, exposure to chemicals, and home-based workers.

---

10. "Sourcing From India's Informal Sector Homeware Industry," Levi Strauss & Company, Homeware Meeting summary, March 1, 2002.

TABLE 3-1 The Supply Chain Analyzed

Company	Own production capacity	Sub-contract using own overseas office	Supply via agent	Contract direct to overseas supplier	Supplier sub-contracts inputs	Supplier takes product from family smallholders	Supply from UK-based firm, which may in turn subcontract to overseas	Produce purchased at auction	Percentage of supply-base evaluated
A	✓			✓			✓		
B		✓	✓	✓	✓		✓		
C			✓	✓			✓		
D				✓			✓		
E		✓	✓	✓	✓	✓		✓	
F			✓		✓				
G			✓	✓			✓		
H			✓	✓	✓		✓		
I	✓	✓	✓	✓	✓				
J			✓	✓			✓		

(continues)

TABLE 3-1 (Continued.)

K					✓	✓	✓		
L				✓	✓	✓			
M		✓		✓	✓				
N		✓		✓	✓	✓			✓
O				✓	✓	✓	✓	✓	✓
P				✓	✓	✓			
Q				✓	✓		✓		

NB Company A was also supplied by overseas joint ventures; company G purchased supplier-branded products; company I had suppliers with home workers; company N had a licensing agreement covering marketing and manufacture and company Q purchased from an overseas producer board.

Source: The Ethical Trading Initiative's 2000–2001 Annual Report, at *www.eti.org.uk/pub/publications/annrep/2000_en/page04.shtml.*

Textile, Garment, and Footwear Industries

Probably no other sector has become more closely associated with the sins of their suppliers than the clothing and footwear industry. There are many inherent problems with this area, which is still labor intensive, with little plant or heavy equipment needed. In a global marketplace, the poorest—those that will accept the lowest pay and yet are able to produce a quality product—will be sought out, and that usually means low pay, poor working conditions, and few environmental protections. Sewing garments or assembling a football can be done at home, and a great portion of this work falls into that multitiered network of unmonitored, often individual subcontractors, too often including children and involving long and unregulated hours of work with little safety supervision. Of course, garment factories themselves are notorious for their difficult working conditions, poor safety records, low wages, exploitative hours, and sloppy employment practices. Toxic dyes and other chemicals are often used in the manufacturing process, and equally, fiber development and disposal, the use of pesticides in cotton cultivation, and uncontrolled water pollution that comes about during the washing and dyeing processes all create potential environmental and health problems.

The severe criticism that large retailers such as Nike, Gap Inc., or Reebok have received from activists for supporting, or at least permitting, "sweatshop" conditions in this area has had two effects. In the first place, as the single most vilified industry, the clothing industry—the "rag trade"—has essentially provided the momentum for the development of the Social and Ethical Accounting and Reporting movement that has become the foundation of CSR (which we will explore in the next two chapters).

Second, many of these companies are at the forefront of innovative new programs for improving working conditions in these factories, and for generally improving supplier management performance. Well-known brand names that for the past few years have been harangued by activists—Levi Strauss, Nike, Gap Inc.—have in fact been fairly instrumental in developing codes of conduct for better supplier behavior. Gap Inc., for example, now has more than 80 employees dedicated to its ethical sourcing and supplier monitoring program. Nike has more than 60. In fact, more than a quarter of the companies currently involved in the Ethical Trading Initiative (see Chapter Ten) are garment or footwear companies.[11]

Moreover, under pressure from these key corporate buyers, there is evidence of a greater appreciation for the need to improve these types

11. Sarah Roberts, op. cit.

of factory conditions by developing-world governments themselves. Cambodia, for instance, under the pressure from increased ILO factory inspections and the withdrawal of several large retailers (including Nike for two years) from the country because of its poor labor standards, has now reached an agreement with Washington D.C., in which Cambodia will receive an annual 18 percent textile quota as long as the garment industry improves its labor conditions. Accordingly, many Cambodian factories have made substantial improvements to their employment and environmental policies.[12]

Automotive Manufacturing

In the midst of global relocation and poised on the edge of a significant new demand for cars and trucks in competitive developing economies (estimates are that the number of automobiles and trucks globally will jump from 700 million today to over a billion by 2050), the automotive industry is already confronted with many of these same employment, environmental, and health and safety issues. Moreover, with its enormous network of suppliers and business partners, the automotive industry is particularly susceptible to criticism.

"The automobile industry is strongly motivated to manage EHS impacts in its supply chain," says Ram Narasimhan, Professor of Marketing and Supply Chain Management at Michigan State University Eli Broad College of Business. "The industry attracts attention from many stakeholders including regulators concerned with gas mileage, emissions, and recovery of material from retired vehicles. Its processes involve many safety and environmental risks, and it relies on multiple first tier suppliers for a steady flow of components and for quick time to market."[13]

In fact, the automobile industry, because of its multiple levels of risk exposure, leads in many aspects of environmental supply chain management. Toyota, GM, and Ford, for example, require thousands of their first- and second-tier suppliers to gain ISO 14001 environmental standards certification. Many observers believe that further improvements in the social and environmental standards of suppliers will come as the automotive industry, with its enormous influence and relentless drive for efficiencies, becomes more and more entrenched in developing economies.

---

12. Amy Kazmin, "U.S. Sportswear Giant May Be Ready for a Cambodia Comeback," *The Financial Times,* June 18, 2002.

13. Ram Narasimhan and Joseph Carter, "Environmental Supply Chain Management," *Center for Advanced Purchasing Studies,* 1998, p. 12.

Forest Products, Pulp, and Paper

As we have already seen, on the environmental side, particularly, the combined forest, pulp, and paper industry has become an area that attracts high levels of NGO involvement and concern. Deforestation particularly of rainforests, has become a significant problem, and NGOs have been focused on this area since the 1980s, one of their longest-running campaigns. Unrestricted logging and deforestation programs have left an estimated 30 percent of the world's remaining forests "seriously degraded," and despite efforts to slow the destruction, trees are being cut down at the rate of 130,000 sq km each year. Wetlands have been reduced by 50 percent over the last 100 years. It is a significant problem, made more difficult by the very low cost of labor required to cut the timber, and the enormous markups available to finishers and retailers for quality (e.g., mahogany) furniture.

A good example of this deforestation can be seen in Paragominas, Brazil, where for the past 15 years suppliers have been clearing the Amazon forest remorselessly, at a rate of nearly $1 billion worth of timber each year. What was once a thick forest is today unused, unkempt fields. Brazil banned logging of mahogany (which can bring up to $1,500 per every square foot) in October 2001 fearing that at current rates of deforestation, most reserves of mahogany would be wiped out in a few more years; yet it continues to be cut down and sold illegally. Greenpeace has named almost 100 companies that it contends deal in this illegal mahogany to meet a growing demand from American furniture makers.[14]

Similarly, the Three Gorges dam project in China (financed in large part by well-known U.S. and European banking groups) has seen the forest cover of the Yangtze River catchment area reduced from 45 to 16 percent over the last 20 years. Much to environmentalists' dismay, this included approximately 40 percent of the habitat of the Giant Panda. The project also promises to flood more than 100 towns and cities, causing the displacement of 1.3 million people, resulting in untold environmental harm to the Yangtze River valley. Although reforestation efforts have been partly successful, the project may have been one of the greatest environmental catastrophes of all time.[15]

Much of the focus of activist attention in this area has been on the do-it-yourself home improvement marketplace. These are the public-facing companies such as Homebase and B&Q in the United Kingdom and Home Depot and Lowe's in the United States that provide retail

---

14. Larry Rohter, "Brazil's Prized Exports Rely on Slaves and Scorched Land," *The New York Times,* March 25, 2002; and "2003 State of the World Report," Worldwatch Institute.

15. "China's Bio-diversity," Introduction at *www.chinabiodiversity.com/shengwudyx2/vegetation-en/1p.htm.*

sales of lumber products. They also provide both higher profile reputations and more vulnerable targets for protest.

The Forest Stewardship Council's (FSC) forest certification program, for example, launched in Britain in 1993, was one of the first and most effective NGO-sponsored campaigns that advocated ethical sourcing and focused not on pressuring the suppliers, but on pressuring the retail providers. Faced with mounting public and NGO protests about deforestation, and confounded by an inability to explain where their lumber products originated, these large retailers quickly began to require their suppliers to offer only FSC-certified goods. That meant extending the labeling and certification process through the distributors, manufacturers, sawmills, and ultimately, to the forest owners themselves, so that every item could be accounted for.[16]

Devised entirely by NGOs, the FSC program is a standard that contains 10 principles for good forest management, and a supply "chain of custody" certification process that provides for much more accurate tracking of sources throughout the extended supply chain. The FSC has developed a set of core principles that are concerned with important areas such as timber management, pesticide use, erosion control, and harvesting operations. To receive FSC approval, companies are required to be audited by accreditation firms.

Both Home Depot (August 1999) and Lowe's (August 2000) have now declared acceptance of the FSC certification program, and even Staples—the office supply store—has a formal "environmental paper procurement policy" which pledges to protect forest resources by purchasing postconsumer, recycled products. Similarly, Kinko's has a strong dual environmental procurement policy that incorporates sustainable forest management practices and uses recycling and alternative fibers technologies. The company was one of the first retail firms in America to prohibit the use of paper from "old-growth" forests in 1997, and in 2003 adopted a strict set of vendor requirements in which suppliers must guarantee and document that none of their supply sources or operations result in the logging of old growth or endangered forests.[17]

Horticulture/Agriculture

There are many other industries where NGO and investor pressure is just beginning to take effect. Coffee growers, for example, have come under fire recently for the poor labor conditions of pickers. Even Starbucks—once

---

16. Sarah Roberts, op. cit.

17. "Kinko's Adopts New Forest-Based Products Purchasing Policy," *Greenbiz.com,* March 24, 2003 at *www.greenbiz.com/news/news_third.cfm?NewsID=24236&CFID =7169687&CFTOKEN=16723084.*

thought to be immune to criticism because of its strong social and environmental core values—has come under scrutiny for buying coffee that involved child labor, poor working conditions, and low wages. In fact, the food and agricultural industries—from strawberries to bananas, confectionary to tea and coffee—are likely to be the next major area of activist focus. There are many reasons for this.

"In the past 30 years there has been a tenfold increase in the global export of agricultural products," says Nick Blowfield, from the Natural Resources Institute. "This increased reliance on food grown in other countries, is giving the supply chain—from producer to retailer—and regulators a host of new challenges . . . The initial concern was for the environmental and food safety impacts of farms and plantations where unsanitary practices and uncontrolled chemical usage were perceived as common-place. More recently, concerns about human rights, worker welfare, and biodiversity loss have become determinants of the success of a product, a company and sometimes even a country in the global marketplace."[18]

Utilizing the Internet, activists have moved quickly to highlight the exploitation of fruit and agricultural workers, among the most poorly paid and downtrodden workers in the world. Web sites such as VINET have become a communication hub for activists to trade stories and bring to light issues.

There are many other industries with similar concerns: conflict diamonds, silk, brass, cosmetics, waste management, building, and construction. The list goes on and on, and promises to grow as activists continue to target industry retail leaders.

---

18. Mick Blowfield, "Fundamentals of Ethical Trading/Sourcing in Poorer Countries," *The World Bank Group* at *http://wbln0018.worldbank.org/ESSD/essdext.nsf/26By DocName/FundamentalsofEthicalTradingSourcinginPoorerCountries.*

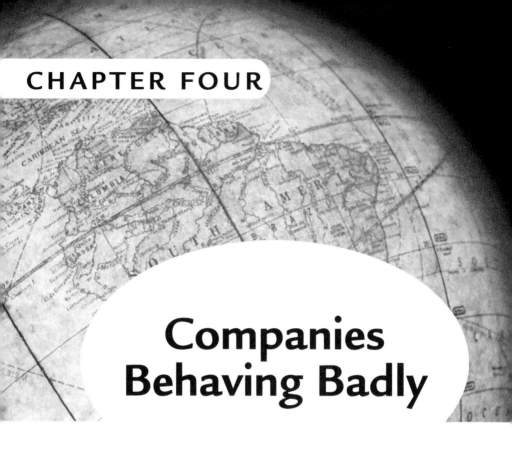

CHAPTER FOUR

Companies Behaving Badly

*E*fficiency and overhead reduction was
the rationale for the dramatic shift of production and logistics responsibility
to third parties, and measured by these standards, outsourcing to third-
party vendors in developing economies has worked remarkably well.
Consumer prices have dropped dramatically, while productivity and profits
have soared. But in the last five years, particularly, many companies have
gone through a painful learning process that has moved from early denial,
through half-baked methods intended to force better behavior among their
suppliers, to fully developed supplier management programs.

Initially, relocating and outsourcing production in order to take advantage of low labor costs and loose environmental and safety regulations seemed to be a perfect solution for everyone concerned—corporations, consumers, investors, and those employed in developing economies (although U.S. unions weren't too pleased). In fact, it made such perfect operational sense that it took some time for companies to realize that there might be a down side to this supply chain revolution. Even as late as 1995, mentioning social responsibility issues in a company's annual report, emerging Web sites, or in advertising or marketing campaigns—particularly those involving labor or environmental activities of a supplier in a developing country—was practically unheard of. Even in 1997, despite stiffer EPA rules and penalties for violations, only 32 percent of procurement departments surveyed admitted to having questioned their suppliers during the strategic sourcing process about their environmental activities.[1]

It therefore came as a surprise to analysts and business leaders that the same parties that benefited from these lower costs—the consumers and investors—would actually come to join sides with human rights and environmentalist pressure groups to demand that buying corporations continue to assume responsibility over employment and environmental actions of their suppliers. In short, what was never considered as this supply chain revolution was taking place was that shifting responsibilities for production to third parties did not fully abrogate the parent companies from ethical and social responsibilities that came with that production.

Denial, Obfuscation, and Half-Baked Measures

So how have companies dealt with pressure to take on accountability for their often wayward suppliers over the past decade?

The initial reaction of most companies to charges that they were sponsoring, dependent upon, and benefiting from low-wage, unsafe, and environmentally unfriendly production methods was one of incredulity and denial. After all, corporate leaders explained, a company cannot be held responsible for actions taken by a subcontractor in a foreign country. As late as September 1997, Nike was still producing a press release that dismissed critics of its supplier policies as "fringe groups."[2] The obvious

---

1. Ram Narasimhan and Joseph Carter, "Environmental Supply Chain Management," *Center for Advanced Purchasing Studies*, 1998, p. 12.

2. John Samuel, "Sites for Sore Consumers," *The Washington Post*, March 29, 1998 at *www.infochangeindia.com*.

answer was for local governments to maintain higher standards of labor and environmental law and enforcement. In the early phases of this transition, companies disclaimed any control or responsibility over the process at all.

"Many companies back then like Nike—which are essentially design and marketing companies—could have a top grade 'A' rating by us or the Europeans, or the Japanese CSR Research groups," says Alice Tepper Marlin, President of Social Accountability International. "But the data we got was all on what was happening in our own borders . . . and so we ran into many companies that got excellent evaluations on the environment and on employment issues, but they weren't doing any of their own production. We would only find out through somebody's exposé that the employment situation [overseas] was horrendous."[3]

But as groups such as the International Labor Organization and Societé Generale de Surveillance began to actively inspect factories, it soon became apparent that high-profile brand name companies that had contracts with suppliers were going to be exposed anyway. As high-profile cases began to emerge, activists asserted that, given that developing-world governments provided little protection to workers, responsibility for the subcontractors' social and environmental policy rested squarely on the company ordering and purchasing the product. After all, they reasoned, the buyer–supplier relationship meant that companies were much more influential than local government in demanding high standards or monitoring compliance. As companies were the ones that requested, directed, and paid for the production, and benefited from the contract, their responsibilities logically extended to the behavior of their subcontractors. If major buying corporations couldn't twist a supplier's arm to make it behave, who could?

"The corporate world has demonstrable global reach and capacity," says John Ruggie, from Harvard University's Center for Business and Government. "It can make and act on a decision far faster than governments or agencies. And parts of it—particularly such brand-sensitive companies such as Coca-Cola—are vulnerable to external pressure. Society, therefore, has come to demand help from the corporate sector in coping with adversity."[4]

This reasoning was even more persuasive given the power that U.S. companies, in particular, wielded over suppliers in developing economies. As we have already seen, in 2002 the United States imported more than one-third (36 percent) of China's total exports, including 1.2 billion

3. Interview, June 24, 2003.

4. John Ruggie, "Managing Corporate Social Responsibility," *The Financial Times,* October 25, 2002.

garments that accounted for $39 billion in U.S. retail sales. Nearly 30 percent ($22.5 billion) of all of India's exports fall into the category of housewares and the U.S. market alone (a $67 billion industry in the United States) accounts for nearly one-third of all of those exports. If any single group had power over the standards of behavior of these suppliers, it seemed to be the multinationals that contracted the manufacturing of the goods in these massive markets.[5]

And as the press continually points out, many of the most influential companies are more powerful in economic terms than the developing nations whose factories they use. According to the United Nations Conference on Trade and Development (UNCTAD), 29 of the world's largest economic entities are multinationals, led by ExxonMobil, a company that was larger than all but 44 national economies, and had an economic equivalent of Pakistan. The UNCTAD report concluded that the economic importance of the largest 100 multinational firms compared to national economies had grown significantly during the past decade.[6] The logic of the purchasing company having responsibility for suppliers might be tenuous under international law, but it has held great sway with pressure groups, consumers, and investors concerned about labor and environmental exploitation.

What is more, growing evidence indicated that consumers and investors not only supported this point of view, but were potentially liable to act to punish companies that they felt were misbehaving. A Millennium poll on Corporate Social Responsibility of 22,000 consumers across 23 nations on six continents, for example, found that 90 percent of consumers worldwide agreed that large companies should do more than focus on profitability.[7] A similar survey by Burson-Marsteller found that 64 percent of European opinion leaders—media, politicians, church leaders, NGOs, and institutional investors—said that a company's reputation for social responsibility would affect their buying behavior, and over 40 percent of those polled said that a company's social and environmental behavior would affect share prices. A recent European survey found that 86 percent of those interviewed said they would have a preference for purchasing a product from a company that was actively engaged in a CSR program,[8] and 60 percent of consumers said they formed their impression based

---

5. "Sourcing from India's Informal Sector Homeware Industry," Levi Strauss & Company, Homeware Meeting summary, March 1, 2002.

6. Guy De Jonquieres, "Companies 'Bigger Than Many Nations,'" *The Financial Times* and *www.unctad.org.*

7. Teresa Fabian, "Supply Chain Management in an Era of Social and Environmental Accountability" at *www.sustdev.org/journals/edition.02/download/sdi2_1_5.pdf.*

8. John Samuel, op. cit.

upon "labor practices, business ethics, responsibility to society at large, or environmental impacts."[9]

But it was not liberal Europe alone that felt corporations should behave better. A U.S. survey by Harris Interactive found that 79 percent of Americans said they considered corporate citizenship when they made purchasing decisions, and 71 percent considered corporate citizenship when they made investment decisions. Twelve percent said that they would purchase a less profitable stock if it had better corporate citizenship performance.

Yet in a Hill & Knowleton poll, 73 percent of Americans rated U.S. companies as "below average" when it came to corporate citizenship.[10] A PricewaterhouseCoopers survey in 1999 found that nearly a quarter of Americans during the year had boycotted a company's products, or urged others to do so, because they didn't agree with the company's policies or activities. The survey found that nearly 90 percent of Americans held companies totally or partially responsible for keeping operations and supply chains free of child labor, and 95 percent said companies were responsible for preventing discrimination, protecting worker health and safety, and not harming the environment.[11] Nine of ten opinion leaders in Europe and America believe companies should continue efforts to become more socially responsible despite recession.[12]

Compounded by a seemingly unending spate of corporate scandal that began in 2001, the people's verdict was becoming clear, and it was soon obvious that complete denial of responsibility for the actions of their suppliers was simply an unworkable strategy, particularly for companies in vulnerable industries. As activists relentlessly exposed sweatshop conditions in overseas factories and the anti-globalization movement began to grow, several prominent companies began shifting their focus somewhat. By the late-1990s, even the companies that had at first stridently resisted efforts to make them assume responsibility for the activities in their supply chain—particularly in the light manufacturing, garment, and footwear industries—had begun to accept the need to make some effort toward controlling suppliers.

---

9. "Surveys Find Many Consumers Hold Companies Responsible for Their Actions," September 30, 1999, from *Press Room* on the PricewaterhouseCoopers Web site at *www.pwcglobal.com.*

10. "Consumers Skeptical of Corporate Citizenship Activities," *Holmes Report,* p. 1 at *www.holmesreport.com.*

11. "Surveys Find Many Consumers Hold Companies Responsible For Their Actions," op. cit.

12. "U.S. Attitudes on CSR Move Closer to Europe's," *Holmes Report,* April 25, 2002, p. 2, at *www.holmesreport.com.*

Early Efforts

Early efforts to force suppliers to take responsibility for their actions centered on the simple requirement for suppliers to sign a contract saying that they adhered to all national and local laws concerning employment and environmental policies. After all, most nations including China, India, Indonesia, El Salvador, or Mexico have at least nominal labor and environmental laws on the books, even if they are not well enforced. There are minimum wage laws in China, for example (about 30 cents an hour), and China officially restricts overtime to 36 hours per month. They also prohibit arbitrary fines, physical punishment, and pay reductions. There seemed to be ample numbers of laws; all companies needed to do was to make certain that their suppliers adhered to them.

This, of course, is the practical crux of the issue. As we have already seen in many examples, simply getting a supplier in a foreign country to sign a piece of paper saying that it does not break the law has obvious shortcomings. After all, most factories in China, India, Thailand, or Indonesia knew very well that inspections were unlikely and penalties would be nonexistent. It soon became apparent that whatever suppliers agreed to, without heavy pressure from the buying company enforced by independent inspection, such pledges usually had little practical effect on the way the factories actually conducted operations.

There were many obvious reasons for this. Governments often lack the resources and desire to enforce laws. The requirement for inspections is time consuming and costly and requires resources that most developing-country governments do not have. Bribery and corruption mean that it is not uncommon for local inspectors to ignore issues by failing to inspect factories or limiting their visits to preannounced tours or paper-based surveys. Above all, both suppliers and government officials too often feel that adhering to these laws will make them uncompetitive and erode their profits. Developing-world governments want to encourage foreign investment and continue to expand exports. What incentive would they have to apply laws that might, by their reckoning, increase wages and company costs and make their industries less competitive?

The Failure of Company Codes of Conduct

As it became more and more apparent that these national and local laws were unlikely to be enforced in developing economies, many companies changed tactics and began to require their key suppliers to agree to their own corporate codes of supplier conduct. By 2000, nearly every major multinational had begun to develop their own codes of conduct (which, pointlessly, usually required suppliers to comply with local labor and environmental laws), and set other requirements for livable wages, unionization rights, health and safety, and protection of the environment.

Most prominent companies were soon caught up in this rush toward developing individual company codes of conduct. "Five years ago, only a handful of companies addressed human rights," says BSR, the American research group and consultancy. "Today hundreds of companies have developed codes of conduct governing global labor practices, and policies integrating the Universal Declaration of Human Rights into their operations."[13]

But pursuing a supply chain policy limited to high-level and inherently unenforceable codes of conduct ultimately proved unworkable. It soon became obvious that simply asking subcontractors to enforce company codes of conduct was in effect no different than requiring them to obey national laws—unenforceable without independent monitoring, and unlikely to provide any real measure of protection for workers or the environment. Gap's Code of Vendor Conduct admitted openly that "People shouldn't assume that because we have a code, the garment manufacturers that get our business are in 100 percent compliance with its provisions 100 percent of the time; they are not."[14]

Wal-Mart provides a good example of the failure of suppliers to obey these codes of conduct. Following a three-month investigation, *Business Week* reported that employees in Zhongshan, China that were working for a supplier making Wal-Mart handbags, were forced to work extended hours at poverty wages and endure beatings as well as ruinous fines for small infractions. This despite the fact that these problems were in violation of Wal-Mart's vendor standards agreement, and the fact that Wal-Mart's hired auditors "missed most of the more serious abuses, including beatings and confiscated identity papers." Activists, such as the Shareholder Action Network, complained that Wal-Mart's monitoring program was dependent on auditors who had neither the trust of the workers nor the ability to complete an accurate audit, and called for "independent monitoring programs with local non-governmental and independent labor rights groups."[15]

---

13. "Introduction to Corporate Social Responsibility," *BSR White Papers*, May 2, 2002, at *www.bsr.org/BSRResources/WhitePaperDetail.*

14. Laura Slattery, "Codes of Conduct Not Preventing Worker Abuse," *The Irish Times*, March 15, 2002 as cited by the "Clean Clothes Campaign" Web site at *www.cleanclothes.org/codes/02-03-15.htm.*

15. "Vendor Standards Resolution Filed at Wal-Mart," Shareholder Action Network at *www.shareholderaction.org/walmart_res.cfm.*

Similarly, in 2000, Nike decided to discontinue all its contracts with factories in Cambodia after a television documentary asserted that these factories were using child labor. Although the company insisted that all of its suppliers had agreed to strict codes of conduct regulating underage employment, the company nonetheless was forced to withdraw from the country after the embarrassing revelations.[16]

"The codes show that companies are feeling the pressure of consumer concern," explained Grace Lally, a spokesperson for Globalise Resistance, reflecting the skepticism felt by many. "But they are a PR stunt for consumers in the West. I doubt the workers in sweatshops in China ever hear of the codes of conduct." Having already published their codes of conduct, however, companies were forced to act.[17]

"It is all exacerbated by the buying company's requirements for quality, their price pressure, and the turn-around time," says John Brookes, a veteran of many supplier audits and CEO of Manaxis. "A supplier organization will say, yes, they can meet any contract . . . but then they have to do whatever they can to get it done. They don't have the excess capacity, they don't have the people on the street that they can just pull in on a temporary basis to fulfill an order. The factory owners in China and in Asia and in Central America—they are not without morals and ethics—but they have a very real business necessity to make ends meet. And sometimes when corners are cut it is the workers and the environment that are exploited."[18]

Coming Clean

By 2001, it had become clear to most parties involved that something radical was required to end these types of supplier abuses. Companies were being criticized remorselessly and yet had found that their efforts to make their suppliers adhere to national laws or codes of conduct were largely unsuccessful. In 2002, Gap Inc. was forced to withdraw contracts from more than 120 factories worldwide because of compliance-related issues.[19] Something more had to be done.

One of the first companies to accept the need for a more honest appraisal of supplier performance, was ironically Nike, so often vilified for its supply chain policies. In cooperation with the Global Alliance for

---

16. Amy Kazmin, "U.S. Sportswear Giant May Be Ready for a Cambodia Comeback," *The Financial Times,* June 18, 2002.

17. Laura Slattery, op. cit.

18. Interview, August 15, 2003.

19. See "Our Program" at *www.gapinc.com/social_resp/sourcing/program.htm.*

Workers and Communities, they requisitioned a report on working conditions in nine Nike subcontractor factories in Indonesia. The results, openly published, were not good.

"The report detailed a variety of labor problems," says Gary Gereffi, professor of sociology and director of the Markets and Management Studies Program at Duke University, "including low wages, denial of the right to unionize, verbal and physical abuse by supervisors, sexual harassment, and forced overtime. The contents of the report are not surprising; similar findings were asserted throughout the 1990s."

"What is new about this report," explains Gereffi, "is that Nike paid for it, released it—and can't deny it. Nike's response to these problems will set new benchmarks that other apparel and footwear companies must match or else risk incurring relentless scrutiny by industry critics."[20]

This admission by companies of their implied responsibility and their acceptance of the need to fund and support supplier monitoring was a watershed, and began a new era of openness in reporting. A good example of this new movement can be seen when garment and sporting goods companies such as Eddie Bauer, Liz Claibourne, Nike, Reebok, Adidas-Salomon, and Levi Strauss became members of organizations such as the Fair Labor Association (FLA), a coalition of unions, consumer groups, NGOs, activists, and universities that was founded in 2001 to help companies monitor global supply chains. Having audited almost 50 factories around the world, the FLA's first account, published in 2003, provided a new level of honesty that, although still highly critical of supplier activities, has actually reflected well, rather than ill, on most of the companies involved.

"The companies deserve a lot of credit," says Michael Posner, an FLA board member and executive director of the Lawyers Committee for Human Rights, "for trusting the public with the grit as well as the gloss."[21]

Social and Environmental Reporting

Even while these early efforts to force suppliers to behave better continued, companies sought to demonstrate to investors and consumers that they were addressing these supply chain issues by issuing independent

---

20. Gary Gereffi, Ronie Garcia-Johnson, and Erika Sasser, "The NGO-Industrial Complex," *Foreign Policy,* no. 125, July/August, 2001, at *www.foreignpolicy.com*. Copyright 2001, Carnegie Endowment for International Peace.

21. Alison Maitland, "Big Brands Come Clean on Sweatshop Labour," *The Financial Times,* June 10, 2003, and *www.fairlabor.org*.

reports on their social and environmental policies and performance. It was one thing, after all, to inspect suppliers, but it was another thing entirely to report on corporate inspections procedures and their results so that the world would know of those efforts.

But with no internationally applicable standards upon which to be judged, and no real method for reporting their efforts, companies were free to design their own social accountability reports, which they began to do feverishly from the late 1990s forward. In fact, so rapid was the scramble to show participation that the number of companies providing some type of nonfinancial reporting leapt from a handful of companies (such as the Body Shop) in 1997 to more than 2,500 in 2003. A KPMG survey, for example, found that all of the chemicals and synthetics companies listed in the Global Financial Times 250 provided some type of SEAAR (Social and Ethical Accounting, Auditing, and Reporting) reporting in 2002; as did 86 percent of petrochemical companies, 84 percent of electronics and computer firms, 73 percent of automotive, and 58 percent of all oil and gas companies. The number of top FT 100 companies in Britain issuing reports increased from 24 percent in 1999 to 30 percent in 2002.[22]

Yet although the enthusiasm with which companies adopted nonfinancial reporting was welcomed by all parties, the results of these reporting efforts has often been less than satisfactory. The problem has been that these reports are too often a hodge-podge of self-serving and badly designed efforts, varying from a few pages littered with inspirational slogans and pictures to hundreds of pages containing dry and unrevealing environmental emissions data.

"By far the largest number of corporate responsibility reports," says Geoff Lane of PricewaterhouseCoopers, "deal exclusively with environmental issues such as air emissions, water discharges, use of natural resources and impacts on biodiversity and landscape. Some reports include detailed statistics showing emissions of a wide range of compounds, but little contextual information to help the reader judge the significance of those emissions; others concentrate on global environmental problems such as climate change without providing any information on their own greenhouse gas emissions. On the whole, these reports provide few clues as to the creation or destruction of environmental capital by the individual business."[23]

---

22. "Beyond Numbers," *KPMG Assurance and Advisory Services Booklet,* p. 17.

23. Geoff Lane and Melissa Carrington, "Measuring the Triple Bottom Line," *PricewaterhouseCoopers,* at *www.pwc.com/extweb/manissue.nsf/ 2e7e9636c6b92859852565e00073d2fd/dee94804c6db148685256cdf0036db78/$FILE/ TripleBtmLine.pdf.*

Alarmed by the hundreds of company codes of conduct and reports that were appearing, the Council of Economic Priorities, a nonprofit research group, examined 360 company codes of conduct. Their conclusions were highly critical of the movement toward individual codes and reports:

- "Internal codes are inherently expensive and inefficient to develop and monitor due to duplication of effort.
- Codes lack consistency, so consumers can't easily distinguish between strong and weak codes.
- The codes are rarely monitored, and if so, often not robustly.
- They tend to be unclear about interfacing with laws and customers that vary widely by country and region.
- Workers do not know about the codes."[24]

A survey completed by the OECD in 2002 found similarly dismal results when it came to company self-reporting efforts on supply chain activities. Of the 147 companies that they interviewed, only one of the companies provided detailed and independently verified reports on labor conditions within its supply chain. Many more (21) produced what the OECD termed "intermediate or limited reports" which failed to provide "substantive details on labour conditions in its supply chain."[25]

As SustainAbility authors noted in their 2001 report, "Corporate sustainability reporting is in danger of hitting a quality plateau." The average sustainability report, for example, jumped from 59 pages to 86 pages between 1999 and 2001 (which may not seem much unless you try to read them). SustainAbility calls this "carpet bombing" because readers are bombarded with huge amounts of information, much of which is of questionable relevance.[26]

The carpet bombing issue, the general criticism about the quality and veracity of most company nonfinancial sustainability reports, and the rapidity with which so many independent reporting initiatives were developing combined to make a single, consistent reporting method seem the only logical alternative.

24. Teresa Fabian, op. cit.

25. "Managing Working Conditions in the Supply Chain," *OECD Directorate for Financial, Fiscal and Enterprise Affairs Working Paper on International Investment*, no. 2002/2, June 2002, p. 4.

26. Alison Maitland, "Truants, Nerds and Supersonics," *The Financial Times*, November 18, 2002.

The Explosion of the SEAAR Movement

With this tormented history, by 2003 it was becoming obvious to all parties involved that what was required to ensure that developing world suppliers did not exploit their workers or the environment and that high-profile companies could avoid relentless criticism for those activities was for companies to take a standardized approach to judging supplier performance, to be independently verified and reported in an easily comparable, and readable format. This combined approach to supply chain monitoring and reporting is still referred to by many names—sustainability reporting, CSR, nonfinancial performance assessment, or triple-bottom-line accounting—but the movement is not nearly as indistinct or amorphous as the variety of names implies. Probably the most accurate title is social and ethical accounting, auditing, and reporting (SEAAR).

A consensus around this reporting framework has begun to grow rapidly, particularly in Europe. So rapidly in fact, that the Pricewaterhouse-Coopers' Reputation Assurance practice has predicted several key trends that reflect this consensus, which include:

- Within the next 10 years, the valuation methods used by Wall Street analysts will include new metrics—such as social performance and intellectual capital—to assess more accurately the net worth of a company.

- Within the next 5 years, 70 percent of North American and European companies will assign Board responsibility for areas of reputation and social responsibility.

- Within the next 10 years, the majority of global multinationals will publish a broader range of key nonfinancial information alongside financial data, covering areas such as environment, diversity, community development, and anti-corruption.

- The future credibility of audits will depend on the audit firm's ability to review and give opinions on nonfinancial performance, inevitably in conjunction with non-audit professionals, including nongovernmental organizations."[27]

There are many obvious benefits to this monitoring and reporting framework. A standardized approach ensures that suppliers share certification

---

27. "Surveys Find Many Consumers Hold Companies Responsible for Their Actions," September 30, 1999, from Press Room on the PricewaterhouseCoopers Web site at *www.pwcglobal.com.*

among the various buyers, each beginning to demand that they adhere to the respective buying company's independent requirements. Certification itself will be more meaningful, because it will incorporate leading practices and concepts, as will company reports to analysts and concerned investors.

Possibly most important of all, a standardized approach to reporting is beginning to bring benefits to purchasing companies themselves. Without accurate information on policies and performance, the media up until now has been left free to simply accept at times sensationalizing corporate misbehavior. Only third-party verification based on a standardized reporting process can provide companies with a strong defense when wrongly accused. Of course, accurate reporting also means that companies will no longer have "wiggle room" against accusations of poor employment or environmental practices, and therefore it will become even more imperative that they actually do begin to apply these codes of conduct—and monitor supplier performance—much more effectively.

The Mandatory Versus Voluntary Debate

In many ways, the rise of international standards and certification bodies has suddenly transformed the entire debate as to the respective responsibilities of government and business. Over the past five years, companies lobbied strongly to resist mandatory reporting or independent auditing, citing fears of bureaucracy, cost, and lack of valid comparisons. And although several national governments and even supranational groups such as the EU Commission have moved toward requiring nonfinancial reporting (as we see in the next chapter), companies have so far been successful in arguing that so many standards exist that it is unworkable until a preferred set of performance and process standards become recognized by the international community. Those in favor of mandatory reporting requirements argue that with the level of privatization and deregulation occurring in most developed economies, the corporate community can't have it both ways—they must accept some form of mandatory regulation, or create an acceptable system for protecting workers and the environment themselves.

Ultimately, the argument may have already been resolved simply by *fiat,* for two reasons. First, the combined effect of NGO, investor, and consumer pressure has forced companies to appreciate the value of more meaningful—less easily criticized—reports on the social and environmental supply chain performance. Companies have suddenly become aware that their efforts at selective reporting are not only not helping them, but effectively making things worse, laying them open to greater criticism for hypocrisy.

Second, and equally important, the standards movement has coalesced around several major performance and process standards and reporting processes much more quickly than anyone could have anticipated. Today, a handful of these (Chapter Ten) have emerged as leaders, and are quickly being adopted by the most progressive multinationals. And as a 2002 OECD survey revealed, for those companies that do have codes of labor and employment practice, the "vast majority of these companies mention all of the core labour standards." They concluded that this convergence was surprising given the wide variety of codes being developed by companies just three years ago.[28] Growing acceptance of these standardized codes of supplier conduct is creating a *de facto* requirement for companies to adopt these standards as a matter of competition, thereby undermining the need for states to make such reporting mandatory.

In fact, this certification process brings many benefits to the governments of third-world economies as well. "In countries with stringent, rigorously-enforced labor and environmental laws," says Gary Gereffi, professor of sociology and director of the Markets and Management Studies Program at Duke University, "certification provides a private layer of governance that moves beyond state borders to shape global supply chains. In countries with nascent or ineffective labor and environmental legislation, certification can draw attention to uneven standards and help mitigate these disparities. The challenge is for states to accept certification not as a threat but as an opportunity to reinforce labor and environmental goals within their sovereign territory and beyond."

Finally, this type of standards certification process can help to ensure that global trade remains unfettered. "While certification will never replace the state," says Gereffi, "it is quickly becoming a powerful tool for promoting worker rights and protecting the environment in an era of free trade. These new mechanisms of transnational private governance exist alongside and within national and international regimes like the North American Free Trade Agreement, complementing and, in some cases, bolstering their efforts."[29]

These emerging standards, codes, and reporting guidelines then promise to revolutionize the relationship between companies and their suppliers, and are rapidly becoming an important strategic concern for companies worldwide. Importantly, as we will see, this standardization and reporting framework is taking on great momentum, particularly in Europe and Japan, with a level of enthusiasm that is largely unappreciated in the United States. How that dramatic shift occurred and why it is so important to U.S. corporations is what we explore next.

---

28. "Managing Working Conditions in the Supply Chain," OECD Directorate for Financial, Fiscal and Enterprise Affairs Working Paper on International Investment, no. 2002/2, June 2002, p. 1.

29. Gary Gereffi, Ronie Garcia-Johnson, and Erika Sasser, op. cit.

CHAPTER FIVE

The SEAAR Movement

*A*s a result of these various internal
and external pressures, many progressive companies in the United States,
but particularly in Europe, Japan, and Australia, have chosen to implement
broad programs of supplier monitoring and auditing. Equally important, as
part of the movement toward greater corporate social responsibility that is
occurring worldwide, many companies (more than 2,500) have begun to
publish reports that detail their social and environmental policies and
activities (as well as those of their suppliers). This reporting movement,
known as SEAAR — Social and Ethical Accounting, Auditing, and
Reporting — promises to have a profound effect on how companies in the
future will manage their extended supply chain.

Although the SEAAR movement in the United States still remains less well developed or recognized, the shift in focus toward this social and environmental reporting framework, particularly in Europe over the last three years, has been nothing short of remarkable. In fact, such has been the pressure and enthusiasm for corporate social responsibility among the European business community, that most major corporations have developed some type of SEAAR-based CSR programs (and, unlike in the United States, in the European context the two terms, Corporate Social Responsibility and SEAAR, are used almost interchangeably).

These efforts span the full gamut of corporate dedication, from simple and unenforceable pledges to adhere to recognized labor and environmental codes of conduct through to the adoption of international standards covering social and environmental behavior, with full and audited reporting. And the numbers continue to grow. The World Business Council for Sustainable Development, based in Geneva, has over 160 multinationals as members. CSR Europe, one of the most influential forums for education and dialogue on the subject, has 59 company members and 16 national partnership organizations, with a total membership of 500,000.[1] The Global Reporting Initiative, as we have seen, listed more than 2500 companies filing some type of social and environmental reports in 2002 (see Figure 5-1).

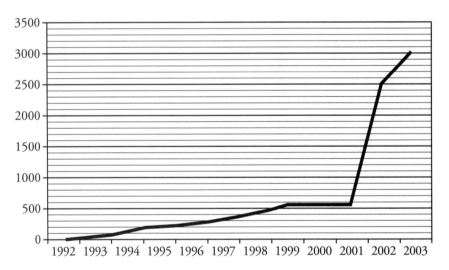

Source: Corporate Register at *www.corporateregister.com/pdf/Guide.pdf.*

FIGURE 5-1 International Nonfinancial Reports in the Last Decade

---

1. CSR Web site at *www.csreurope.org/whatwedo/default.asp.*

What is more, corporate social and environmental reporting, at least in Europe, is no longer the domain only of large and international companies. A recent survey by the European Commission of 7,600 companies in 19 European nations, found that 50 percent of all European SMEs (small- and medium-size enterprises) have now adopted some type of CSR program.[2] A similar survey by Grant Thornton found that European SMEs have moved much more quickly to adopt advanced CSR standards than previously thought. The survey indicates that 41 percent of small- and medium-size companies in Europe have a formal environmental responsibility program in place, with many more having policies in place to cover social and corporate governance issues.

"We were surprised about the extent to which corporate social responsibility has been embraced by SMEs across Europe, especially the number of companies that have formal policies in place in a number of areas ranging from environmental responsibility to ethical sourcing," says Andrew Godfrey, Head of European services for Grant Thornton.

"SMEs have done this quietly, without hype and without much support. And as CSR continues to climb up the boardroom agenda in listed companies, we believe we will see further growth of social responsibility in the SME sector."[3]

So why have European companies adopted SEAAR in such a robust and enthusiastic way? There are many reasons.

EU Government Legislation

First, for the past several years in Europe, the government has supported strongly, if not actually led, the CSR initiative. The **European Union** has pressed for corporations to provide wider reporting on such issues as environmental and social performance, and has set up a forum for promoting CSR programs throughout Europe, with the EU Commission in July of 2001 calling for voluntary "triple-bottom-line" reporting from all EU companies. The Commission also approved a resolution on CSR in 2002 that proposes the creation of a standardized multistakeholder platform for judging CSR criteria, and has provided funding to study the possibility of developing an EU Ombudsman for monitoring and assessing European company social and environmental activities in developing countries.

---

2. *www.ethicalcorp.com/NewsTemplate.asp?IDNum=243*.

3. "Formal Environmental Policies in Place at 41% of Companies," Grant Thornton International Press Release, June 2002, from *www.gti.org/press/pressrelease_june.htm*.

Similarly, in 2001 the **French National Assembly** passed a mandatory requirement for nonfinancial reporting, that came as a surprise to many observers. Always strong on workers rights, of course, with its history of powerful trade unions and close corporate and government ties, France has nonetheless not traditionally been known for this type of corporate transparency or concern for the environment in the past. But in 2001, the French Parliament passed the Nouvelles Régulations Economiques (NRE), a set of French laws that requires French corporations listed on the "premier marché" (first league) of the CAC to make mandatory disclosure on social and environmental issues in their annual reports against a template of community, labor, and environmental standards.[4] The NRE went into effect in 2003, and made reporting on issues such as labor policies, water and energy use, and emissions of greenhouse gasses obligatory as part of a company's annual report. Organizations are also required to explain their social and environmental programs and their efforts to educate and train employees about good environmental and ethical management.

Britain, too, has moved toward enshrining at least the reporting requirements of corporate social responsibility in law. In 2002, the Trade and Industry Secretary, a British cabinet-level post, officially took on the job for advocating corporate social responsibility (the British remain the only nation to have a cabinet-level position officially dedicated to CSR), and the government has made a straightforward case for the use of public policies to promote standard codes of conduct and to encourage social and environmental reporting.

This government effort came on the back of moves by the British insurance industry—representing corporations that control 20 percent of the UK stock market—to require British companies to report on their policies for managing risks in social and environmental policies. As part of a move toward greater transparency and disclosure, British law also now requires pension fund trustees to declare to what extent they take into account social, environmental, and ethical issues when making their investment decisions.

These moves by the government to support social and environmental reporting were a direct reflection of the British public's demand for higher standards of corporate behavior. Half those responding to Mori's 2002 UK corporate responsibility study, for example, said that business should pay as much attention to society and the environment as it does to financial performance. Almost half of those interviewed (44 percent) said that social

---

4. For a detailed explanation and critique see *www.sa-intl.org/press_releases/NRE_PressRelease.pdf.*

responsibility played a very important part in their purchasing decisions. This number has almost doubled in the past five years.[5]

With an extraordinarily active group of consultancies, forums, initiatives, and advocates, Britain is very much at the center of the SEAAR movement. UK companies are now pioneering new levels of transparency and reporting, with corporations such as British Telecom, Diageo, British Airways, and even Shell and BP/Amoco joining innovative companies such as the Body Shop and Co-Operative Bank in providing clear and detailed company reports on environmental and employment policies. In SustainAbility's recent "Top 50 Sustainability Companies," the top seven companies were all British.

Possibly the most important contribution to CSR made by the British has been the development of the Ethical Trading Initiative in 1997, a collaborative effort between the UK government, British industry, and various NGOs and standards development bodies. The ETI (see Chapter Ten) encourages adoption of agreed labor and environmental standards, and promotes open social and environmental reporting, and is quickly becoming one of the de facto cornerstones of the European SEAAR framework.

One of the most progressive countries in terms of environmental policies and SEAAR reporting, **Germany** is also a leader in reporting initiatives, accounting for nearly 80 percent of the Eco-Management and Audit Scheme (EMAS) reports filed in 2002. Similarly, over half of Europe's 40 facilities that have received SA 8000 certification (guaranteeing that the facilities meet high social and labor rights standards) are in **Italy,** and the Italians have recently launched the Italian Resource Centre on Corporate Social Responsibility, an online database providing best practices and a guide to university and business school CSR courses.[6]

Many other EU countries have also taken measures toward requiring mandatory SEAAR reporting. For example, since 1995 **Denmark** has required "green accounting" by its top 3,000 firms, those that have significant environmental impacts. **The Netherlands** passed legislation in 1999 that requires several hundred of its companies to report on their environmental management systems. **Norway** passed the Accounting Act (Regnskapsloven) in 1999 that requires all companies to include health, safety, and environmental information in their annual financial reports, and **Sweden** has required that environmental performance information from 20,000 companies be included in their annual reports.[7] In total, companies

---

5. Alison Maitland, "Social Reporting: Pressures Mount for Greater Disclosure," *FT.com,* December 10, 2002.

6. Italy Country Profile, CSR Europe Web site at *www.csreurope.org/partners/default. asp?pageid=256.*

7. Paul Scott, "The Pitfalls in Mandatory Reporting," *Environmental Finance,* April 2001, p. 24.

from more than 13 EU countries were providing reports in 2002. (For a good summary of the many corporate responsibility and reporting initiatives now flourishing in Europe, see Appendix A).

On top of this flurry of European business and government activity in the area, the academic community has also rallied strongly in support of the CSR and nonfinancial reporting movement. Beginning with a group of prominent academics calling for a wholesale rethinking of the way business education was being offered in European universities, the result is a collaborative effort among major **European business schools,** the EU, and several major multinationals to integrate the core principles and values of CSR into European business school MBA and executive course curriculum.

One of the most important efforts in this area is the European Academy on Corporate Social Responsibility, an initiative that involves many of the major business schools in Europe: Copenhagen Business School, Cranfield University School of Management, ESADE Business School, ASHRIDGE, INSEAD, and many others. The academy's eventual goal is to persuade some 250 business schools and universities in Europe to adopt their CSR curriculum. Their stated mission is to "help companies achieve profitability, sustainable growth and human progress by placing Corporate Social Responsibility (CSR) in the mainstream of business practice." Supporting them in this effort are many of the world's most powerful corporations, including GM, Volkswagen AG, Nike, Danone, Coca- Cola, IBM, Levi Strauss, Motorola, Microsoft, and many others.

"The greatest critique of MBA training at the moment is that it is out of date," says Etienne Davignon, the director of the Academy. "If teaching on CSR doesn't come fairly soon, businesses will lose interest—not in the topic but in the business schools."[8]

Accordingly, the academy is sponsoring a series of research programs, funded by the EU Commission and with additional support from European corporations, that will help better define CSR, setting parameters around its activities, and helping companies apply policies and principles effectively.[9]

This push to incorporate CSR into a core curriculum promises to revolutionize European business education, instilling in future business leaders new views on the role of business in sustainability and social and environmental policies. The new coursework will include classes to help future managers deal with pressure groups and NGOs, to learn new accounting and reporting requirements, and to appreciate the complexities inherent in a global supply chain.

---

8. Roger Cowe, "Embracing Companies' Social Role," *The Financial Times,* May 10, 2002, p. 6.

9. Ibid.

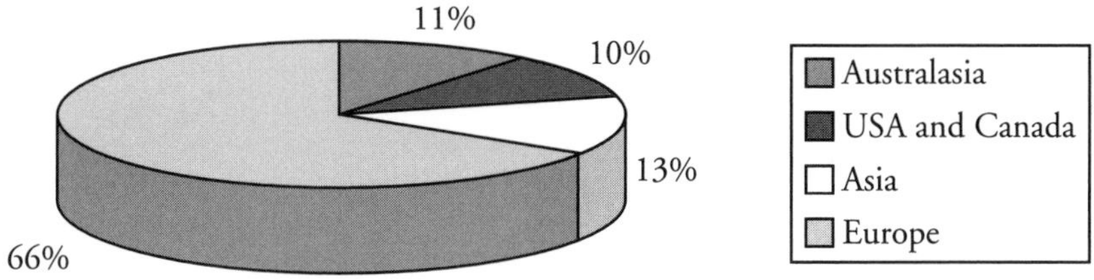
11%
10%
13%
66%
Australasia
USA and Canada
Asia
Europe

Source: Corporate Register at *www.corporateregister.com/pdf/Guide.pdf.*

FIGURE 5-2 Nonfinancial Reporting by Region in 2000

Moreover, this business and government-sponsored drive to adopt CSR programs is not limited to the European Union. **Japan,** itself going through a similar exercise in SEAAR realization, has the highest level of social and environmental reporting by companies in the world, with strong reports coming from powerful multinationals such as Toyota and Honda. Japan has the highest number of companies (more than 2,000 in 2001) that have been certified to the ISO 14001 environmental standard (see Chapter Ten). **Australia,** a strong proponent of SEAAR, particularly in their mining sector, has begun to provide tax incentives to companies that demonstrate that they have strong environmental and social policies, and under their new Financial Services Reform Act (March 2003), now requires investment firms to disclose the extent to which labor standards or environmental, social, or ethical considerations are taken into account by analysts (see Figure 5-2).[10]

The United Nations

Equally important, in terms of an endorsement for SEAAR, in August of 2003, the United Nations issued their "Draft Norms on the Responsibilities of Transnational Corporations and Other Business Enterprises with Regard to Human Rights," which describes in detail the responsibilities of companies for human and labor rights. Although not binding in law, the standards are intended to be adopted by governments and then used as a basis for corporate behavior. Their sanction is at this point limited to a

10. William Baue, "Australia to Require Investment Firms to Disclose How They Take SRI into Account," *Social Funds.com,* January 3, 2003 at *www.socialfunds.com/news/print.cgi?sfArticleId=998;* Paul Scott, "Reporting All Over the World," *Environmental Finance,* December 2000–January 2001, p. 36 at *www.nextstep.co.uk/uploadedfiles/pdf/article5.pdf.*

range of "mechanisms" (mostly techniques for naming and shaming through investigation and censuring companies violating human rights policies), but the "norms" are probably most valuable in that they incorporate best practice thinking in terms of human rights laws, standards implementation, and best practices for monitoring and coaching suppliers, and complement the U.N.'s Global Compact by adding important new levels of detail.

The SEAAR Movement in the United States

Possibly even more remarkable than this rapid acceptance of nonfinancial reporting in Europe, Japan, and Australia is the fact that, with a few notable exceptions, on our side of the Atlantic this SEAAR movement has largely failed to materialize. Although most U.S. companies now boast a strong program of corporate social responsibility, the approach by both government and the business community in the United States is on the whole markedly different from that found in Europe, Japan, and Australia.

Coming off of a series of devastating corporate scandals, when U.S. business leaders, politicians, and the media continually refer to the need for greater "corporate social responsibility," the phrase has widely been interpreted to mean better corporate governance—in terms of excessive executive stock options, off-balance sheet investments, or touting worthless stocks to investors. This emphasis on corporate corruption, however, can be misleading. It is true, of course, that many of the early tenets of corporate social responsibility originated in the United States, and certainly most U.S. companies use the phrase commonly on their Web sites and in their public relations announcements. Yet almost universally, these programs tend to have a strong emphasis on philanthropy and a marketing "message" of integrity that can appear disingenuous to skeptics.

Pointing out the growing gap in perception and enthusiasm for the SEAAR-type of CSR in the United Kingdom and the United States, the Holmes Report notes that "It seems inconceivable that the U.S. administration—particularly the Bush administration—would create a cabinet level position devoted to corporate ethics. But that's just one difference between the approach to corporate social responsibility here and the approach in the UK."[11]

---

11. "In the UK, a More Formal Approach to Social Responsibility," *Holmes Report*, p. 3 at *www.holmesreport.com.*

In fact, when President George W. Bush launched his initiative for Corporate Social Responsibility with much fanfare in the autumn of 2002, he did not mention nonfinancial reporting, the environment, labor or employment rights, or the growing responsibility for a global supply chain. The administration's focus (now sadly relegated to a URL link from the Whitehouse Web page), was exclusively on the corporate accounting fraud that had rocked the markets and discredited the SEC. Unlike the accepted wisdom among the rest of the OECD economies (with the possible exception of Canada), few U.S. company leaders seem to understand CSR to primarily involve applying international labor or environmental standards throughout their supply chain, or reporting on their social and environmental performance as part of their annual report.

Accordingly, comparatively few U.S. companies have adopted international standards or vigorous program of nonfinancial reporting. Of the more than 200 largest multinationals that are members of the United Nation's Global Compact, a forum designed to help corporations agree on standards of social and environmental policies in developing nations (see Chapter Eight), only five of the major U.S. companies—Cisco Systems, Dupont, Hewlett-Packard, Nike, and Pfizer—have joined.[12]

Similarly, in a joint 2002 study by the United Nations Environmental Program (UNEP) and the NGO SustainAbility, which ranked corporations according to the quality of their reporting on corporate governance, environmental and social polices, U.S. companies fared badly. Only seven of the top 50 reporting companies were American-based, and these tended to be well-established transnational companies (see Figure 5-3).

Moreover, except for those given by the Conference Board or BSR (Business for Social Responsibility), the two major U.S. forums in this area, there are comparatively few U.S. conferences concerned with CSR or SEAAR, and most U.S. business schools remain focused on traditional business accounting and ethics courses. Almost none of the major universities or business schools offer any courses on triple-bottom-line accounting. There are a few notable exceptions. Alice Tepper Marlin, the President of Social Accountability International, and her husband teach a course on CSR and SA 8000 at New York's Stern Business School, and Elliot Schrage, former Vice-President for Corporate Affairs at Gap, provides a seminar on CSR issues at Columbia. For most universities and business schools, however, CSR or ethical supply chain issues are usually omitted altogether, or else

---

12. Laura Turengano, "UN Global Compact: Many US Companies in Wait-and-See Mode," *Inside Giving,* July 22, 2002 at *www.globalpolicy.org/reform/business/2002/0722insidegiving.htm;* see also "Newsroom: Press Releases and Announcements," CERES, August 17, 2003 at *www.ceres.org/newsroom/press/ceresirrcrel.htm.*

1	The Co-operative Bank	26	British Airways
2	Novo Nordisk	27	SAS
3	BAA	28	Alcan
4	BT	29	General Motors
5	Rio Tinto	30	Henkel
6	Royal Dutch/Shell	31	Kesko
7	BP	32	Novartis International
8	Bristol-Meyers Squibb	33	Unilever
9	ITT Flygt	34	RWE
10	South African Breweries	35	Bayer
11	BASF	36	Deutsche Telekom
12	Volkswagen	37	Procter & Gamble
13	WIMC	38	Swiss Re
14	CIS Co-operative Insurance	39	Toyota
15	Baxter International	40	BMW
16	Cable and Wireless	41	Tesco
17	Ricoh Japan	42	AWG
18	Kirin Brewery	43	Danone
19	Chiquita Brands International	44	AWG
20	United Utilities	45	Aracruz Celulose
21	Suncor Energy	46	Sony
22	BC Hydro	47	Tepco
23	Eskom	48	Suez
24	Matsushita Electric	49	Credit-Suisse
25	Manaaki Whenua	50	Adidas-Salomon

FIGURE 5-3   SustainAbility's Top 50 Companies, 2002

integrated loosely into other philosophy or management courses. And as the Holmes Report astutely noted, it is hard to imagine the Bush Administration pressing for a cabinet-level position for corporate social responsibility or mandatory triple-bottom-line reporting.

It is not that U.S. companies are not taking the issue of an ethical supply chain seriously—most U.S. companies have during the past decade put in place often very sophisticated processes and systems to demonstrate compliance with OSHA (Occupational Safety and Health Administration), EOE (Equal Opportunity Employment), or EHS (Environmental Health and Safety) regulations. The Global Environmental Management Initiative (GEMI), for example, is a nonprofit organization of leading companies dedicated to fostering environmental, health, and safety excellence and corporate citizenship worldwide. Through the collaborative efforts of its members, GEMI also promotes a worldwide business ethic for environmental, health, and safety management and sustainable development through example and leadership. Over the last 10 years, GEMI has developed a series of documents, reports, and tools that help business achieve environmental, health, and safety (EHS) excellence.[13]

It is simply that the vast majority of U.S. companies do not at this time seem to accept that the same level of monitoring, adherence, and reporting necessary for OSHA or EHS in the United States should apply to overseas operations, particularly if those operations are merely outsourced or subcontracted. Nor, in any case, do they see these types of activities, at home or abroad, as falling under the umbrella of corporate social responsibility. More to the point, in a litigious society, many companies in the United States are still simply hesitant to admit any relationship—much less responsibility—for overseas activities with regard to subcontractors or an extended supply chain and labor or environmental practices.

"Over the past decade," says Paul Scott, Director at Next Step Consulting, "it has become apparent that U.S. companies are reluctant to publish any environmental information not already in the public domain, or required by law. This is largely due to corporate lawyers protecting their companies from potential lawsuits by restricting the flow of such information—considered necessary in view of the litigious nature of American culture, and the high costs associated with losing claims brought in U.S. courts."

"This has had the unfortunate effect," concludes Scott, "of discouraging even progressive, innovative companies from publishing anything more than generalized, anodyne reports with a strong public relations focus."[14]

The Director of Corporate Social Responsibility for one major U.S. multinational that is leading the way in European-style SEAAR in the United States recently described the differences between the European and U.S. approaches to sustainability issues as being like "night and day." "Although things have changed somewhat in the last 6 months," he concluded, "sustainability, as a concept, is still not really understood in the U.S."

"There is a lot of pressure for this type of work to be done in Europe," he contends. "The standards setting is being done over there; GRI has moved over there . . . they wish they had more visibility from their U.S. counterparts . . . but there is this huge disconnect in terms of the people in Brussels [and the U.S.]."

The Holmes Report agrees: "In the U.S., there's a greater focus on human resources issues, like diversity, or equal opportunity for women, and

---

13. See "New Paths to Business Value: Strategic Sourcing—Environment, Health and Safety," *The Global Environmental Management Initiative,* March 2001 at *www.gemi.org/newpath.pdf.*

14. Paul Scott, "Reporting All Over The World," *Environmental Finance,* December 2000–January 2001, p. 36 at *www.nextstep.co.uk/uploadedfiles/pdf/article5.pdf.*

there's more direct corporate philanthropy. In the UK and Europe, it's more formalized, and there's more rigor applied to reporting social performance."[15]

That difference in perception and approach extends to the environmental side of the equation as well. In July of 2003, CERES, the U.S.-based coalition of NGOs, unions, and investors that founded the Global Reporting Initiative, surveyed 20 of the world's largest companies on their attempts to monitor performance and to put in place environmental policies that would reduce the risk of climate change. The results showed again that U.S. companies fell well behind the activities of their European counterparts. Based on an assessment of 14 different key activities that companies should be taking to help monitor and address environmental risk—board-level reviews, performance monitoring, producing SEAAR reports—the survey showed the dramatic divergence between the way that U.S. and European companies were approaching these issues. Among the petroleum producers, British Petroleum and Royal Dutch Schell had completed all of the 14 activities, but ChevronTexaco, ExxonMobil, and ConocoPhillips had only completed three or four of those activities each. GE and ExxonMobil had never even conducted a board-level review.[16]

"In Europe," says Allen White, the cofounder and former acting CEO of the Global Reporting Initiative, "you can talk about CSR reporting and be very comfortable that a) people understand it, and b) they are not afraid of it, and c) they are ready to go. There exists a common understanding. In the U.S. there is no such common understanding."[17]

The CSR Schism

It is this very different approach to CSR that is already causing a good deal of confusion and friction between the U.S. and European business communities. Although it is not by any means an absolute—not all European companies are adopting SEAAR programs, and several U.S. multinationals are leading the SEAAR cause—there is still an enormous gap in the way that the vast majority of businessmen in the United States and in Europe understand the direction of the CSR movement.

15. "In the UK, A More Formal Approach to Social Responsibility," *Holmes Report*, pp. 3–4 at *www.holmesreport.com.*

16. Tony Tassell, "U.S. Groups 'Worst' at Tackling Climate Change," *The Financial Times,* July 10, 2003, p. 16; see also "Corporate Governance and Climate Change: Making the Connection," CERES at *www.ceres.org/newsroom/press/ceresirrcrel.htm.*

17. Interview on August 12, 2003.

At the heart of this widely differing emphasis is a fundamentally different view of what corporate social responsibility means. Unlike most European companies who view CSR policy through the lens of reporting on a company's social and environmental performance in its extended supply chain, U.S. companies tend to see CSR as almost a domestic and financial accounting-based issue. Very few U.S. companies understand CSR to primarily involve applying international labor or environmental standards throughout their supply chain, or reporting on their social and environmental performance as part of their annual report.

Instead, most U.S. companies still seem to be interpreting CSR to mean a combination of good deeds and improved corporate governance. In fact, few U.S. executives, according to all evidence, seem to appreciate these differing interpretations, or the rapid emergence of international standards and reporting frameworks that will soon become as common and expected (if not required by law in many nations) as normal financial reporting in Europe and Japan.

What is possibly more important and revealing is that the press in the United States, still broadly seems to perceive CSR in the context of corporate governance and recent accounting scandals, or more broadly as a company's responsibility for assisting in global issues such as the AIDS/HIV pandemic, free trade, or debt relief policies. In many ways, because there is such a wide difference in understanding and interpretation, U.S. business leaders seem not to be appreciating how seriously the European governments, businesses, investment community, and general population are taking this drive toward transparency and social and environmental accountability and reporting.

Why has the U.S. business community on the whole been so different in its approach to CSR and SEAAR? Like most of us who see evidence of this remarkable schism daily, Frank Vogl, from Transparency International, believes that the U.S. business community has failed to appreciate this rapidly expanding SEAAR movement in Europe, remaining largely oblivious to the likely repercussions of such divergent policies. He blames this difference in approach on four things:

- **Ignorance.** Many CEOs do not know what is happening in Europe, they do not adequately understand the NGO pressures, they do not appreciate the range of stakeholder concerns and, unlike Jack Welch, they do not see the power of a focus on values for their business survival.
- **Complacency.** Many business leaders believe they are doing a great job on the ethics front. After all, their firms have not had a major public crisis—yet. CEOs feel peer pressure on business profits, not on integrity performance. CEOs take great pride in being listed in the annual surveys by *Fortune* magazine and by *The Financial*

Times/PriceWaterhouseCoopers of the most respected companies. Issues of corporate integrity and accountability are not criteria that feature prominently in these surveys, which tend to focus on financial performance.

- **U.S. Government and Public Pressure Has Been Modest in a Number of Integrity Areas.** U.S. companies have not faced the same levels of governmental pressure and public outcry in many of the social responsibility areas, as have the Europeans. Respect for capitalism's virtues sometimes runs deeper on this side of the Atlantic. Americans appear more tolerant, for example, about the massive remuneration given to U.S. CEOs, which dwarfs compensation to top European and Japanese business leaders. In Europe top executive pay is often seen as an ethics issue—in this country we accept it just as business as usual.

- **Mistaking PR for Integrity Management.** Misunderstandings about the importance of social responsibility issues have led corporations to view them in purely public relations and advertising terms. . . . Many firms wrongly believe that PR and advertising can secure their integrity reputations. Frequently, this muddled thinking is the product of efforts by consulting firms, who promote "reputation management" and "reputation assurance" services by highlighting the negatives and the scandal stories (Nike, Exxon and so forth). Moreover, by striving to substitute PR and advertising for substantive integrity management, companies evidently fail to see that their action can serve only to strengthen public distrust over time, while adding credibility to NGOs who, by similar advertising means, attack global corporations.[18]

Alice Tepper Marlin, President of Social Accountability International, thinks this yawning gap in perceptions regarding CSR and SEAAR in Europe and the United States has only been further hampered by the lack of media attention on these types of CSR-related issues.

"One problem in the U.S. over the past two years," says Marlin, "is that terrorism and the two wars has dominated the news so strongly that there isn't room for much other news—so it is very, very hard to get a different news story in now. So people are thinking much less about policy issues and human rights issues, there is very little written and very little attention other than terrorism and Iraq, the Middle East and Afghanistan right now."

"That is not true in Europe," she concludes, "where there is a much wider variety of stories and greater coverage."[19]

---

18. Frank Vogl, "Corporate Integrity and Globalization: The Dawning of a New Era of Accountability & Transparency," a speech to The G. Albert Shoemaker Program in Business Ethics at the Smeal College of Business Administration, Pennsylvania State University, March 23, 2001 at *www.transparency.org/speeches/vogl_shoemaker.html*.

19. Interview, June 24, 2003.

Many activists take a more cynical view, claiming that the reason U.S. companies don't want to accept transparent, third-party reporting is because they have too often made extravagant and emotion-ridden claims about their dedication to corporate responsibility and the environment, and are afraid that open reporting will prove that those claims were simply marketing hype. CorpWatch even awards "green Oscars" for companies that have excelled in this type of deceit, "giving human rights, social and environmental abuses a patina of respectability." Nike, under criticism for alleged inaccuracies in its claims of activities that it was pursuing in Asia to stop child labor during the events that lead up to the *Nike* v. *Kasky* lawsuit, even decided to withhold its yearly corporate social responsibility report in 2002, only further fueling allegations that it was because they had misrepresented their actions in the report in the first place.[20]

Whatever the true reasons for U.S. corporate reticence, these broadly different interpretations of CSR mean that too often the two business communities—European and American—are talking at cross purposes. To illustrate the point, when I mention CSR to a European businessman, he or she inevitably assumes that I will be concerned about what standards or certifications they have. They are thoroughly familiar with ISO 14001, SA 8000, the Ethical Trading Initiative, or the Global Reporting Initiative. Adoption of triple-bottom-line accounting is generally accepted as the future norm.

When, on the other hand, I mention CSR to a U.S. business audience, I inevitably get a response concerned with what steps the company is taking to avoid corporate accounting scandals, what Sarbanes-Oxley will mean to them, how much the company gives to the local community, or its sponsorship of the local soccer league. The mention of SA 8000 or the GRI is almost uniformly met with total incomprehension.

The Repercussions of the Conflicting Interpretations

So what are the possible repercussions of this growing chasm of understanding and application?

Skeptics contend that the enormously different interpretations of CSR will only add to the friction that has recently been witnessed between the United States on issues as far ranging as farm support, steel subsidies, corporate taxation, war in Iraq, and the development of the International

---

20. Vanessa Houlder, "Shades of Green," *The Financial Times,* August 19, 2002, p. 10.

Criminal Court. With the European Union quickly moving—both by legislation and through consensus—toward requiring companies to provide accurate reports on social and environmental performance (including contract and supplier performance), the issue may have important political and economic repercussions in the near future.

After all, this new European and Japanese approach to SEAAR requires a fundamental rethinking of how a company manages its supply chain policies, particularly when it comes to suppliers and subcontractors in foreign markets. The European approach to nonfinancial reporting accepts that transparency and rigor of reporting will mean companies really must change their policies to reflect what they say, and therefore must develop new ways of influencing, monitoring, and reporting on subcontractors.

This dilemma can have two obvious results. First, it can be disruptive, creating a further divide between the Euro/Japanese approach and that of the United States. The European interpretation, by all logic, will soon by necessity be forced upon the American companies doing business in the European Union. Because it is government driven, EU directives will quickly move all EU companies toward this higher standard, and presumably investors and consumers will reward them accordingly. By all accounts, within the next few years, triple-bottom-line accounting and SEAAR-type reporting will become a minimum and expected standard. If U.S. companies, in turn, are required to comply with these reporting regulations, it could precipitate a WTO-type crisis, with these reporting requirements labeled as a form of tariff against imports—both between the EU and the United States, and also between the EU and developing labor markets.

"Probably it will be a trade issue, eventually," says John Brookes of Manaxis. "Because just as with ISO 9000, and ISO 14000 before, European customers will put pressure on American suppliers, and American suppliers will be encouraged and eventually comply."[21]

This dividing effect may already be apparent. "This Anglo/European drive toward CSR and triple-bottom-line reporting is beginning to bring pressure on U.S. companies, as well," points out Jim Kartalia, President of Entegra Corporation and a specialist on risk and reputation management. "Any American corporation that wants to do business globally is going to be forced to address these issues. The EU is pushing this legislation," he concludes, "and they are going to force American companies to comply or else they are not going to get business."[22]

---

21. Interview, August 15, 2003.
22. Interview, January 23, 2002.

"In Europe, trends toward environmental supply chain management are already visible," says Joseph Carter, Professor of Supply Management at Arizona State University. "Although, an average U.S.-based firm may not be thinking along environmental issues while developing corporate strategy, pressures from global firms, including those based in the United States, are likely to influence other firms to follow the European trend."[23]

Dr. Judy Henderson, Chair of the Global Reporting Initiative, thinks the two different approaches to SEAAR may have a more contentious result. "What I would be more concerned about," she says, "is that we get to the situation which we have with financial accounting, where Europe goes in one direction and the U.S. goes in the other . . . and then 70 years down the track they are trying desperately to harmonize the reporting framework and standards. That is why we thought with the GRI that we could get in on the ground floor as an international framework, and we could sort of leapfrog that dichotomy between the U.S. and Europe."[24]

Either way, it is not inconceivable that by mandating SEAAR, European and Japanese governments are moving quickly to what could be another dramatic ideological trade conflict with the U.S. government and business community.

On the other hand, a more optimistic view holds that the drive toward mandatory SEAAR, particularly if it is accompanied by competition, and a general acceptance by NGOs, consumers, and investors that this level is good and necessary, may simply become a part of how all business is conducted in the future, and may rapidly be adopted by U.S. businesses as well. On an organizational level, these standards will turn out to be "leading practice" both in terms of investment and in terms of risk and reputation management. European companies will set new standards for "transparency" through their third-party auditing and verified social and environmental reporting that initially will provide a certain competitive edge to European multinationals, forcing U.S. multinationals to eventually apply those standards as well.

"I think a lot of companies are doing very good and very interesting work [in the U.S.] behind the scenes," says John Queenan from PricewaterhouseCoopers' Advisory Services. "But they are just not being very transparent to the public about it . . . My opinion is that the gap is not necessarily as wide as people think . . . and U.S. companies are catching up quickly."[25]

---

23. Joseph Carter, and Ram Narasimhan, "Environmental Supply Chain Management," *Center for Advanced Purchasing Studies*, 1998, Focus Study (Executive Summary).

24. Interview, July 29, 2003.

25. Interview, November 6, 2003.

Boston-based Allen White, the GRI's cofounder and former acting CEO, agrees. "My own view is that we are on a road to convergence, inexorably—not divergence . . ." he says. "I say this because the forces of globalization, by definition, will tend to level the playing field in terms of international standards. It won't matter, or will matter less over time, whether General Motors or Ford or Du Pont, or whatever company in the U.S. thinks or doesn't think about a particular CSR aspect—whether it is reporting or assurance or labor standards. This is the case because these companies already are so closely integrated into the European economy and the global economy through their operations and subsidiaries, partnerships and alliances, that they will be forced to adopt best practices in non-financial reporting."[26]

Of course, based on the issues raised in earlier chapters, there is a strong business case to be made for closer monitoring and reporting on ethical supply chain policies even without this European SEAAR initiative, based simply on the protection of a corporation's reputation in light of increased investors, NGO, consumer, and legal pressures.

"I think the European Reporting movement will, to some extent, move the Americans along," concludes Alice Tepper Marlin. "It also depends how global American companies are. Some companies that you would identify as American right away, really are very international companies. And they have to be influenced by what is happening in Europe, and they do take a global perspective."[27]

Home-Grown Pressures on U.S. Companies

But the pressure on U.S. companies to monitor and take ethical responsibility for their overseas supplier connections does not simply end with consumer, NGO, or investor pressures, or with European governments that promise to put great pressure on U.S. multinational corporations, by law and by competition, to also provide audited reports of their supply chain policies. Possibly more important, there are also some significant and ominous lawsuits moving through the U.S. court system that potentially may have a significant effect on how companies interpret their responsibilities with regard to their extended supply chain.

Many states, of course, already require all government purchases to conform to "anti-sweatshop" requirements, and the federal government has a plethora of social and environmental procurement policies in force for

---

26. Interview, August 12, 2003.
27. Interview, June 24, 2003.

government purchases. Although there has been little discussion of social and environmental reporting in Congress—certainly nothing on the scale now taking place in Europe and Japan—in July 2003, a symposium hosted by Senator John Corzine, entitled "Environmental and Social Disclosure and the Securities and Exchange Commission: Meeting the Information Needs of Today's Investors," may mark the beginning of a new level of concern and awareness and activity by Congress. Although mostly focused on the potential for environmental liabilities of listed corporations, the symposium did include SEC Commissioner Harvey Goldschmid, and congressional speakers revealed a new level of concern for social and environmental reporting.

"Not only can corporate decisions cause substantial and often irreparable harm to our natural resources and public health," warned Texas Representative Lloyd Doggett, co-sponsor of the symposium, "they can expose a company to costly civil and criminal liabilities."

"American investors have been denied crucial information about the companies in which they have invested," agreed Representative Barbara Lee, from California. "Consumers want to both protect the environment and understand their own [risk] in this process through socially and environmentally responsible investing. For that, we need the SEC to ensure better corporate disclosure of relevant information." Some speakers called for a Blue Ribbon Panel to be formed to study the issue and to recommend how the SEC should promote this type of social and environmental reporting.[28]

Litigation

One of the most important legal issues facing modern U.S. corporations and their leadership comes from an obscure law established in 1789 known as the **Alien Claims Tort Act (ACTA),** which may potentially form the basis for an important precedent in international litigation.

The ACTA is potentially important for three reasons. First, under the statute, U.S. companies and their executives may be held liable for transgressions committed by foreign organizations or governments in another country if it can be proven that the American company encouraged or abetted those actually guilty of the activities. Second, it opens the door for companies themselves (as opposed to governments) to be held responsible for human rights violations. Finally, and possibly most important, the statute allows non-U.S. residents to sue U.S. companies in U.S. courts for violations that they may have committed overseas.

---

28. "News Release," *Friends of the Earth,* July 10, 2003 at *www.foe.org/new/releases/0703secsymp.html.*

The obscure ACTA statute, originally intended as a remedy for representatives of the young United States when foreign companies or individuals (i.e., pirates) violated diplomatic safe conduct agreements for protecting U.S. diplomatic staff in the early years after the American Revolution, is only now making its way through the U.S. Federal Court system for validation and interpretation, but is attracting considerable attention in the corporate supply chain world because of a spate of major cases that involve major U.S. corporations and serious accusations of human rights violations. These cases include examples such as:

• *Wiwa* v. *Royal Dutch Petroleum Co.*, which involves a civil lawsuit filed against Shell Oil company, alleging that the giant multinational was complicit in human rights violations—specifically the persecution and execution of environmental activists—by the government security forces in Nigeria.

• *Doe* v. *Unocal*, a similar scenario, where the energy giant Unocal is accused of being complicit in human rights violations in Burma, and is concerned with events that occurred during the construction of the Yadana natural gas pipeline in the south of the country. The plaintiffs contend that Unocal, a company based in the United States, colluded with the Burmese military to force villagers through violence and intimidation to work against their will on the pipeline—and subjected opponents of the pipeline to threats, rape, and murder. Given the reputation of the Burmese military (under the argument that even if Unocal didn't know, they should have suspected), Unocal is accused of standing by while knowing that the abuses were occurring, and in fact benefiting from the brutality. Hundreds of witnesses testified in the case that the Burmese military not only provided "security" for the building of the pipeline, but also forced many villagers at gunpoint to work as unpaid labor. In March of 2002, the U.S. Court of Appeals for the Ninth Circuit in California agreed, in a landmark decision, that Unocal could be tried under the ACTA statute.[29]

As Terry Collingsworth, General Counsel of *International Labor Rights Fund,* explains, "A verdict of significant monetary damages against Unocal could also serve as a warning to investors, including large institutional funds, that companies at risk of exposure for human rights violations may not be a good investment."[30]

"The decision of the Appeals Court," says Kenny Bruno, writing for the *The Bangkok Post,* "comports with what most people believe: a company

---

29. Terry Collingsworth, "Holding Businesses and Burma's Government Responsible for Human Rights Abuses," *Open Society News,* Fall–Winter 2002/2003 at *www.soros.org/osn/fall2002/holding.html.*

30. Ibid.

that knows of abhorrent and illegal practices and provides assistance to the perpetrators while reaping economic benefits, is culpable."[31]

- A third lawsuit, filed in California by the International Labor Rights Fund and the Center for Human Rights at Northwestern University Law School in the summer of 2003, claims that Occidental Petroleum knew of, supported, and possibly paid for an aerial assault against a small village of Santo Domingo, Columbia in December 1998 which killed 19 civilians.

Once again demonstrating the new rules of the extended global supply chain, companies are finding themselves suddenly confronted with their past activities. "This case builds upon the success we have had in using the Alien Tort Claims Act (ATCA) to address egregious human rights violations committed by U.S. companies in their overseas operations," said Terry Collingsworth, ILRF's Executive Director. "The ILRF has made it a priority to focus on human rights violations in Colombia, and based on recent decisions in cases brought against Coca-Cola and Drummond Coal, we are confident that our case against OXY will go forward. Companies should not be profiting from murder. This case is the first of several we envision against OXY for its ongoing and willful participation in murder and other human rights violations in Colombia."[32]

Moreover, these may not simply be isolated cases. "In a potentially devastating footnote for global business," warns Elliot Schrage, former Senior Vice President for Global Affairs at Gap and an adjunct senior fellow at the Council on Foreign Relations, "the court acknowledged that other theories of third-party liability beyond aiding and abetting, such as negligence, could be used to link the violations of a state actor to a private corporation. This interpretation would dramatically increase a company's exposure to ATS [ATCA] liability by calling into question all sorts of relationships that it has with government officials and agencies and state enterprises."[33]

At this point, no case has gone to trial under the ACTA statute, but whatever the merits of the individual cases, the ATCA is a sobering and important new development in U.S. law, and promises to focus even more attention in the future on new corporate responsibilities in developing nations.

Possibly even more important, a re-run of the *Nike* v. *Kasky* lawsuit settled out of court in October 2003 when Nike agreed to pay $1.5 million to the Fair Labor Association to be used on programs for improving and

---

31. Kenny Bruno and John Cheverie, *The Bangkok Post,* September 28, 2002.

32. "Lawsuit filed against Occidental for involvement in Colombian massacre," *Alexander's Gas and Oil Connections,* April 24, 2003 at *www.gasandoil.com/goc/company/cnl32386.htm.*

33. Elliot Schrage, "Emerging Threat: Human Rights Claims," *Harvard Business Review,* August 2003, p. 1.

monitoring supplier factories, could potentially redefine the notion of corporate free speech and fundamentally affect the future of nonfinancial reporting in America. The case, which had been making its way through the U.S. court system for two years, reached the Supreme Court in June of 2003 but was left unresolved when Nike decided to settle out of court.

The case involved a situation in which Nike, in defending itself in a letter-to-the-editor war in *The New York Times,* made claims defending its employment policies in Vietnam, that, if found to be false, would have put them in violation of California's truth in advertising laws. Nike claimed that they were merely responding to charges made against them, that they replied in general terms, and were using the media as a tool for their right to defend their reputation. Kasky, an activist, claimed that whatever their response, because they were discussing company-related issues, Nike was still trying to entice consumers to buy their products, and therefore should be held to the high standards of truth normally applied in commercial speech. If their claims could be proved to be untrue, claimed Kasky (and he contended they were), Nike had potentially violated California's advertising laws, which require companies to be truthful when making public commercial speech.

The case constituted a minefield of difficult legal and ethical issues. Can a company only speak out in the media if it can quantify and prove its claims? Does the fact that the debate took place in a newspaper change a company's legal responsibilities for accurate advertising and disclosure? On the other hand, if corporations can say anything in the name of First Amendment freedoms, how can the consumer be sure companies are telling the truth?

Equally important, for many activists and supporters of social and environmental reporting, the suit represented one more reason why companies should begin to accept greater responsibility for their overseas suppliers—and for accurately reporting on their efforts in this area. "The ruling," says Elliot Schrage, "invites the establishment of a framework to monitor corporate reporting on social performance, comparable with the regulatory framework that governs companies' disclosure of financial and business performance." Seen in this light, even with the out of court settlement, the case still constitutes another strong reason why companies should begin legitimate, standardized, easily compared reporting of ethical, social, and environmental activities, in that through a similar case brought in the future against other companies, corporations could potentially be compelled to prove that claims of good social and environmental behavior in their supply chain *are actually true.* This could revolutionize corporate attitudes about nonfinancial reporting, forcing companies to move toward formal monitoring, third-party auditing, and reporting on their suppliers' behavior. "The message to multinational business—and to global regulators," concludes Schrage, "is that social accountability demands the same kind of independent scrutiny as financial auditing."[34]

On the other hand, even with the settlement, this litigious approach could still backfire on activists and advocates of SEAAR. The obvious concern of many observers is that U.S. companies, fearing prosecution for false or unverified claims about the good behavior of their suppliers, will simply assume that they are safer saying absolutely nothing about the activities of their suppliers and avoiding protracted and expensive litigation. This could mean, worry some activists, the abrupt end, not the beginning, of open social and environmental reporting, as companies close their shutters in response. As we have seen, Nike themselves, for example, in response to the case had already withdrawn its social responsibility report for 2002, explaining that to say anything about their ethical supply chain policies was too provocative and legally dangerous.

Whatever the outcome of similar cases in the future, however, in many ways the *Nike* v. *Kasky* case may mark a fundamental turning point in social and environmental reporting for U.S. companies. After all, the time when a company can choose the option of silence and stonewalling is well past. Activists, NGOs, politicians, consumers, and investors can investigate factory conditions for themselves these days, and the companies involved risk exposure whether they produce social and environmental reports or not. Silence alone will provide little comfort for a company in the future.

As we saw in Chapter Four, the more sensible reaction by Nike (and one that they have already partially taken) is to simply admit to supplier problems "warts and all" in their reports and to work with NGOs, other companies, and the factories themselves to improve on those conditions. It is therefore likely that the case will ultimately be seen as one more important reason for companies to move toward taking greater responsibility for their extended supply chain, and for more formal and audited efforts on those efforts.

As we have seen, much of the imperative for companies to adopt a SEAAR program depends on where they are located, the nature of their industry, what their company is doing in terms of social and environmental activities, and the relative risk that they face from employment or environmental violations in their extended supply chain. For those companies that will eventually adopt this framework (and by all accounts that will soon be many), it is important to understand the key features—the codes, standards, and approaches—that are emerging.

---

34. Elliot Schrage, "A New Model for Social Auditing," *The Financial Times*, May 27, 2002.

CHAPTER SIX

Who Is in Charge Here? Organizational Responsibilities for an Ethical Supply Chain Program

*D*espite the combined effects of the supply chain revolution and the new levels of responsibility being forced on companies for monitoring the social and environmental behavior of their suppliers, most companies still have no formal program that ties together the various key activities required for maintaining an ethical supply chain: a strategic company ethical framework, environmental and social supplier sourcing programs, supplier inspection, and nonfinancial reporting regimes.

D espite globalization of the supply chain, even in large and sophisticated companies, ethical supply chain activities are often spread among many departments, at many different levels and locations in the company, with little coordination or strategic focus. In most companies, for example, the procurement department is still expected to take an entirely independent role in creating and developing supplier sourcing and management policies. Supplier selection criteria is still focused almost exclusively on price and quality issues, and many companies still do not attempt to screen suppliers—particularly overseas suppliers—for serious employment or environmental issues beyond what is the minimum required by U.S. law. What screening that does take place is usually completed by paper-based survey, with general questions and little or no verification or follow-up. Human Resources usually has responsibility for addressing hiring and domestic employment issues and enforcing EOE (Equal Opportunity Employment) guidelines, but will have very little influence over supplier employment policies. Few companies have created a coordinated and strategic framework for social or environmental sourcing, and only the most innovative of U.S. companies have a program in place to monitor use and disposal of company products by customers, or to ensure that they are purchasing nontoxic and environmentally friendly materials.

"We are working with a couple of different clients now," says Stephanie Meyer, a Principal at Stratos, the Canadian CSR consultancy and research group based in Ottawa, "who have a number of different CSR initiatives [ongoing]. They are managed by different parts in the organization, and have never really been seen as a cohesive whole before. 'Yes,' [they say] we are looking at workplace health and safety. 'Yes' we are looking at human resources policy and trying to make a good place to work. 'Yes' we've got these different environmental programs internally and we've got this external giving program, and one part of that goes toward environmental organizations.

They have a lot of pieces in place," she says, "so we are helping their executives to understand how it might look if you pulled it together into more of a cohesive strategy where the parts are complementing each other."[1]

What is more, despite the enterprise information systems revolution, most U.S. companies have not yet attempted to apply advanced information technology platforms to coordinate the myriad information sources that make such a program possible: supplier employment and environmental performance information, product incident history, monitoring ever-changing environmental codes, energy use and emissions information, product wastage and disposal, coordinating incident reports from

---

1. Interview, September 2, 2003.

overseas suppliers, or monitoring the Web for early reputation warning signs. Yet these are exactly the types of applications that should be used to help corporate leaders understand and manage their ethical supply chain responsibilities.

"Congress in this country in the 1970s," says Nicholas Eisenberg, CEO of Ecos Technologies, "saw there was a broad societal reaction against pollution, and knew that there were a lot of technologies out there that could help us reduce pollution, and so they said to industry, 'thou shall not pollute . . . thou shall adopt the best available technologies to curtail that pollution.'

Companies spent the next several decades," he contends "investing in people, systems, process, data bases and applications, to ensure that they were conforming with an increasingly complex set of regulations on a national and international basis.

Yet over the last decade, in particular, the drivers have changed from being strictly regulatory, government regulations, and have become more and more tied to business drivers—risk, cost, productivity, efficiency, competition and reputation—and so a lot of the . . . effort has changed from a focus on [conformance] to asking 'how can we derive business value from this?'

But the underlying infrastructure to do that," explains Eisenberg, "to execute effectively against that is very poor, because it was designed for a different purpose. It was designed to ensure compliance with government regulations—it wasn't designed to retain, create and avoid the loss of business value. And so what you have in most companies is a hodge-podge of hundreds of different applications that are uncoordinated, working on similar problems, similar issues, but with no ability to communicate with each other or to leverage the value that has been created . . ."[2]

Lacking Strategic Focus or Coordination

Why have companies, on the whole, been so slow in developing a more coordinated company-wide program for ensuring an ethical supply chain? There are many reasons.

First, despite the growing number of supplier-related incidents, many companies have no resources specifically allocated to dealing with overseas supplier relations. Even strategic sourcing exercises are often completed in a cursory way, or, too often, not done at all, as harried purchasing staff deal with minute-to-minute changes to orders, missed

2. Interview, August 25, 2003.

delivery, or quality control issues. The Director of Procurement, quite understandably, still sees his/her role almost entirely as focusing on ensuring low price and high quality goods, and an uninterrupted supply chain—a full-time job in most companies. In short, despite the traditional assumption that the responsibility for supplier management falls within the procurement function, far too often strategic sourcing and supplier qualifications—let alone supplier inspection—remains a low priority. In many ways, this simply reflects the former separate roles of the pre-1990s "supply chain revolution," where planning, warehousing, logistics, manufacturing, and procurement were all separate departments, with unique incentive programs and targets.

Consider, for example, the many separate, but related, initiatives that exist in the typical company:

- The **Environmental Health and Safety** group—usually focused exclusively on corporate office and domestic operations compliance issues—sees its role as monitoring compliance to U.S. laws, not monitoring the social and environmental performance of overseas suppliers.

- **Sales** staff want high quality goods available at all times for customers, and have less concern about inventory levels, carrying costs, or supplier behavior (unless their customers are requiring, as is increasingly the case, the company to explain and verify its position concerning poor supplier behavior).

- **Operations**—warehousing, logistics, assembly—want to contain costs, and purchasing wants to negotiate with suppliers to provide goods on time and at a good price—but don't want to assume the role of EHS policeman with those suppliers and have little time for organizing detailed interviews or inspections.

- **Corporate affairs** knows little of operational issues, but is concerned with communicating a strong corporate responsibility message.

- **Human resources** is more concerned with benefits and EOE issues than with administering foreign supplier site inspections for employment violations.

In short, there is often not one single corporate group that has been given responsibility for ensuring that suppliers in the extended supply chain adhere to standards of environmental health and safety. In many ways it is just the age-old problem of no one knowing who is responsible.

"I don't think that the output is the true value of [SEAAR] reporting," says Stephanie Meyer of Stratos. The real value "is the process and how that can help you to move toward a better understanding of all of the impacts in the organization. What I am hearing from clients," she says, "is that [a CSR project] is often one of the first times that they have had a truly cross-functional team pull together [in this area]. And it is by necessity, because they realize that they need to talk to 'so-and-so' in purchasing, and 'so-and-so' down the hall for this piece, or for that piece. It is the first time that a lot of these people are talking, and if you can get them together and working on a team in this area, they can look for other opportunities for synergy . . . that is what really helps them to understand that they can operate in a better, more effective way . . . and makes them more open for looking at some of these broader organizational strategies for improvement."[3]

"At present, most companies are not managing risks in their supply chain in a systematic way," agrees Teresa Fabian of Pricewaterhouse Coopers. "While some companies [for example] have excellent systems for ensuring they are sourcing from sustainable forests, they may not have considered the issue of poor workplace conditions and vice versa."[4]

Not only do most companies lack strategic focus when it comes to an ethical supply chain policy, but as we have seen, many companies simply don't see overseas supplier management as part of their responsibility at all. Often company leaders still see outsourced or overseas contract operations as outside their sphere of control or responsibility, to be left with Corporate Affairs staff to smooth the ruffled feathers of NGOs or the press. As we have seen, however, supplier issues have become too important for companies simply to ignore, or to approach in an uncoordinated or haphazard manner any more.

Activities Necessary to Monitor and Manage the Ethical Supply Chain

What does this trend toward responsibility sharing along an extended supply chain mean to the modern company? For one thing, it means that the social and environmental supply chain issues need to be given much higher priority in the organization. It also means new organizational structures, and dedicated resources. Consider, for example, the number and variety of duties and activities that now need to be done as a unique operational process in order to ensure ethical behavior and strong risk management in a typical company:

---

3. Interview, September 2, 2003.

4. Teresa Fabien, "Supply Chain Management in an Era of Social and Environmental Accountability," *Sustainable Development International,* Edition 1, p. 29, from the Sustainable Development Commission at *www.sustdev.org/journals/edition.02/download/sdi2_1_5.pdf.*

- **Policy Creation and Ongoing Risk Assessment.** Someone in the organization needs to be responsible for the initial and ongoing creation of a corporate ethical supply chain policy, including a value statement, appropriate codes of conduct, and a framework for analyzing and reacting to supply chain risks. In order to make that policy reflect reality, someone will need to be responsible for an analysis of the socioeconomic impacts and the relative risks that the company faces, by country, by contractors, and by product. These policy advisors will also need to be involved in the planning and oversight of ongoing or planned projects, particularly focusing on the expectations of other stakeholders such as the local community, the government, activists, or business partners.

- **Managing the Supplier Program.** This effort, going well beyond a strategic sourcing regime, requires incorporating social and environmental selection and monitoring criteria into an ongoing supplier evaluation program. It will also require resources to create and maintain education programs, to draw up and negotiate relevant contracts, and to collect performance information through a variety of sources, including internal systems that can record historical performance data, and through both written and in-person surveys. And because of the need for verification, a modern supplier program will need to move beyond the simple "by-mail" surveys of the past, requiring much greater levels of contact and collaboration with overseas suppliers. The process will also need to incorporate often-overlooked sources of risk such as waste and recycling vendors.

- **Document Management.** Establishing a central database of audit information is critical, both in terms of effective management and in providing legitimate, verifiable information to investors and NGOs. This involves systems for collecting information, for data management and data mining, and for historical data retention and analysis. It may also require supporting or overseeing a program for supplier data retention—not an easy thing to enforce among suppliers in developing countries unfamiliar with collecting performance data, and often unwilling to admit, much less record, faults or failures.

- **Training and Education.** A supplier program also requires an ongoing program of education and training for both company and supplier employees that covers company policy, the organization's process for risk and supplier assessment, social and environmental performance codes and expectations, and the reporting process.

- **Communication.** A strong communication program is necessary, both internally concerning policies and resources, and externally to corporate stakeholders: NGOs, pressure groups, the media, and investment and consumer groups. Someone knowledgeable about the company ethics policies, supplier evaluation program, and the reporting process will need to create a credible communications program for NGOs, investors, and government agencies that will adequately explain the value and legitimacy of the company's ethical supply chain process. Much of that communication will need to be person-to-person, keeping open channels with various stakeholders—NGOs, investment analysts, and the press.

- **Gaining Internal Commitment and Corporate Alignment.** The process also requires a very important change in management effort in order to communicate the business case for supplier management and SEAAR to leaders throughout the organization, and to gain the endorsement and active participation of senior corporate executives in creating policy and regularly monitoring risk issues when they arise. Someone—with both political clout and sufficient tact—will need to make certain that mid- and lower-level managers are aligned and support these policies actively. At the heart of this process will be creating and explaining the case for action—something that will be made much easier if a credible business case for policies can be made and convincingly argued.

- **Complete the Reporting Process.** Finally, the process will require special and dedicated resources not only to manage the supplier program, but to collect accurate data and to develop the publishable corporate SEAAR report. This will also mean surveying and selecting the most appropriate standards and reporting processes among the many that exist today, and coordinating information collection and sharing among quality and other standards projects ongoing in the company. And, of course, someone has to actually write the report in a complete, accurate, and coherent way.

Who Is in Charge at the Organizational Level?

"Managing sustainability issues is difficult enough at the best of times," explains Sarah Roberts from the National Centre for Business and Sustainability, "so spending time trying to get other companies operating in distant countries to improve their sustainability performance is not usually top of managers' agendas. However, the need to find effective mechanisms to do just that is increasingly rising to the top of staff priority lists in departments as diverse as public affairs and procurement, due to the potential reputational risks to brand owners of poor environmental or social performance in their supply chains."[5]

So where does the organizational responsibility for managing these various tasks lie? Leading practices seem to demonstrate that to develop this type of ethical supply chain program, a company needs resources that come from four key areas.

---

5. Sarah Roberts, "Analysis: Ethical Sourcing Codes—the Answer to Supply Chain Sustainability Concerns?" *Ethical Corporation,* August 1, 2002.

Executive and Board Sponsorship

One thing we have learned from enterprise-wide change projects in the past is that successful deployment depends on strong, visible, and active leadership. Not only is visible and consistent senior leadership important in convincing employees and suppliers of the value of ethical behavior, but only senior leadership has the span of organizational control to cover the many areas—supplier engagement, materials sourcing, manufacturing, logistics, product distribution, and sales—that are involved in the company's extended supply chain. This in itself is an important departure for most companies, where the senior executive team and the board seldom consider either the company's strategic ethical framework or specific supply chain related codes of conduct or supplier issues.

"Top management involvement in the process of establishing and implementing a responsibility vision," agrees Sandra Waddock from the Carroll School of Management at Boston College, in her collaborative 2002 study with the ILO of over 120 managers in the apparel and footwear sectors, "is absolutely critical. Employees typically seek guidance from management, attempting to understand what senior management wants and what management will reward. As many managers interviewed emphasized, if management does not believe in the vision being articulated or sees it as merely a public relations exercise, then there is little hope for its becoming part of operating practices.

On the other hand," explains Waddock, "if top management is involved in the development of a vision and communicates that commitment on a regular basis, if vision is supported through reward systems, allocations of resources and changes in procedures, then the vision will move forward."

Most large or international corporations, of course, may have many layers of "senior management," reflecting geographical and organizational levels within the overall company pyramid. "The interviews," stresses Waddock, "indicate that management commitment at each of these levels is crucial; a senior manager in charge of country level operations, in charge of quality control, in charge of purchasing, who does not believe in the principles outlined can lead to a breakdown of support for corporate responsibility objectives within his or her area of responsibility. Support needs to be generated at all levels in a cascade fashion from the top of the organization all the way down and through supply chain operations to supervisors and workers on the production lines."[6]

---

6. Sandra Waddock and Charles Bodwell, "From TQM to TRM: Emerging Total Responsibility Management Approaches," *Journal of Corporate Citizenship,* Summer 2002, p. 9.

A Corporate Ethics Office Lead By a Chief Ethics and Risk Officer (CERO)

The entire process ultimately needs someone to coordinate and lead the SEAAR effort. For many companies, that role does not really exist at this time, but for many progressive organizations it essentially expands on the role of the Chief Risk and Ethics Officer. This position, focused specifically on leading the types of activities that we have been describing, is certain to expand into an ever-more prominent senior role in companies, becoming as strategically important as the CFO or the COO positions are today. The position carries various titles—Chief Ethics Officer, Chief Corporate Social Responsibility Officer, or Chief Risk Officer—depending on the emphasis of the program, but they all have in common an important set of responsibilities:

- Implementing ethics and risk management policy throughout the organization
- Selecting and implementing process and performance standards
- Communicating ethics and risk policy among employees and stakeholders
- Overseeing the supplier management program
- Developing education and training programs
- Providing guidance and advice on ethical and risk issues
- Confirmation and monitoring of compliance, adherence/oversight
- Directing the "risk" scanning exercise
- Tracking to resolution identified risks
- Overseeing the development of the company's social and environmental reporting

In order to be able to oversee these significant duties, the Chief Ethics and Risk Officer or CSR Manager needs to be invested with significant authority, and will need to have the political presence and personality to act as a liaison between employees, suppliers, the CEO, and the board. Most importantly, the CERO will usually also be responsible for setting up, or at least advising on, and supervising implementation of the important aspects of an ethical supply chain program, including, signing up for "aspirational" codes of conduct, selecting and implementing social and environmental standards, negotiating with and monitoring the performance of suppliers, and creating the company's social and environmental "sustainability" report. Playing a lead role in supplier selection, the CERO will need to understand fair labor practices, and will need to be able to perform and oversee credible social audits in factories that may have a strong incentive to doctor the results. They will also need to understand best practices in environmental packaging, in materials labeling, and other environmentally sound logistics practices.

An Ethics Committee

Many progressive companies have formed a corporate ethics committee that includes senior leadership, the CERO, representation from the Board, legal counsel, human resources, and the different functional areas within the company, including manufacturing operations, procurement, and corporate relations. This committee not only helps to create and implement corporate ethical policies, but reviews potential incidents and makes recommendations to the CEO and the board on ethics-related policy. Under the guidance of the CERO, this committee has responsibility for reviewing not only the ethical issues that arise with major suppliers, but any significant project or incident that involves health, safety, employment, or the environment within the entire supply chain process.

The program should be supported by an **ethical supply chain team** dedicated to overseeing suppliers and other business partners in the supply chain. This team will be responsible for ensuring that the company's supply chain operations on a day-to-day basis identifies and deals appropriately with risks that might harm the company's reputation. Their duties include responsibility for providing advice on environmental and purchasing issues and on workplace environmental, health, and safety policies in both domestic and overseas operations. They will also be responsible for selecting, monitoring, and reporting on the social and environmental performance of suppliers, for the supplier management program, and for creating and administering the social and environmental report for the company.

This is a cross-functional team, made up of a combination of organizational leaders and experts from areas such as procurement, legal, supply chain operations, and occasionally third-party specialists. These specialists may work with suppliers around the world, establishing close working relationships with NGOs, government agencies, suppliers, and unions.

Of course there will also be support required from **specialist groups.** These include legal, strategic planning, EHS, human resources, and corporate affairs, as well as design engineers and operational and product specialists. Each of these groups, including the executive leadership, needs to be involved both in making policy and in making decisions once a potential incident has arisen.

H&M, the European clothing retailers, provide a good example of the CSR reporting structure in a modern global company. The company has 30 employees designated as "Code of Conduct Inspectors," who carry out supplier monitoring and inspections. In addition, the company has 110 quality controllers working in their 21 production offices, each tasked with reporting any infringements that they encounter of the Code of Conduct. Inspection results are reported both at the local office and corporate

CSR Reporting Structure

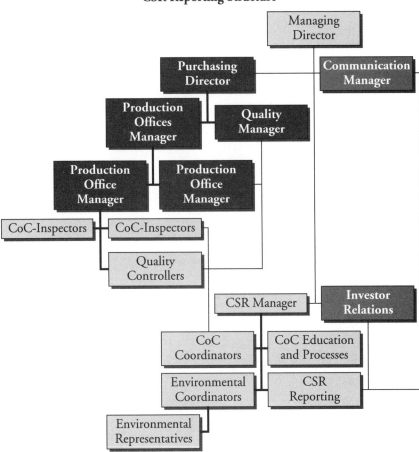

Source: www.hm.com/corporate/pdf/social/csr_report_social.pdf.

FIGURE 6-1   H&M's CSR Reporting Structure

office, with all results registered in the code of conduct database. The CSR department is led by a dedicated corporate manager who reports directly to the company's CEO (see Figure 6-1).

This is the type of dedicated resource and organizational structure that a good ethical supply chain program demands.

So what does this dedicated resource have to do, and how do they do it? There are a series of key activities and processes, explored in the next chapters, that leading companies are beginning to develop that are key to a strong ethical supply chain program.

CHAPTER SEVEN

The Corporate Ethics and Risk Management Framework

*R*eflecting the importance of ethical behavior, this process should be sponsored and endorsed by all company leaders, should involve the board in a way that guarantees that members are both informed and independent, and ideally, should be lead by a new and important role — the company's Chief Ethics and Risk Officer. The framework should be built on traditional value statements and the types of internationally recognized codes of conduct that we discuss in Chapter Eight, but should move beyond passive efforts and involve a formal system for identifying and reacting to potential supplier social and environmental issues.

In fact, although most of the Corporate Social Responsibility debate (at least in Europe) is today focused on how to monitor and verify company and supplier performance, monitoring and reporting are only the end result of a much more important processs—or framework—that needs to be initiated, not in the supplier organization, but in the buying organization itself. The key features of this ethical and risk management corporate framework include:

- A corporate value statement and aspirational **code of conduct**
- A strong **business case**
- The selection and adoption of internationally accepted social and environmental **performance standards**
- Measurable and verifiable **indicators of performance**
- A program to build **awareness and support**
- A **supplier program** that includes education, training, and communications activities, and monitoring and auditing of supplier performance
- A **SEAAR-based reporting structure**
- Supporting **IT systems**

Finally, in order to leverage new knowledge and information management systems and techniques, a company needs to develop its **"Research and Analysis" Capabilities,** in order to capture, organize, and distribute information gleaned from sources external to the company—the Internet, government agencies, suppliers, NGOs—concerning local political, cultural, and legal concerns. This helps company leaders not only understand what potential problem areas or incidents are arising in the supply chain and what the company is doing to deal with those issues, but more generally to monitor the company's reputation in the media, relevant political, cultural, or legislative changes, or NGO actions launched against the company.

Today, the modern company should be collecting information concerning their corporate reputation and risk from a wide variety of sources, including:

- Current and proposed legislation in all operating and sales areas
- Leading and expected industry social and environmental practices
- The adoption of standards by competitors and by the industry
- Trade union positions and concerns
- Press, NGO, and activist positions concerning the company or competition
- The social and environmental records of individual suppliers
- Customer expectations and concerns with regard to product safety, packaging, and disposability

"This systematic scanning and prioritizing exercise should be repeated or reviewed every year or two," suggests GEMI, "because EHS regulations, liability concepts, market preferences, competitor positioning, and information are rapidly evolving."[1]

The Benefits of Creating a Company-Wide Ethics and Risk Management Framework

There are many benefits to this type of formal, enterprise-wide approach to ethics and risk management. A formal written policy, dedicated resource, and high-level sponsorship all help to create a framework for differentiating between acceptable and unacceptable behavior, and for demonstrating to employees, suppliers, investors, and customers the company's intentions to require their suppliers to behave in an ethical way. It also ensures that company employees understand the importance of corporate ethical values and are actively encouraged to identify potential risks in the supply chain as they arise.

In short, this type of formal ethical framework is a company's best opportunity for early identification of risk, and its first line of defense against accusations of indifference or unethical behavior. After all, employees, particularly in the procurement and sourcing functions, are a company's closest contact with suppliers and business partners, and need to understand that as front-line employees

---

Intel's Ethical Supply Chain Framework

Intel provides a good example of this type of ethical supply chain framework. The company's board and senior management have been actively engaged in the development and implementation of their CSR program, and they have a dedicated CSR Manager to coordinate and champion all ethical supply chain activities. The company has had various long-standing environmental, health, and safety programs, and has already been completing some form of compliance auditing for some time, including some 200 assessments done each year worldwide on their suppliers. They already maintain control of waste products, and ship these back from their various sites in developing countries in order to avoid having to burn the materials. Their Product Ecology group looks at all issues concerning manufacturing, use, and

---

1. "New Paths to Business Value," the Global Environmental Management Initiative at *www.gemi.org/newpath.pdf.*, p. 20. The Global Environmental Management Initiative (GEMI) is a non-profit organization of leading companies dedicated to fostering envi-

disposal of products, and these efforts are coordinated with their "Issues Prevention and Management" group, which serves as the company's risk management function, providing both the early alert and incident management activities for the company. That group is also tied directly into Intel's customer service centers, which screen for any social, environmental, or ethical issues, and forward those issues on to the Issues Prevention group and other appropriate departments. These several departments then meet with the Corporate Social Responsibility department on a regular basis to coordinate activities company-wide.

they have a responsibility to identify social or environmental issues in the supply chain.

Let's turn now to the specific elements of this ethical framework.

---

ronmental, health, and safety excellence, and corporate citizenship worldwide. Through the collaborative efforts of its members, GEMI also promotes a worldwide business ethic for environmental, health, and safety management and sustainable development through example and leadership. The guidance included in this [footnoted] document is based on the professional judgment of the individual collaborators listed in the acknowledgements. The ideas in the document are those of the individual collaborators and not necessarily their organizations. Neither GEMI nor its consultants are responsible for any form of damage that may result from the application of the guidance contained in this document. This document [footnoted] has been produced by GEMI and is solely the property of the organization. This document may not be reproduced or translated without express written permission of GEMI, except for use by member companies or for strictly educational purposes.

CHAPTER EIGHT

Choosing an Aspirational Code of Conduct

*A*s an early step to the development of
an ethical supply chain, most companies will want to consider adopting one
of the several "aspirational" codes of conduct that have become so widely
accepted globally. As appropriate, a company will want to become a
signatory of an active compact, or may simply want to adopt the principles
as part of their own company ethical policy, incorporating it into the current
company code of conduct.

Over the past two decades, as growing globalization trends and pressures have emerged, a variety of NGOs, churches, and international forums have proposed a number of codes of conduct for companies, particularly with regard to labor rights issues in developing countries. The best known of these early codes included the Rutgers Principles, the Global Sullivan Principles, the OECD Guidelines for Multinational Enterprises, and the Interfaith Center on Corporate Responsibility, all of which set the initial tone and quality standards for the more formalized codes of conduct that were to follow.

These codes did not require any formal certification (although the Global Sullivan Principles now requires companies to complete a yearly, unaudited performance report), but encouraged companies to "aspire" to work toward common goals of human rights, social justice, and economic opportunity. And although these early codes of conduct came about far too early in the development of the global SEAAR movement to have widespread influence, they nonetheless had some notable successes. One of these was the Global Sullivan Principles, lead by the Rev. Leon Sullivan in South Africa, which helped persuade 11 major corporations, including General Motors, to withdraw from South Africa in protest against the government's policy of apartheid.

"Aspirational" Codes of Conduct

These include the many forums and international codes for labor rights and environmental sustainability that serve as pledges — to which companies "aspire" to adhere. These codes usually reflect similar values — protection of human rights, outlawing bribes, providing safe and healthy working conditions for employees, or actively protecting the environment. Although seldom enforceable, and often based on elastic clauses such as "a living wage" or "do no harm to the environment," they nonetheless provide a loose but growing coalition of willing companies with broad guidelines for behavior.

Today, five of these important "aspirational" codes of conduct have become dominant, each more or less reflecting the same social and environmental principles — support for human rights, protection of the environment, promoting equal opportunity employment, respecting employees' freedom of association, and providing a safe and healthy workplace — but each with its own separate emphasis or approach.

The ILO

One of the most important groups in the field of labor rights, of course, is the International Labor Organization, an agency of the United Nations and a strong advocate of labor standards and principles worldwide. Originally established to help cope with the crisis of labor conditions ("injustice, hardship and privation") in 1919 following World War I, the ILO became the UN's first specialized agency in 1946. In 1998 they adopted the Declaration of Fundamental Principles and Rights at work, which today sets the standard for employment rights throughout the world.

ILO principles and recommendations cover a broad range of labor-related issues such as the right to organize, freedom of association, equality of opportunity, and worker health and safety rights, including elimination of forced or compulsory labor and abolition of child labor. Although primarily a forum for national governments, they also provide technical assistance to member nations and provide an inspection service for investigating human rights and labor violations.[1]

The UN Global Compact

The United Nations Global Compact was launched in April 2000 as a coordinating forum for UN agencies, NGOs, and the global business community with a goal of helping member organizations complete joint initiatives and gather to discuss global issues. Focused on improving environmental and employment standards in developing countries, the Compact is based upon nine principles that businesses should follow:

1. Support and respect the protection of internationally proclaimed human rights.
2. Make sure they are not complicit in human rights abuses.
3. Uphold the freedom of association and the effective recognition of the right to collective bargaining.
4. Eliminate all forms of forced and compulsory labor.
5. Effect the abolition of child labor.
6. Eliminate discrimination in respect of employment and occupation.
7. Support a precautionary approach to environmental challenges.
8. Undertake initiatives to promote greater environmental responsibility.
9. Encourage the development and diffusion of environmentally friendly technologies.[2]

---

1. See *www.ilo.org*.
2. "The Global Compact: Corporate Leadership in the World Economy," *Global Compact Office*, The United Nations, January 2001.

Although admirable in its intentions, as with most of these aspirational initiatives, signing up to the Compact merely asserts that signatory companies agree with these principles, and there are no mechanisms to ensure that companies adhere to high social and environmental standards. Critics argue that the Compact, although valuable as a discussion forum and for publicizing key principles, nonetheless suffers from two key weaknesses. First, there is no attempt to require companies that join the Compact to demonstrate—through audits or any other mechanism—that they actually are adhering to any of these principles.

"Given the structure of the compact," says Oliver Williams, director of the University of Notre Dame Center for Ethics and Religious Values in Business, "it is quite possible for a company with a poor record in labor or the environment to highlight another area of corporate citizenship in its annual report where its record is superlative. The general public will only receive the information about a company that the company chooses to report."[3]

The second weakness of the Compact is that the principles are worded at such a high level, and the choice of words allows such flexibility, that it would be impossible to hold member companies to any auditable standard even if they did require proof of good behavior.

Spokesmen for the Compact explain that they do not wish to provide an enforcement mechanism, or become entangled in assessing the performance of companies. They instead see the Compact as merely a moral framework that also provides a useful forum for companies to gather and discuss issues. That is all right, as far as it goes, but the problem with this approach is obvious. Without any inspection or enforcement mechanisms for membership, the Compact provides little in the way of "teeth" to their conviction that companies should adhere to these standards. What is worse, of course, this type of approach leaves the Compact open to abuse by companies that sign up to the forum as part of a public relations strategy, even while blatantly ignoring those principles throughout their supply chain.

Still, aware of these issues, the Compact has encouraged (but not required) member companies to also participate in the Global Reporting Initiative (see Chapter Sixteen), hoping that the GRI process would provide the needed inspection and enforcement services, allowing the Compact to remain above the fray. Whatever its limitations, the Compact nonetheless has provided much-needed endorsement and publicity

---

3. Oliver Williams, "Major U.S. Companies Doubt Global Compact Credentials," *Business Day,* April 22, 2003 at *www.bday.co.za/bday/content/direct/1,3523,1330151-6096-0,00.html.*

for social and environmental performance and reporting, and there are now around 500 signatory companies participating from around the world.

Oddly, considering the undemanding nature of the Compact, very few U.S. companies have chosen to participate. This may be a reflection of fears of litigation, as U.S. companies are uniquely wary of signing up to what might be interpreted as a contract that governs their conduct—particularly with regard to human rights. Given the elasticity of the phrasing in the principles, it is hard to imagine any company worrying about a genuine legal risk, but it is apparent that many U.S. companies are avoiding the Compact for some reason.

More likely, say skeptics, companies simply don't want to be accused of hypocrisy if caught out violating these principles by NGOs. There are reasons to be wary for companies that don't have a good understanding of the activities within their supply chain, warns Jim Kartalia, President of Entegra. "Once a company becomes a signatory," he explains, "their reputation risk has jumped through the roof, because as signatories they are saying they want to be a good corporate citizen. If they don't then have the systems to help them know where they are succeeding or failing, they risk looking hypocritical—and the media is going to tear them apart."[4]

The CERES Principles

Created by a coalition of U.S. environmental groups and the socially responsible investment community, the 10 CERES principles cover the gamut of sustainability issues, including reduction and disposal of wastes, energy conservation, the creation of safe products, company transparency, reporting, and management commitment. In many ways, the CERES coalition is a good example of the new pressures that are being brought to bear on today's corporations. Leveraging shareholder authority, the coalition uses shareholder resolution to push companies toward endorsing these environmental principles, with the expectation that CERES signatories will publish public reports on their progress in these areas.

CSR Europe

CSR Europe was created in 1995 by the former president of the European Commission, Jacques Delors, and is a networking forum and

---

4. Interview with Jim Kartalia, January 23, 2003.

think tank covering a broad range of corporate social responsibility issues. Its membership includes 16 national government partners, and 59 corporations, for which CSR Europe provides information through publications, benchmarking standards, and leading practice tools and techniques. Their goal is to provide a forum that brings together governmental policy makers, investors, businesses, NGOs, labor unions, and academics, and as with similar forums, they have a set of aspirational principles that define their purpose. According to their guidelines, organizations should:

- "Conduct business responsibly by contributing to the economic health and sustainable development of the communities in which we operate.

- Offer our employees healthy and safe working conditions, ensure fair compensation, good communication as well as equal opportunity for employment and development.

- Offer quality, safe products and services at competitive prices, meet customers' needs promptly and accurately and work responsibly with our business partners.

- Minimize the negative impacts our activities can have on the environment and its resources, while striving to provide our customers with products and services that take sustainable consumption into account.

- Be accountable to key stakeholders through dialogue and transparency regarding the economic, social and environmental impacts of our business activities.

- Operate a good governance structure and uphold the highest standards in business ethics.

- Provide a fair return to our shareholders while fulfilling the above principles."[5]

The Pros and Cons of Aspirational Codes

Ironically, given that these aspirational codes are dedicated to helping both workers and the environment, there has been much criticism by all parties during their recent proliferation. Activists are often unhappy

---

5. *www.csreurope.org/aboutus/default.aspx.*

because these codes remain largely unenforceable and can be used as "greenwash" by corporations (there are many examples of this). It can also be argued that these codes are offering a public relations alternative to the more serious and meaningful standards and reporting frameworks that have recently emerged.

More to the point, these aspirational codes of conduct, though a valuable first step in creating an ethical supply chain, are by their nature elastic and voluntary, and are now seen by advanced companies only as a first step in establishing a broader ethical supply chain framework. These high-level codes are therefore usually more a reflection of good intentions than of any commitment to specific actions, but they do provide sensible guidelines for developing principles in areas such as environmental policy, child labor, decent wage policies, and freedom of association that reflect a concern for workers in the extended supply chain, and at least a partial acceptance of responsibility by companies to oversee good behavior by their subcontractors and suppliers in the developing world.

Combining a Corporate Value Statement and Company Code of Ethical Conduct

Even if companies are going to sign up to international labor codes of conduct or social and environmental standards, a company first needs to create a set of written principles that reflect the ethical values of the company. These need to be more than the often vacuous platitudes that are reflected in most company vision statements or a limited focus on customer service, product safety, or conflict of interest guidelines. The value statement should reflect, among other things, the company leadership's position on social and environmental policy within their extended supply chain, and the code of conduct should be a detailed set of principles that specifically describes the company's position on issues such as energy usage, recycling, working hours, wages, child labor, and other key issues that plague supplier operations in the extended supply chain.

This broad policy statement should form the basis of a company's ethical supply chain planning process, providing at least a "moral minimum" standard of behavior for management, employees, suppliers, and other stakeholders who will benefit from a clear view of a company's ethical position. Northern Telecom provides a good example of a strong statement of ethical policy and objectives.

CASE STUDY

Northern Telecom's Code of Conduct

Recognizing the critical link between a healthy environment and sustained economic growth, we are committed to leading the telecommunications industry in protecting and enhancing the environment. Such stewardship is indispensable to our continued business success. Therefore, wherever we do business, we will take the initiative in developing innovative solutions to those environmental issues that affect our business.

We will:

- Integrate environmental considerations into our business planning and decision making processes, including product research and development, new manufacturing methods, and acquisitions/divestitures.
- Identify, assess, and manage environmental risks associated with our operations and products throughout their life cycle, to reduce or eliminate the likelihood of adverse consequences.
- Comply with all applicable legal and regulatory requirements and, to the extent we determine it appropriate, adopt more stringent standards for the protection of our employees and the communities in which we operate.
- Establish a formal Environmental Protection Program, and set specific, measurable goals.
- Establish assurance programs, including regular audits, to assess the success of the Environmental Protection Program in meeting regulatory requirements, program goals, and good practices.
- To the extent that proven technology will allow, eliminate, or reduce harmful discharges, hazardous materials, and waste.
- Make reduction, reuse, and recycling the guiding principles and means by which we achieve our goals.
- Prepare and make public an annual report summarizing our environmental activities.
- Work as advocates with our suppliers, customers, and business partners to jointly achieve the highest possible environmental standards.
- Build relationships with other environmental stakeholders—including governments, the scientific community, educational institutions, public interest groups, and the general public—to promote the development and communication of innovative solutions to industry environmental problems.
- Provide regular communications to, and training for, employees to heighten awareness of, and pride in, environmental issues.

Source: "Business Strategy for Sustainable Development," the International Institute for Sustainable Development (IISD), from BSDglobal.com/tools/strategies.asp. See also "Business Strategy for Sustainable Development," at www.iisd.org/publications/publication.asp?pno=242.

HP provides a good example of a code of conduct for its suppliers that is a combination of specific HP values and standard labor and environmental aspirational codes. "We expect our product material suppliers," says HP, "to act as responsible corporate citizens and take a positive, proactive stance regarding social and environmental issues. We ask that they pursue a policy of continuous improvement and be forthright in sharing relevant information with us. Suppliers need to understand HP's expectations and manage to them. HP suppliers must comply with all national and other applicable laws and regulations, and they must require their suppliers do the same. Suppliers must comply with HP's requirements specified in the Supplier Code of Conduct and the product content environmental guidelines found in the General Specification for the Environment (GSE)."[6]

CASE STUDY

Combined Aspirational and Company Code of Conduct: HP

HP SUPPLIER CODE OF CONDUCT

At HP, we work collaboratively with our suppliers to ensure compliance with our Supplier Code of Conduct. While we recognize that there are different legal and cultural environments in which suppliers operate throughout the world, this Code of Conduct sets forth the minimum requirements that all suppliers must meet in doing business with HP.

Specifically we expect our suppliers to:

1. **Adhere to all national and other applicable laws and regulations** governing protection of the environment, worker health & safety, and labor and employment practices wherever they do business.

2. **Establish management systems** (policies, plans and performance measures) that are designed to implement these requirements, and to provide for compliance assurance and continual improvement.

We require our suppliers to sign a Supplier Agreement that says they agree with HP's Supplier Code of Conduct. If a supplier identifies areas

---

6. See *www.hp.com/hpinfo/globalcitizenship/environment/supplychain/scserfaqs.html.*

that do not comply, the supplier agrees to implement and monitor improvements.

We use our Supplier Management Process to assess our suppliers' performance. This process uses questionnaires, reviews, and on-site supplier visits. We may also use independent verification where appropriate. We are committed to working with our suppliers to address any deviations quickly and effectively.

1.0   Compliance with Laws

HP suppliers must comply with all national and other applicable laws and regulations, and they must require their suppliers do the same. This includes laws and regulations relating to environmental, occupational health and safety, and labor practices.

1.1   Environmental Practices

HP expects our suppliers to provide products to HP and to conduct their business operations in a way that protects and sustains the environment in accordance with applicable laws and regulations.

1.1.1   Products

Products supplied to HP must comply with HP specifications and all applicable legal requirements. Among these, is General Specification for Environment (GSE), *www.hp.com/hpinfo/community/environment/pdf/gse.pdf* which include the following:

- **Product Content Restrictions**
  Comply with laws and regulations that restrict or prohibit certain chemical compounds as constituents of products, as specified in HP's General Specification for Environment (GSE).

- **Product Labeling for Recycling and Disposal**
  Comply with all laws and regulations regarding product labeling for recycling and disposal, as specified in HP's General Specification for Environment (GSE).

1.1.2   Operations

HP suppliers are expected to comply with applicable environmental laws and regulations in all of their operations worldwide. Specifically, suppliers are expected to conform to these requirements in each of the following areas:

- **Environmental Permits and Reports**
  Obtaining and maintaining environmental permits and registrations for operations and facilities and fulfilling reporting obligations.

- **Hazardous Materials and Waste Management**
  Managing hazardous materials used in operations and disposing of hazardous waste generated from operations.
- **Industrial Wastewater Discharge and Air Emissions Management**
  Monitoring, controlling and treating wastewater and air emissions generated from operations.

1.2 **Occupational Health and Safety Practices**
HP suppliers are expected to provide a safe and healthy working environment for their workers in accordance with laws and regulations in all of their operations worldwide. Specifically, suppliers are expected to conform to these requirements in each of the following areas:

- **Employee OHS Training**
  Providing workers with the training they need to understand the health and safety hazards in their jobs and the protective measures and work practices appropriate to control those hazards.
- **Occupational Injury and Illness Reporting and Management**
  Encouraging workers to report occupational injuries and illnesses to their employer and providing workers with medical treatment and management of occupational illness and injury to enable them to return to work.
- **Machine Safeguarding**
  Providing and maintaining operating machinery and equipment with guarding or other protective measures as necessary to prevent injury to workers.
- **Industrial Hygiene**
  Identifying, evaluating and controlling workplace exposures to chemical, biological and physical agents to prevent worker illness and injury.
- **Workplace Ergonomics**
  Controlling ergonomic hazards in manual handling, machine operation, and other physically demanding jobs to prevent work-related musculoskeletal disorders.[7]

---

7. Safety and health references that address training, injury/illness reporting, machine safeguarding, industrial hygiene and ergonomics can be found on the following Web sites: *www.osha.gov*; *http://europe.osha.eu.int*; *www.osha.gov/us-eu/index.html*; and *www.ilo.org/public/english/protection/safework/index.htm*.

1.3 Labor Practices

HP suppliers are expected to adopt sound labor practices and treat their workers fairly in accordance with local laws and regulations in all of their operations worldwide. Specifically, suppliers are expected to conform to these requirements in each of the following areas:

- **Freely Chosen Employment**
  Ensuring no forced, bonded or involuntary prison labor is used in the production of HP products or services. Ensuring that the overall terms of employment are voluntary.

- **No Child Labor**
  Complying with local minimum working age laws and requirements, and not employing child labor.

- **Minimum Wages**
  Providing wages and benefits that meet or exceed legal requirements.

- **Working Hours**
  Not requiring workers to work more than the maximum hours of daily labor set by local laws, and ensuring the overtime is voluntary and paid in accordance with local laws and regulations.

- **No Discrimination**
  Prohibiting legal discrimination based on race, color, age, gender, sexual orientation, ethnicity, religion, disability, union membership or political affiliation.

- **No Harsh or Inhumane Treatment**
  Prohibiting physical abuse, harassment or the threat of either.

- **Freedom of Association**
  Respecting the rights of workers to organize in labor unions in accordance with local labor laws and established practices.

2.0 Management Systems

HP suppliers are expected to maintain management systems that measure, improve and communicate to interested parties the environmental, occupational health and safety and labor performance of the company's operations in a systematic way. Specifically, HP suppliers are expected to maintain management systems in these areas that contain each of the following components:

- **Policy**
  Written statement of the company's commitments and objectives for its environmental, health and safety, and labor practices.
- **Performance Objectives with Implementation Plan, and Measures**
  Written performance objectives, targets and implementation plans, as decided and adopted by the company for itself, with a plan for assessing the company's performance against those objectives.
- **Assigned Company Representatives**
  Identified company representative[s] responsible for implementation of the company's environmental, health and safety and labor programs.

Source: *www.hp.com/hpinfo/globalcitizenship/environment/pdf/supcode.pdf.*

Whatever the real or imagined legal obligations that come with membership of these types of compacts, or the development of these types of aspirational codes of conduct, pledges to adhere to these principles can hardly be taken lightly. It is an important part of the role of the CERO to weigh up the pros and cons of membership of the various codes, and this assessment should be completed as part of the process of building the business case for action and creating the "moral minimum" framework for a company's ethical supply chain policies.

CHAPTER NINE

Creating a Case for Action

O*ne of the most important functions of
the ethics committee, led by the Chief Ethics and Risk Officer, should be to
develop a credible ethical supply chain business case for the company. It is
a critical exercise, not only in producing the supporting financial data to
justify an ethical supply chain initiative, but also because the process of
building a business case itself will provide improved insight into the
strengths and weaknesses of the current company processes and potential
supplier-related vulnerabilities. The business case should be as comprehensive and strategic as possible, taking into account many of the quantitative
and qualitative arguments for and against various elements of a full ethical
supply chain program that we have made already in this book.*

A company's motivation to ensure that its suppliers are adhering to sound employment and environmental policies might be altruism, or equally it might stem from a legitimate need to avoid being seen as "socially irresponsible" by investors and consumers. Or a company's motivation may simply be enlightened self-interest—realizing that a better managed supplier is likely to provide higher quality goods, dependable delivery, and lower prices in the end. Whatever the motivation, however, in order to better understand the relative costs and benefits of adopting various aspects of an external supply chain framework (and for explaining these to interested and sometimes skeptical stakeholders, including senior management), it is important to build a strong business case for action.

Savings and Benefits

First, it should be said that when calculating the savings and intangible benefits for an ethical supply chain framework, it is worthwhile keeping in mind—and giving proper weight to—the liability costs of inaction, particularly given the catastrophic possible outcomes of becoming a target of an NGO campaign or a government investigation. After all, the fact that a serious social or environmental incident can create lasting damage to a company's reputation means that the exercise needs to be something more than simply weighing up the relative cost versus benefit dollar figures.

With this in mind, and although difficult to calculate objectively with any accuracy, it is important to take into account the contingency costs of damage to the company's reputation—a run on the share price, consumer boycotts, legal fees, fines, and environmental clean-up costs—that a crisis in the supply chain may provoke. In many ways, these areas tend to dwarf the typical day-to-day "hard costs" that are used to calculate normal costs and savings in studies such as these. When potential liabilities or reputation damage are involved, day-to-day costs can become suddenly very insignificant in comparison.

"For example," says GEMI, "Intel recently decided to join many other companies in agreeing to buy only wood products certified to come from well-managed second-growth forests. Intel buys few wood products, so the cost consequences were small. To protect reputation, a decision was quickly made without a detailed calculation of pencil prices."[1] Too often, companies still resist change simply because there is a visible, if relatively small investment cost involved, overlooking the potentially devastating costs of being blind-sided by a reputation-damaging disaster.

---

1. Global Environmental Management Initiative, p. 22.

Putting aside the critical issue of reputation damage, at the most practical level, there is growing evidence that basic improvements in the health, safety, and environmental policies of developing world suppliers can mean significant return on investment. There is, after all, also a positive side to managing suppliers proactively and helping them improve their performance.

First, as we have seen, though less easily quantifiable, given the multiple pressures of globalization, strategic sourcing, and the continuous quality improvement movement, closer integration, at least with selected suppliers, is necessary for more efficient supply chain collaboration. Closer monitoring and audits lead to collaborative planning, rethinking inefficient or dangerous processes, to closer levels of communication and cooperation, and to generally higher expectations for performance all around.

More important, of course, are the straightforward productivity increases that come from better management and more efficient working methods at the supplier level. After all, supplier workplace injuries, low pay, and poor equipment maintenance, even in developing markets, are hardly a good foundation for efficient production. Purchasing illegal or toxic ingredients can shut down an entire production process, or lead to later recalls. Low wages and bad working conditions tend to produce low performance—waste, late deliveries, rework—and poor quality products. Reducing toxins in supplier facilities reduces their health and safety costs (protective equipment, employee turnover and retraining, employee compensation), wherever the plant is located, and recycling not only reduces waste but can often significantly reduce disposal costs.

Too often, U.S. companies tend to focus only on the negative—that is, bureaucratic—side of the equation, emphasizing only the costs associated with these types of programs, say experts. Again, reflecting the different perceptions discussed in Chapter Five, this seems to be less the case in European companies. "I believe that companies in Europe see those kinds of activities as a way of increasing their competitiveness," says Tomasz Kobus, from PricewaterhouseCoopers' Assurance/Business Advisory Services in New York. "Aside from just being responsible, it means selling more and being more competitive in the market."[2]

Many would argue that if exceeding minimum standards of employee treatment—training, pay, conditions, working hours—was effective for industry in U.S. or European production sites, it follows that similar improvements will increase productivity, reduce workplace injuries, and reduce training costs from turnover in developing labor markets. There is an ever-growing body of evidence to support these real business benefits. John Brookes, CEO of Manaxis and an experienced social and environ-

---

2. Interview, November 6, 2003.

mental auditor, contends that high expectations of supplier performance and good overall supply chain management go hand in hand. "Leading edge companies tend to manage everything well," he suggests. For example, "it would be unusual for a company to manage quality well, but not their environmental issues. Companies that have the right culture, driven from the top, tend to be doing the right thing . . . I think the same companies that have lead in other areas are leading in corporate social responsibility areas."[3]

Equally important, in terms of productivity increases, is helping developing world suppliers understand the value of modern organizational and employee management techniques. "For example," explains Michael Allen, Director of External Affairs with the Global Alliance for Workers and Communities, "supervisory skills training helps line managers fully understand that abusive management practices are not only morally unacceptable code violations, but that they are also bad management . . . a skills-based approach draws out the business case for worker-friendly management practices: that well-treated workers are more productive, loyal and creative."

In recent training sessions with supplier managers and supervisors that Global Alliance had in Indonesia, for example, participant comments reflected that important link between improved management training and greater productivity:

- "Quality problems are now responded to much more quickly."
- Managers "give more opportunity for 'subordinates' to express ideas."
- "Problem-solving meetings are now held . . . Improved communication about work processes is resulting in positive impact on work quality."
- "Greater delegation by department heads and supervisors has prompted higher performance and discipline standards from operators."[4]

Those same factory managers report improvements in quality and customer satisfaction, and employees interviewed spoke of the improved working conditions, better treatment by supervisors, and a greater sense of participation.

"This is a mutual gains agenda that invests in training and employee welfare that in turn enhances worker performance," concludes Mike Allen. "A sustainable approach to 'supply change' is only feasible through equip-

3. Interview, August 15, 2003.
4. Allen Michael, "Analysis: Increasing Standards in the Supply Chain," *Ethical Corporation*, October 2002, pp. 34–36.

ping managers and workers with the tools, skills and incentives to take ownership of the issues at workplace level. The associated business benefits of enhanced employee motivation, retention and performance at least hold out the promise of building on the essential compliance agenda and moving from minimum standards to high performance."[5]

Stratos, the Canadian-based sustainability consultancy, asked Canadian companies in a 2002 survey what they believed were the benefits of sustainability reporting. Their responses:

- Improves reputation (74 percent).
- Aids stakeholder communications (56 percent).
- Improves performance (54 percent).
- Improves management of risk (54 percent).
- Strengthens management systems (54 percent).
- Motivates employees (50 percent).
- Attracts investment (43 percent).
- Identifies opportunities for savings (30 percent).
- Increases access to markets (30 percent).[6]

More objective savings can be calculated—even if only indirectly through improved social and environmental policies by company suppliers—from reduced health care or insurance pay-outs to injured workers, lower recruitment and retraining costs for replacing employees, less downtime lost to union efforts, reducing the cost of protective garments when using unsafe materials, decreasing hazardous disposal costs, or myriad other practices that are now considered necessary to productive working environment.

"These jobs are relatively highly skilled," contends John Brookes, highlighting a widely held misperception. "Although they are minimum wage jobs, needlecraft is not an unskilled job, believe me."

"Even though they might only get paid four dollars a day," he explains, "they have to invest in training people, and it is not as straightforward [as it seems]. Yes, they will bring people in from the provinces, and yes, there are people knocking on the door waiting to take these positions, but there are training costs involved, so reducing turnover is one of the major issues for supplying companies . . . and one of the things that actually can drive the tangible benefits from an SA 8000-type system.

---

5. Allen, pp. 34–36.

6. "Corporate Sustainability Reporting: Adding Business Value," *Stratos, Inc.,* August 2002, p. 4 at *www.stratos-sts.com.*

"The quality demands of western purchasing organizations are extremely high," maintains Brookes. "You remember when you were a kid, anything made in Japan was ridiculed—then it was Taiwan, then Korea. Today that kind of thing doesn't exist anywhere anymore. Reebok, Chiquita, Nike, whoever," he suggests, "all western buyers have the same quality demands from Chinese factories as they would from everywhere else. And there are skill levels associated with that quality. It is manual labor, to be sure, but it is semi-skilled and there is a major investment in training for suppliers."[7]

There are many good examples of how applying higher standards has improved supplier productivity:

• A recent study conducted by the World Bank's private sector lending arm (the International Finance Corporation) and the consultancy SustainAbility, found that of the 176 companies surveyed in 60 different countries, "sustainable practices can be linked with lower costs, higher revenues, reduced risk, better reputation and staff morale, and greater access to capital."[8]

• The Thai Garment Manufacturing Association implemented a series of social responsibility policies pressed upon it by various international corporations. Applying SA 8000 (see Chapter Ten), the company limited its overtime to a maximum of 12 hours a week (well below the 36 hours allowed under Thai law). Yet even as overtime was cut by nearly one half, a combination of better working practices and an employee incentive plan meant that productivity rose 21 percent and employee pay rose 10 percent.[9]

• Rewriting their code of conduct and based on the SA 8000 standard, Chiquita began working toward certification in 2000. In 2001 they began a collaborative program with banana growers to provide greatly improved working conditions for the pickers, including rebuilding facilities and initiating modern health and safety programs, helping to provide a school and daycare center for workers' children, and building affordable housing around the processing sites for the workers and their families. In their 2001 Social Responsibility report, Chiquita lists the soft benefits that come from their efforts as greatly improved employee morale and trust. But there are "hard" benefits, as well. Recycling policies have saved the company millions of dollars, with savings on agrochemicals alone amounting to 14 percent, or $4.8 million a year. Similarly, pallet recycling (before, they were simply thrown away) saved $3 million, and health and safety

---

7. Interview, August 15, 2003.

8. Alison Maitland, "Developing Nations Win by Getting Greener," *The Financial Times,* June 27, 2002.

9. Somporn Thapanachai, "Accountability Essential," *The Bangkok Post,* November 16, 2002.

costs were reduced by $513,000 per year in one division. Able to better retain trained employees, and essentially ensure an efficient, loyal workforce, the policies help them avoid underage employment, and better worker conditions have meant that they have avoided the perennial and crippling strikes that typically plague the industry.[10]

- Ron Nielsen, Manager of Environment and Sustainability at Alcan, a company that was listed by the Dow Jones Sustainability Index in 2000 as among the top 10 percent of companies in its sector in terms of economic, environmental, and social policies, recently listed 10 reasons why these types of sustainability are beneficial:

1. Finding new approaches to operations that raise productivity and conserve resources
2. Developing new profitable products and alliances because of improved stakeholder, customer, and supplier relations and intelligence
3. Fostering increased loyalty and improved relationships with suppliers, contractors, and customers due to the focus on these relationships
4. Longer tenure and increased attraction of high quality workers due to company reputation, values, and focus
5. Increased worker productivity and innovation due to a focus on workplace and employee issues
6. Improved relations with communities and governments because of proactive, responsible, and ethical approaches
7. Increased demand for a product or service because of consumer support for sustainability
8. Improved management and increased mitigation of risks and liabilities through a business decision-making model that reinforces sustainability principles
9. Increased access to capital as markets begin to value sustainability performance
10. Better use of resources—R&D, investment, business planning—on those parts of the business that demonstrate long term, sustainable opportunity[11]

---

10. Conference Presentation by Jeff Zalla, Corporate Responsibility Officer and Vice President, Corporate Communications, at "How to Manage Corporate Responsibility" seminar, October 3, 2002; and "2000 Corporate Responsibility Report," *Chiquita Brands International, Inc.*

11. Toby Kent, "Alcan and Sustainable Development," Conference Report for the "How to Manage Corporate Responsibility Conference," *Ethical Corporation Magazine,* October 2–4, 2002 and at *www.ethicalcorp.com/confreport_usa2002.asp.*

"Companies that manage and report on sustainability issues," says Geoff Lane of PricewaterhouseCoopers, "typically cite improved financial performance, reduced operating costs, improved operational efficiency, enhanced brand image and reputation, increased sales and customer loyalty, increased ability to attract and retain employees, reduced regulatory oversight and improved access to capital.

"A growing body of academic evidence," he concludes, "suggests the benefits are tangible."[12]

There are also potentially considerable savings to be achieved, if the company is requiring its suppliers to become certified in quality processes such as ISO 9000. The current trend is to combine important aspects of the ISO 9000 quality standard certification process (now almost ubiquitous even in developing world manufacturing sites), with the ISO 14001 environmental standard certification process. Both have been designed by the International Standards Organization (OSI), and the two process approaches have many aspects in common (similar audit processes, document control requirements, management review, etc.), and the audit and certification process can often be combined for cost savings and efficiencies. These types of productivity results are not that unusual, and the relative costs of implementing a standard such as SA 8000 to the buying company are not as onerous as often thought.

"In terms of SA 8000," explains John Brookes, a certified auditor and CEO of Manaxis, "there should be relatively little cost in terms of maintaining the system. SA 8000 was designed (as was ISO 14000) to be able to be implemented by companies in all industry sectors, all countries, all shapes and sizes—even not-for-profit organizations. The requirements were written with the idea that they should not become too onerous or too expensive for the smaller company to implement.

"The cost of SA 8000 for most businesses," he contends, "would be minimal. They are required to create some records, to be able to demonstrate to the outside world that management principles are being adhered to, and there will be some monitoring costs—but relatively little, and those costs can really be offset very quickly against the company's needs and risk management, since they need to be doing this anyway."[13]

Finally, it is important not to overlook the "soft benefits" that come from these types of programs. These types of savings come not from the bottom line (increased productivity, less spent on overtime, legal fees, penalties, etc.), but rather from top line benefits (increased sales because of

---

12. Geoff Lane and Melissa Carrington, "Measuring the Triple Bottom Line," PricewaterhouseCoopers Web site at *www.pwc.com/extweb/manissue. nsf/2e7e9636c6b92859852565 e00073d2fd/dee94804c6db148685256cdf0036db78/$FILE/TripleBtmLine.pdf.*
13. Interview, August 15, 2003.

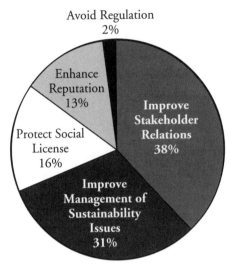

Avoid Regulation
2%

Enhance
Reputation
13%

Improve
Stakeholder
Relations
38%

Protect Social
License
16%

Improve
Management of
Sustainability
Issues
31%

FIGURE 9-1　Benefits from
SEAAR

Source: GlobeScan August 2002.

high NGO or Socially Responsible Investment Indices ratings, good press, or a "top 100" CSR rating, etc.).

In short, as many companies such as Chiquita, Apparel Avenue, and Gap have found, the same principles of quality and good management that are valid in domestic operations also apply to developing labor markets, and improving conditions and pay can contribute both directly and indirectly to the bottom line through productivity increases and reduced costs (see Figure 9-1).

Potential Costs

On the opposite side of the ledger, the team will need to consider the costs associated with dedicating resource and time to the supply chain program, developing education and training programs, monitoring suppliers, and developing a company report. These efforts all cost money. As we have seen, Nike now has a team of 85 working full-time on SEAAR-related monitoring and reporting; Gap has a team of 90. Ford reported in 2001 that it was spending between $27,000 and $85,000 per manufacturing plant in order to attain certification in ISO 14001.[14] Baxter

---

14. "New Paths to Business Value," the Global Environmental Management Initiative at *www.gemi.org/newpath.pdf.*

International, the healthcare company, reported spending $625,000 over two years on its social reporting exercise.[15]

With commercial auditors charging $1,500 a day, it is not uncommon for a buying company to spend $10,000–15,000 each year on inspectors and coaches for each supplier. When dealing with thousands of suppliers, these monitoring and inspection costs can soon add up.[16] And, of course, what companies do not want, is to lose their cost savings and the advantages of outsourcing by having to spend enormous sums of money to improve subcontractor operations.

These costs will vary significantly, of course, depending on the effort undertaken, the size and location of the company, and the relative cost sharing formula agreed on between company and supplier. Some companies may limit themselves to paying for the audits and certification process, expecting supplier factories or farms to fund the improvement process itself. In other cases, that arrangement may be reversed, particularly where multiple companies buy from the same factory, competitors and industry groups often collaborate in funding improvements according to their relative percentage of yearly purchase from the supplier.

Tools and Methods for Compiling the Business Case

One of the best ways to begin developing a business case for action is for the CERO and his or her team to use a **self-assessment tool** that can help them benchmark the company's current state against their stated goals and the performance indicators that they have selected and the stakeholder expectations they have developed. These self-assessment tools help the company understand the gap between stated policy and reality in areas such as:

- Levels of employee "buy-in" to high standards of ethical behavior
- Board and senior management perceptions and degrees of support
- Stakeholder expectations

---

15. Alison Maitland, "Social Reporting: Pressures Mount for Greater Disclosure," *FT.com*, December 10, 2002.

16. "Supply Chains and the OECD Guidelines for Multinational Enterprises," BIAC Discussion Paper on Supply Chain Management," OECD, June 19, 2002 at *http://216.239.51.100/search?q=cache:4HIg_TX2Fi8C:www.uscib.org/docs/ CR-biacscm.pdf+ethical+supply+chain&hl=en&ie=UTF-8.*

- The information gathering capabilities and general "risk awareness" of the company
- Potential areas of concern throughout the extended supply chain, including supplier behavior

There are many good examples of these self-assessment tools, including those from CERES, the Global Environmental Management Initiative (GEMI), the Sustainable Development Commission in the United Kingdom (see Appendix D), or from pioneering companies such as Sustainability Northwest (see Appendix E), which can be used to judge the quality of a company's "sustainability" or ethical supply chain strategy.

Following this type of self-assessment, a company will be in a better position to develop an implementation plan and to gauge the spending and resource requirements that make up the cost side of the business case.

Creating a Formal Implementation Plan

Finally, the CERO and his or her staff should create a detailed implementation plan highlighting key goals, success criteria, and probable required changes to management systems and processes (staffing, inspection team development, new IT systems, education and training needs, etc.) that form the basis of the company's business case for action. The plan should detail responsibility and accountability for successful implementation, and set the basis for a reward and incentive plan to be incorporated into management and employee pay and reward systems (including building accountability into employee job descriptions). It should address items such as:

- The case for action
- The company's ethical supply chain strategy
- Results of the self-assessment tool
- Proposed new policy, operations, and activities tied to specific timelines and milestones
- Immediate and intermediate-term resources required
- Changes to current procedures and likely implications of these changes
- Key performance and success indicators
- Reward and incentive program requirements

- A proposed process for monitoring and assessing success
- Training and education needs and budget
- Expected total costs and benefits assessment

Most companies have found that such an implementation plan works best if developed on two levels: a long-term strategic plan (3–5 years), and a short-term (yearly) plan based on key-date milestones. These plans should be approved and reviewed regularly by senior executives and board members as part of a formal and ongoing risk management process. Once a company self-assessment has been completed and the CERO and his or her team has produced a business case and created a formal implementation plan, a company is in a much better position to move forward with the next important step, choosing internationally accepted social and environmental standards.

CHAPTER TEN

Choosing Performance and Process Standards

*A*s we have seen, the need to create
easily compared, objective, and verifiable standards of social and environmental conduct have prompted the international community to begin
developing corporate integrity guidelines. Supportive groups — and there
are several — have attempted to develop guidelines for nonfinancial, ethical
accounting principles and measurements that corporations can adopt, and
for which certifiable compliance will provide a company with an objective
"stamp of approval" that will be available to consumers and shareholders.

"**W**hether you sell clothing, chocolate, garden furniture or diamonds," says Sarah Roberts from the National Center for Business and Sustainability, "the chances are that your company will have received requests to commit to one of the codes offered by third parties. With outsourcing the norm, all major companies are going to have to find ways to influence the sustainability of their supply networks . . ."[1]

Mick Blowfield, from the Natural Resources Institute (NRI) agrees. "Establishing standards along the value chain," he says "and the monitoring and verification of these standards is an increasingly important part of supply chain management."[2]

As we have seen, beyond the level of aspirational codes, a new set of detailed social and environmental standards have emerged over the past several years. These new standards promise to revolutionize the way companies manage their (and their suppliers') social and environmental practices. These standards—SA 8000, ISO 14001, the Ethical Trading Initiative, AA 1000—are rapidly becoming integral to the ethical supply chain framework of progressive companies worldwide.

But the development of these standards has had its teething problems. As with other quality certification movements—ISO 9000, Six Sigma, Baldrige—there has been a good deal of early chaos as groups have attempted to come to agreement on both the procedures and the measurements that constitute international social and environmental process and performance norms. Accordingly, as pressure on companies to support the standards and reporting movement has grown, there have emerged various options for companies—ranging from simple, unenforceable pledges of good behavior (the aspirational codes we examined in Chapter Eight), to more stringent, and specific, performance standards. It has been confusing, particularly in the past two years, as multiple standards and forums jockeyed for position, and it is only recently that it has become more obvious how to begin to sort the wheat from the chaff.

These more detailed standards emerged in the late 1990s as NGOs, investors, and the public began to demand higher levels of accountability and transparency from multinationals with regard to their social and environmental policies in their extended supply chain. Progressive companies quickly began to supplement their aspirational codes with these more detailed process and performance standards.

---

1. Sarah Roberts, "Analysis: Ethical Sourcing Codes—The Answer to Supply Chain Sustainability Concerns?" *Ethical Corporation,* August 1, 2002.

2. Mick Blowfield, "Fundamentals of Ethical Trading/Sourcing in Poorer Countries," *The World Bank Group* at *http://wbln0018.worldbank.org/ESSD/essdext.nsf/26ByDocName/FundamentalsofEthicalTradingSourcinginPoorerCountries.*

Just as with ISO 9000 and other quality and performance standards, several bodies, including the International Standards Organization itself, have developed more robust sets of environmental and social standards that allow companies, after being inspected and qualifying, to be certified at a higher level of performance in these areas. Some, such as SA 8000 or the ISO 14000 series, are focused broadly on either labor or environmental issues. Others, such as the Forest Stewardship Council or the Worldwide Responsible Apparel Production Principles, deal specifically with unique vertical industries.

In fact, many multinational companies had already begun to create these types of performance standards well before any recognized international standards emerged, in response to the call from pressure groups and investors for greater transparency, standardization, and comparability. But the obvious conflict of interest made self-styled performance standards suspect from the start. It was soon obvious that performance standards that were written by individual companies tended to be inconsistent in their application, and to vary widely, providing cover for policies companies would prefer not to expose. Too often the performance standards would be devised in a way that portrayed the companies in the best possible light, focusing on easily achievable aspects of labor or environmental policy that would appeal to NGOs or investors, while at the same time ignoring the more egregious violations. As we have seen, these self-initiated and self-administered standards provided little dependable information on the company working conditions or environmental policies, and failed to create the trust or reassurance that the companies were hoping for.

Performance Standards

The first important group within this new standards framework is what has become known as "performance standards," because they take the guiding principles for social and environmental performance that are common to the aspirational codes of conduct, and create a level of detail that allows companies to monitor, assess, and report on their performance in these areas much more effectively.

As a result, over the past five years, a number of third-party organizations have scrambled to create performance standards that can be applied to companies more universally, and that will allow outsiders—investors, pressure groups, consumers—to compare activities and performance between companies. There are three key themes at the heart of this performance standards development: transparency, comparability, and quality improvement.

• **Transparency and Comparability.** Adopting recognized performance standards provides the outside world with a verifiable assessment of the company's social and environmental policies. If those policies are superlative, these can serve as a strong sales and marketing tool, providing a favorable comparison with the competition and assuring investors and consumers that there is a strong link between the company's stated values and their actions.

• **Quality Improvement.** Not only do they demonstrate to investors and consumers the company's progressive policies toward labor and environmental policies, but, just as with the ISO 9000 or Baldrige certification processes, these social and environmental performance standards can also be invaluable in helping a company identify and correct the "faults" within their extended supply chain—product wastage, inefficient disposal or reuse polices, unsafe or unhealthy working conditions—that once corrected, can bring significant quality and productivity savings to the supplier, and therefore to the company itself.

If the social or environmental practices within the supply chain are weak, of course, applying standards, just as with applying the Baldrige process, means that a company risks exposure for poor performance. Even so, it also means that problem areas are discovered and can be corrected, and in the long term, as we have seen, all evidence indicates that investors and NGOs are more forgiving of a company that is trying to formally and openly improve on poor policies than of a company that is obfuscating and avoiding exposure or improvement.

These performance standards are usually focused either *horizontally* on broad areas such as environmental policy or labor and employment issues, or focused more *vertically* on industries such as bananas, toys, apparel, and footwear, or forest and lumber. And although there have been many standards and codes to appear in the past five years, consolidation is taking place in which a few well-structured and effective standards have emerged as permanent and preferred leaders.

Horizontal Social Performance Standards

Among these, **Social Accountability 8000 (SA 8000)** is probably the most important workers' rights performance standard to emerge to date, and is clearly destined to evolve into the most widely accepted format for addressing company issues around its social performance. Developed by the Council on Economic Priorities Accreditation Agency (CEPAA), a nonprofit organization, SA 8000 was first published in 1997 as a response to the need for companies to have access to a common, standardized framework for good labor management and workplace environment practices, not only for company-owned facilities, but also latterly to help address labor and employment issues in developing-world factories. Today it is funded from many sources, including grants from foundations, international development organizations, and the U.S. government.

Based on many of the most important ideas taken from the International Labor Organization Conventions, the United Nations Universal Declaration of Human Rights, and the Convention on the Rights of the Child, in 1996 the framework was taken up by Social Accountability International, the New York-based standards and advisory group, which then incorporated various best practice concepts from well-known and widely applied quality standards such as ISO 9000. It is, in their words, a tool for companies to "demonstrate a real and credible commitment to achieving decent working conditions in their supply chains."[3]

In many ways, SA 8000 is both an international human resources standard and a verification tool. Building on accepted international labor rights principles—that employers should provide fair wages and a safe working environment, that labor should be voluntary, should not involve children and should not involve inhumane working hours—the SA 8000 framework also addresses a variety of other important employment issues such as union membership, discrimination, methods of discipline, and the freedom of association. Member companies receive a "Guidance Document" that provides them with the codes and guidelines, as well as a consultancy service, education, and training.

But equally important, implementing the standard means adopting a management system that is designed to help companies enforce these rights and provide workers with education and training on modern management techniques. These include a company communication program and assistance with creating the proper organizational structure so that the company provides the necessary budget allocations, management responsibility, and authority for enforcing the standards. For that reason, a standard such as SA 8000 itself can serve as a good foundation document and guideline for helping companies to create an ethical supply chain program such as the one we are describing.

Although companies themselves can be signatories to its principles, actual certification takes place on a facility-by-facility basis. Social Accountability International does not complete the audits itself, but provides training and accreditation for auditors and auditing firms. These SAI accredited firms—known as certification bodies—can be hired to provide audit and certification of manufacturing facilities.

Aware of the problems inherent in designing a "one-size-fits-all" approach, in developing the SA 8000 standard, Social Accountability International

---

3. Carol Pier, "A Case Study of Corporate Conduct Within the Supply Chain," Human Rights Watch, at *http://216.239.53.100/search?q=cache:OQ0HKPH1fg8C:www.ausncp. gov.au/content/docs/20020901_pier.pdf+supply+chain+supplier+SA+8000+inspec tions&hl=en&ie=UTF-8.*

solicited input from a variety of industry groups, activists, labor rights organizations, and specialists in certification and auditing, and has designed a framework that is both standardized and yet flexible enough to take into account cultural and legal differences of various labor markets around the world.

In many ways, SA 8000 is very similar to standards already developed for the quality movement, and therefore, like any formal Deming-like management system or quality program, inevitably helps a factory identify quality and process "defects" and make productivity improvements.

"It [SA 8000] looks at many of the same processes and requirements that government regulations such as OSHA would ask for," says Fitz Hilaire, Director of Global Supplier Development at Avon. "It looks at the safety procedures. It looks at the policies that govern your hiring and firing, your methods to ensure there is no discrimination, that there is no child labor and those kinds of things."[4]

In fact, *Business Week* has gone so far in its praise of the standard to assert that SA 8000 was: "A potential breakthrough not just on sweatshops, but on common labor standards for the global economy as a whole."[5]

Unlike most other standards, however, SA 8000 has bitten the bullet and requires companies that adopt the framework to demonstrate compliance by submitting to independent audits, completed by third-party certification groups trained in the SA 8000 methodology. There are still some problems, though. Because certification is offered to facilities and not to companies, it is possible to be a member corporation and yet not actually have any company or supplier certification. Moreover, original signatory members still are only required to bring their directly owned and supplier facilities into compliance within an unspecified "reasonable time period." This has lead to criticism of companies such as Dole, which although a signatory member since November 1999, at least according to Human Rights Watch, still has not brought any of its supplier plantations in Ecuador into compliance. "Thus, as an SA 8000 signatory member," says Carol Pier from Human Rights Watch, "Dole pays a $10,000 annual membership fee, can publicize affiliation with 'a global humane workplace standard,' but need not ensure compliance, on its own or its supplier facilities, with SA 8000's terms."[6]

---

4. David Creelman, "Interview: Avon's Fitz Hilaire on Social Accountability," *The Star Tribune* at *http://startribune.hr.com/HRcom/index.cfm/WeeklyMag/F754EEA5-73D8-4CB9-98D56A615F9EBB72?ost=wmFeature.*

5. See Social Accountability International's Web site at *www.cepaa.org/introduction.htm.*

6. Carol Pier, "A Case Study of Corporate Conduct Within the Supply Chain," *Human Rights Watch,* at *http://216.239.53.100/search?q=cache:OQOHKPH1fg8C:www.ausncp.gov. au/content/docs/20020901_pier.pdf+supply+chain+supplier+SA+8000+inspections&hl= en&ie=UTF-8.*

Whatever its limitations in the area of membership versus compliance, the standard is quickly becoming an important force in the emerging social and labor standards market. In 2003 there were 259 facilities currently certified under the SA 8000 standard, from 35 different industries in 36 countries. Signatories include such well-known names as Avon, Dole, Eileen Fisher, Otto Versand, Tex Line, and Toys "R" Us.[7]

CASE STUDY

SA 8000 Efficiency: Apparel Avenue

The Apparel Avenue Co., Ltd., a medium-sized factory in the apparel industry in Thailand, has two manufacturing sites and over 600 employees. It is typical of the type of supplier that we have been examining in this book. Founded in 1988, it produces apparel for international brands including Calvin Klein, Tommy Hilfiger, and Nautica, exporting nearly 75 percent of those garments to the United States.

The company obtained ISO 9002 certification for its production system in 1998, and ISO 14001 certification in 1999 (they claim to be the first garment factory in Asia to have received both certificates). In 2000, the company became the first and only factory in Thailand to earn an SA 8000 certification.

In April 1999, company president Kartchai Jamkajornkeiat initiated the SA 8000 project by appointing a multifunctional working team, representing various departments from throughout the company, led by a senior program manager, Ms. Prawee. She contends that the SA 8000 requirements helped the company greatly improve working conditions, and was widely accepted among employees.

"SA 8000 for Apparel Avenue [was] quite easy to implement," she explained. "Firstly, this is not the first standard that the company has to comply [with]. Secondly, since the employees are familiar with the implementation of quality standards during the last 3 years, they [were] ready to change. Finally, the employees perceive change in a positive way because every time the change takes place, they work in a better condition. Therefore, they believe that this new standard will improve their working environment again."

Still, attaining certification was not easy. A preliminary assessment revealed that company overtime policies would not meet the SA 8000 criteria. Employees worked on a single-shift basis from 8 am to 5 pm, 6 days a week, but also worked overtime, exceeding Thailand's limit of 36 hours per week (under a total Thailand government legal limit of 84 working hours per week). This meant that in order to comply with the

---

7. David Drickhamer, "SA 8000 Sets a Standard," *Industry Week.com,* June 1, 2002 at *www.iwvaluechain.com/Features/articles.asp?ArticleId=1263.*

SA 8000 guideline, the company had to reduce overtime for each employee from 36 to 12 hours per week—a significant hourly reduction that at first appeared impossible, as the company could not afford the loss in productivity, and employees feared the significant loss in pay.

The obvious answer was to improve productivity, and the SA 8000 team essentially began a process improvement investigation that mirrored the business reengineering programs so common in the developed economies in the last decade. They broke down the production process by activity and tasks for each workstation, and then redesigned the workflow process, changing the way work was sequenced, bringing in new tools, and rearranging responsibilities. This new workstation process then became a prototype that was replicated at each workstation throughout the factory.

Within three months, the company had reduced employee overtime by 28.57 percent, and received the SA 8000 certification in August 2000 after an independent audit by Bureau Veritas Quality International (BVQI).

Source: Rohitratana, Kaewta, "How to Effectively Implement SA 8000 in Thailand," Paper presented at the 6th ICIT Conference, Ayr Scotland, 17–19th April, 2001 at *www.mallenbaker.net/csr/CSRfiles/ sa8000_icit.doc.*

The Ethical Trading Initiative

Hand-in-hand with the SA 8000 framework has come the Ethical Trading Initiative, a UK government-funded project that was established in 1998 as a collaborative effort involving more than 30 European companies, various trade union groups, and 19 NGOs. It is a significant initiative, with considerable and growing influence—the combined annual turnover of member companies now exceeding $80 billion.[8]

Unlike many more general labor codes of conduct, the ETI is specifically focused on helping company members "remove risks to their reputation and operations from poor employment conditions in their suppliers."[9]

---

8. Teresa Fabian, "Supply Chain Management in an Era of Social and Environmental Accountability" at *www.sustdev.org/journals/edition.02/download/ sdi2_1_5.pdf.*

9. Peter Burgess, "Pilot Interim Review, Ethical Trading Initiative," SOMO Centre for Research on Multi-National Corporations, November 1999, p. 8 at *www.somo.nl/ monitoring/initiatives/eti-pilotrev.htm;* and also Teresa Fabian at *www.sustdev.org/ journals/edition.02/download/sdi2_1_5.pdf.*

The ETI base code requires that corporate members observe internationally agreed codes of conduct concerning labor and employment standards, including that:

- Employment is freely chosen.
- Freedom of association and the right to collective bargaining are respected.
- Working conditions are safe and hygienic.
- No child labor is used.
- Workers are paid a living wage.
- Working hours are not excessive.
- No discrimination is practiced.
- Regular employment is provided.
- No harsh or inhumane treatment is allowed.[10]

These principles are essentially the same as those found in the SA 8000 standard, and the two groups work hand-in-hand, even sharing common board members. There are important differences, however. SA 8000 is a standard, modeled on the structures of other ISO quality standards such as ISO 9000. This means that it requires that companies be certified by an accredited professional, third-party certification firm. SA 8000 provides a structured method for implementing the principles enshrined in the ETI.

The ETI's approach itself is very different from SA 8000's, and is focused on working with suppliers on experimental programs known as "pilot schemes," which develop new methods for improving working conditions. It is through this exchange of leading practices, they contend, that the ETI brings real value to its members.

Horizontal Environmental Performance Standards

While SA 8000 is often wrongly referred to as a social and environmental standard, in fact it only deals with social and labor-related issues. Following the upsurge in public concern for the environment of the past 10 years, however, several particularly important environmental standards have been developed—both within individual industries and, with the development

---

10. From the Ethical Trade Initiative Web site at *www.ethicaltrade.org/pub/publications/ purprinc/en/index.shtml.*

of the ISO 14000 series, more universally, with one standard applying to all industrial sectors.

ISO 14001

The ISO 14000 series of standards is rapidly becoming the leading international standard for environmental performance. The full 14000 series includes an Environmental Management System (ISO 14001), as well as various other standards for auditing (ISO 14010–14012), performance evaluation (ISO 14031), environmental labeling (ISO 14024), and life-cycle assessment (ISO 14040). As with SA 8000 in the social arena, the 14000 series is a framework that helps companies organize their environmental management systems, providing instructions on how to create an EMS process, how to collect and retain documentation, and how to communicate the process and train employees.

The 14001 series has become extremely popular, particularly in Japan and Europe, where since it was first published in 1996, some 10,000 companies have received certification. As with any ISO framework, the 14000 series is based on the idea that only a worldwide standard can provide the combination of consistency and comparability that are so important for investors, consumers, and NGOs anxious to understand how companies are managing the environment through their extended supply chain. Based in Geneva, Switzerland, the International Organization for Standardization is a nongovernmental organization that has been developing technical standards particularly related to manufacturing, quality assurance, and the supply chain since its establishment in 1947. In developing the ISO 14000 environmental standards, the ISO works with representatives from member countries, which in turn enlist the advice of corporations and government agencies (such as the U.S. Environmental Protection Agency or the U.S. Technical Advisory Group).

Similar in many ways to the EU's Eco-Management and Audit Scheme (EMAS) and the British Standards Institute's BS 7750, the ISO 14001 EMS standard is probably the most highly developed among the many emerging environmental standards, and much like Baldrige's 18 subsection "items," contains 17 key requirements of a company:

1. **Environmental Policy.** Develop a statement of the organization's commitment to the environment.
2. **Environmental Aspects and Impacts.** Identify environmental attributes of products, activities, and services and their effects on the environment.

3. **Legal and Other Requirements.** Identify and ensure access to relevant laws and regulations.

4. **Objectives and Targets.** Set environmental goals for the organization.

5. **Environmental Management Program.** Plan actions to achieve objectives and targets.

6. **Structure and Responsibility.** Establish roles and responsibilities within the organization.

7. **Training, Awareness and Competence.** Ensure that employees are aware of and capable of dealing with their environmental responsibilities.

8. **Communication.** Develop processes for internal and external communication on environmental management issues.

9. **EMS Documentation.** Maintain information about the EMS and related documents.

10. **Document Control.** Ensure effective management of procedures and other documents.

11. **Operational Control.** Identify, plan, and manage the organization's operations and activities in line with the policy, objectives, and targets.

12. **Emergency Preparedness and Response.** Develop procedures for preventing and responding to potential emergencies.

13. **Monitoring and Measuring.** Monitor key activities and track performance.

14. **Nonconformance and Corrective and Preventative Action.** Identify and correct problems and prevent recurrences.

15. **Records.** Keep adequate records of EMS performance.

16. **EMS Audit.** Periodically verify that the EMS is effective and achieving objectives and targets.

17. **Management Review.** Requires top management to periodically review the EMS for effectiveness in achieving the intent of the environmental policy and identify the need for changes to the system.[11]

---

11. See *www.p2pays.org/iso/emsisofaq.asp* or for a full description of the ISO 14000 platform see *www.iso.ch/iso/en/iso9000-4000/basics/general/basics_/.html*.

Vertical or Industry-Specific Environmental Standards

Many standards have developed over the past five years in specific industries—pulp and paper, bananas, furniture—and usually involve a combination of pledges by buying companies to adhere to a set of principles concerned with stopping environmental or social exploitation. There are many examples, but some of the better known and most successful include:

• **The European Community's Eco-Management and Audit Scheme (EMAS).** One of the first and most effective environmental auditing schemes, EMAS is sponsored by the EU and requires signatories to put in place a company environmental policy and to demonstrate senior management commitment. Established in 1995, EMAS is very similar in content to the ISO 14001 standard, and has traditionally been focused on manufacturing and industry in Europe, and though still mostly voluntary, is now mandatory for some industries in Germany and the Netherlands. Unlike ISO 14001, however, EMAS signatories are required to publish performance reports concerning their emissions, waste generation, and water and energy usage.[12]

• **The Better Banana Project, Sponsored by the Rainforest Alliance.** In 1991 the Rainforest Alliance, together with a group of Latin American conservation organizations, formed the Better Banana Project standards in order to help ensure that tropical wildlife and rainforests were protected from poor agricultural policies—pollution, over use of pesticides and agrochemicals, excess soil or water use—and to ensure the health and safety of workers. The effort has helped to alter the way that bananas are farmed by improving soil and water use, reducing rainforest destruction and waste, and promoting reforestation. They also set strict standards for worker health and safety on the farms. Individual farms seek certification under the program, and the Rainforest Alliance helps the farms to create an improvement plan and to become certified under the standards. The certification process can apply to farms, grower cooperatives, and multinationals.[13]

• **The Forest Stewardship Council (FSC).** One of the most effective environmental certification programs, the FSC is an independent NGO (supported by most of the large environmental NGOs such as Greenpeace or the World Wildlife Fund) that provides performance standards and a certification scheme for good environmental and economic forest management.

---

12. "Business Standards and Corporate Governance: Tools and Resources," *Corporate Social Responsibility Forum,* at *www.iblf.org/csr/csrwebassist.nsf/content/a1a2c3d4.html#iso.*

13. See *www.rainforest-alliance.org/programs/cap/program-description2.html.*

One of the first organizations to develop the concept of the "chain of custody," the FSC accredited certification system requires forest products to be labeled and monitored through the various stages of the supply chain, from cutting down the timber through manufacturing and to the point-of-sale by retailers. Forests have been certified in 30 countries, and the FSC is supported by various large corporations in the timber, pulp, and paper industries, including 480 U.S. companies that participate in the FSC's chain of custody program.[14]

Methodologies for Implementing Standard Codes of Conduct

Not only do these codes of conduct, standards, and guidelines demand a high and consistent standard of behavior for organizations, they are all designed to provide a structured framework of behavior for signatory organizations as well as a mechanism for investors who need to be able to measure "comparability" between the principles and activities of companies. As we have seen, however, critics have charged that simply having a guideline, even when combined with performance standards such as SA 8000, tells a company very little about how to actually achieve those goals—or for that matter, whether a company or its suppliers are adhering to those standards or not.

"... The important point is to measure implementation effects," says Robert Pojasek, Adjunct Lecturer on Environmental Science at Harvard University's School of Public Health, "rather than simply reviewing whether the organization has signed a statement." Corporations need specific program guidance, he suggests, such as that found in the Baldrige quality assessment process. Reflecting a widespread feeling among business leaders, he contends that standards and principles "all suffer from the same problem . . . "what" does not necessarily lead to "how.""[15]

To some extent, the response to the "how" question has come in the form of **AccountAbility (AA) 1000,** which, when combined with the provisions of the Global Reporting Initiative (see Chapter Sixteen), is expected to go some way toward resolving those issues. Launched in 1999 by the Institute of Social and Ethical AccountAbility, AA 1000 is not a code of

---

14. "Business Standards and Corporate Governance: Tools and Resources," *Corporate Social Responsibility Forum* at *www.iblf.org/csr/csrwebassist.nsf/content/a1a2c3d4.html#iso.*

15. Robert B. Pojasek, "How Do You Measure Environmental Performance?" *Environmental Quality Management,* October 4, 2001.

conduct or a performance standard but a framework of "best practice" methods in social and ethical accounting, auditing, and reporting. Known as a "process standard," AA 1000 does not tell a company what levels of performance it needs to achieve to be socially responsible (as does SA 8000), but instead focuses on helping companies judge if they have processes in place to monitor and report on their social and environmental performance. In short, unlike codes or standards, AA 1000 does not tell a company what it should do, but instead provides it with a framework to understand how it should be doing it.

Process Standards

Although it does have some elements of performance measurement, unlike SA 8000 or the ISO standards, a process standard such as AA 1000 is designed not to direct companies in terms of what the right thing to do is, but instead to instruct them on the way that they should go about doing the right thing.

AA 1000 has two sets of offerings. The first, the AA 1000 Framework, is a series of modules that provide guidance on how to interact with stakeholders—suppliers, business partners, NGOs, government agencies—in order to create legitimate and worthwhile social and environmental performance indicators.

The second offering, the AA 1000S Assurance Standard, usually implemented in conjunction with a recognized standard such as SA 8000 or ISO 14001, helps organizations evaluate their social and environmental performance against these industry standards. AA 1000S is also specifically designed to be consistent with GRI (the Global Reporting Initiative) guidelines (see Chapter Sixteen), providing guidance to companies on what are known as "assurance principles"—completeness, materiality, accessibility, evidence—when undertaking the reporting process itself. It therefore helps the company ensure that readers of their report can be "assured" of its accuracy and authenticity.

The AA 1000S framework covers five areas:

- **Planning.** Companies work with their stakeholders to create value statements, codes, and objectives, and then develop a social and environmental accounting system, including key performance indicators, measurements, and a reporting process, that reflect those aspirations.
- **Accounting.** The company collects and analyzes information on its social and environmental performance and prepares a report.

- **Auditing.** The performance information and the report are independently audited.
- **Reporting.** The report is published among employees and stakeholders.
- **Embedding.** The company takes lessons learned from the process and makes changes to its policies, procedures, and systems in order to improve their performance.[16]

One of the fundamental tenets of AA 1000 is that a company is very much dependent upon collaboration with its stakeholders in order to create an ethical supply chain, and it is this emphasis on consultation and collaboration with business partners that helps to make implementation of standards such as SA 8000 more effective. Constantly evolving, AA 1000 is in the process of being streamlined, and has recently developed five specialized modules, which include:

- **Assurance Framework.** A GAAP-like set of accounting principles, process standards, and procedures for social and sustainability auditing, important for creating "comparability" between different company reports.
- **Governance and Risk Management.** Designed to help companies develop performance metrics and report to investors on the company's efforts to manage social and environmental risk. This module covers issues such as forms of governance, the composition of various governance brokers within a company, how stakeholders gain access to company leaders, how company leaders are involved with ethical and social performance management, incentive programs for promoting sound and ethical performance among employees, and how ethical and social performance is incorporated in decision making.
- **Integration of AA 1000 Processes with Existing Management and Metrics Systems.** A module that helps match up information-gathering and reporting techniques with standard quality and performance tools such as the Balanced Scorecard. It provides tools for identifying current systems that can provide governance and social and environmental reporting information, with guidance on how to prioritize, embed, and integrate the information. This is an important addition, because it helps to link to other well-respected standards.

---

16. "AA 1000 Assurance Standard: Guiding Principles," Consultation Document, *AccountAbility,* June 2002.

- **Stakeholder Engagement.** This module provides guidance on how to develop a stakeholder program, including guidelines for addressing conflict of interest issues, tools for assessing the effectiveness of stakeholder engagement programs, and guidelines for documenting the outcomes.
- **Accountability in Small and Medium Organizations.** This module modifies other elements of the framework in order to help smaller companies to participate.[17]

Among the benefits that come from this type of a stakeholder-focused approach is the fact that the AA 1000 framework encourages specific dialogue with business partners, activists, and community leaders in a way that tends to quickly identify areas of social or environmental risk or abuse that are often ignored or purposely overlooked through an impersonal survey or questionnaire.

The Gradient Index

In an attempt to provide investors and consumers with information concerning how well companies are performing in social and environmental activities, the Institute for Social and Ethical AccountAbility has also launched the Gradient Index, which uses four areas for rating and ranking organizations. These criteria and standards are expected to be endorsed by the NGO community in the near future. The four areas are:

- **Corporate Understanding.** 'Understanding' focuses on indications that a company truly understands the broad area of supply chain labor standards. Such indicators will include: corporate commitments to International Labour Organisation Core Conventions; membership of multi-stakeholder initiatives that contribute to organizational understanding (e.g., ETI, FLA, SAI); and the existence of senior representatives at an executive and nonexecutive level responsible for ensuring the organization's awareness of supply chain labor issues.
- **Policy.** 'Policy' examines companies' explicit commitment to upholding rights identified by ILO Core Conventions. These conventions form the internationally accepted boundaries for corporate responsibility in this area and should guide corporate activity.

---

17. "AA 1000 Assurance Standard: Guiding Principles," Consultation Brief, *AccountAbility*, March 2002.

- **Management Systems.** 'Management Systems' assesses the processes and structures at operating levels that help to ensure labor policies are implemented and that labor standards are likely to be upheld. These will include: the existence of performance incentives that support good labor practice within buying teams; the existence of performance incentives that support good labor practices for supply factory managers; the provision of funds or specialist advice to assist current or prospective suppliers with improving employment conditions; the communication of policies to sub-contractors and buying teams. Over time, further indicators will deepen understanding in areas such as: job-specific training to relevant business units (e.g. QA, buying etc); the inclusion of supply chain labor considerations in risk assessments; the inclusion of labor considerations in stock management and the inclusion of labor considerations in sales forecasting procedures.

- **Performance and Monitoring.** Lastly 'Performance and Monitoring' seeks evidence on the existence and quality of monitoring mechanisms for evaluating the impact of policies and management systems on supply chain labor standards. These indicators will include: the provision of a whistle-blowing mechanism for contracted workers; the extent of monitoring using internal, independent and trade union/NGO expertise; the existence/extent of monitoring beyond immediate suppliers. Projected future Performance and Monitoring indicators include: the quality of remediation procedures for compliance failures; the quality of monitoring; the quality of mechanisms for identifying high-risk facilities.[18]

Selecting a Standard

There are several approaches to adopting standards a company can take, depending on the results of the business case for action, and an analysis of the areas where a company is vulnerable, or alternatively, wishes to be very progressive. After all, if the company has particularly good environmental practices that are coordinated and enforced with its various suppliers, it may be of a great benefit, both in terms of publicity and also in finding additional productivity improvements, to gain certification in ISO 14001. Alternatively, some companies prefer to begin with the adoption of a high level aspirational code, and then apply industry specific codes, related directly to their immediate needs, before moving toward the

---

18. "Moving Up the Learning Curve—Corporate Management of Supply Chain Labour Standards," *Sustainability* at *www.sustainability.com/news/articles/core-team-and-network/John-Sabapathy-gradient-index-mar-02.asp.*

broader impact codes such as SA 8000. There are any number of approaches that companies are taking.

- ICA Ahold, the Scandinavian grocery retail group, has a multistep supplier program in place, with the ultimate goal of gaining SA 8000 certification at its foreign supplier sites. The company begins by training its buyers in manufacturing-related ethical and human rights issues and providing buyers with the skills and confidence necessary to raise these key issues with their suppliers. The company surveys its international suppliers concerning their policies and working conditions, and then helps them with improvement programs. "We use our influence, where possible, and work with suppliers to systematically improve the social, environmental and ethical quality of their products and services, particularly those sold under Ahold brand names."[19]

- Chiquita, a member of the Ethical Trading Initiative, has certified 100 percent of its company-owned farms in Latin America (though not its contractor farms) under the Rainforest Alliance's Better Banana Project, and has a joint agreement on labor rights with several trade unions, including the International Union of Foodworkers (IUF) and COLSIBA, the union representing banana harvesters in Latin America. They are now working toward site certification in SA 8000.[20]

- H&M's suppliers contractually guarantee not to use certain hazardous or environmentally dangerous chemicals in production, including chemicals that are restricted by national laws (if any nation in which they sell restricts a chemical, H&M uses that same restriction in all other countries), and those that the company has voluntarily chosen to include (particularly substances that might cause skin irritation or allergies or that may be carcinogenic). All suppliers must sign a Chemical Restrictions Compliance Commitment, and tests are regularly performed on the finished clothes to ensure that there are no banned chemicals in the materials. Approximately 30,000 chemical-related tests were performed in 2002, either by H&M or by a third-party laboratory.[21]

The Validity of Standards

Obviously, this level of effort in implementing standards costs money, but supporters respond by asserting that social and environmental performance monitoring and reporting is no more costly—in terms of employee numbers

19. "Sustainable Supply Chain," Ahold Web site at *www.ahold.com/aholdinsociety/food/supplychain.asp.*

20. "Chiquita Joins Ethical Trading Initiative," *PR Newswire,* May 3, 2002.

21. H&M's Social Responsibility Report, pp. 28–30 at *www.hm.com/corporate/pdf/social/csr_report_social.pdf.*

or investment—than financial reporting, and in fact, usually involves much less of an investment in infrastructure (independent auditors, accounting staff, monitoring, reporting, and report production costs), than standard financial reporting requires of firms today. And given that an ethics, human rights, employment, or environmental scandal can mean a precipitous drop in share value, investors need the information and protection that nonfinancial reporting provides. After all, no one contends that companies should be exempt from adhering to Generally Agreed Accounting Principles (GAAP) simply because they may be expensive or burdensome. Many CFOs will contend that financial reporting adds very little value to the company itself, in terms of actual help to management, but nonetheless accept the need for a consistent framework for financial reporting because it is necessary for the investment community. Advocates contend that the two standards areas—financial and nonfinancial—should now be seen as very much equivalent; both necessary to provide monitoring agencies and investors with a more rounded picture of a company's performance.

"The ability to not report [on social and environmental behavior] is not an option any more for a leading company," says Nicholas Eisenberg, CEO of Ecos Technologies, an environmental software and consulting group. "What the NGOs should be pointing out is, 'how can a company be upset about this, when they get skewered about misstatements concerning their financial performance every single day of the year?' And why? Because [that level of accuracy and information] matters."[22]

In fact, there have been real and important improvements in SEAAR during the past two years. First, as we have seen, certain standards, much as with Baldrige, TQM, and ISO 9000 in the quality movement, have quickly taken the lead. SA 8000, ISO 14001, and AA 1000 are all standards that are designed to be universally applied and to offer both a monitoring function (a health check) and structured framework for improvement. Moreover, as we have seen, they are increasingly becoming cost effective, because much of the process for collecting and reporting on performance can be done in tandem with the normal financial and quality information collection process taking place anyway.

"All of these things have pretty much the same concept," explains Martin Ogilvie Brown from PricewaterhouseCoopers' Sustainable Business Solutions Group. "And that is how to improve your processes. [These] are just looking outside of the traditional indicators that you use to manage your company, and using a broader set of indicators, because at the end of the day these influence the major thing that you are worried about, which is your profit and loss."[23]

---

22. Interview, August 25, 2003.
23. Interview, November 6, 2003.

Moreover, it is much less expensive—both in time and money—for suppliers to adhere to a universally accepted standard than to continue to have multiple, often overlapping, surveys and inspections from various buying companies, NGOs, and investors, all requiring different standards and different compliance surveys. One of the most important incentives for suppliers to adopt a single, audited standard is that they are increasingly being swamped by multiple survey and inspection requests from myriad interested parties, each requiring a separate verification of their social and environmental performance.

Finally, having learned from the early struggles and eventual success of the quality standards certification process, the bodies developing SEAAR standards have been purposeful in building and modifying standards according to the concept of "harmonization." This means that not only are standards constructed (SA 8000, ISO 14001, the ETI, AA 1000) in a way that makes them complimentary, but the similarities between these various certifications has been intentionally enhanced, so that any of these leading standards are now quickly becoming recognized as roughly equivalent.

"The strength and influence of certification programs seem to be increasing," contends Gary Gereffi, professor of sociology and director of the Markets and Management Studies Program at Duke University. "Third-party certification and monitoring may soon become the norm in many global industries. The battles over forest-product certification show that consumers and NGOs can quickly delegitimize weak standards and inadequate enforcement mechanisms, and they can also mobilize effectively for more stringent codes of conduct and more reliable monitoring. Corporations in the apparel industry are making concessions that would have been unthinkable just a few years ago as they too advocate third-party arrangements. Even the chemical industry's Responsible Care initiative is considering third-party verification in some countries."[24]

Implementation of Standards

One thing that we have learned over the past decade from Business Process Reengineering and the implementation of quality standards, however, is that the standards process needs to be incorporated into a company's strategic policies and processes, and is seldom successful if administered simply as a "bolt-on." In short, creating an ethical supply chain

---

24. Gary Gereffi, Ronie Garcia-Johnson, and Erika Sasser, "The NGO-Industrial Complex," *Foreign Policy*, no. 125, July/August, 2001 at *www.foreignpolicy.com*. Copyright 2001, Carnegie Endowment for International Peace.

doesn't just happen—it needs to be actively managed and fully integrated with a company's normal day-to-day operations.

"Companies often have problems when they attempt to implement an EMS in isolation," confirms Robert Pojasek, Adjunct lecturer on environmental science at Harvard University's School of Public Health, "because the system does not automatically integrate well into core business practices. Many ISO 14001 implementations have failed because the organization lacked key preconditions, such as widespread environmental concern and awareness within the organization, meaningful management commitment, robust planning, integration of external stakeholders into the process, or a sufficient focus on performance improvement."[25]

These are exactly the sorts of issues that the CERO will have to face in developing an ethical supply chain program, and why it is so important that a company establishes an ethics and risk management framework that includes clear performance indicators, a stakeholder-needs assessment, a supplier management program, and a reporting policy based on GRI standards all of which we explore in the following chapters.

---

25. Robert B. Pojasek, "How Do You Measure Environmental Performance?" *Environmental Quality Management,* October 4, 2001.

CHAPTER ELEVEN

Creating Measurable and Verifiable Indicators of Performance

*W*hether a company chooses to remain
with a high-level code of conduct, or to adopt a more rigorous social or
environmental standard such as SA 8000 or ISO 14001, it is necessary to
assign, whenever possible, specific performance criteria to the supply chain
and supplier assessment process.

As we have seen, even detailed standards or codes often contain "elastic" phrases such as "a living wage" or "safe and hygienic," which will need to be strengthened by developing specific performance criteria. Accurate, timely, and meaningful numbers are important not only for managing the supply chain, but also for company reporting. And because many standards will often duplicate or expand on requirements made by the socially responsible investment indices or local government agencies, it is important that the measures chosen to reflect success in the company are "comparable" with those various requirements.

In fact, there is a logical evolution from high-level codes of conduct and aspirational codes through the medium-level criteria provided in performance standards, and ultimately to more specific and detailed indicators and verifiers of performance. The Natural Resources Institute at the University of Greenwich, in the United Kingdom, for example, has described the hierarchy of the different elements that make this progression from high-level principles to specific detail (see Figure 11-1).

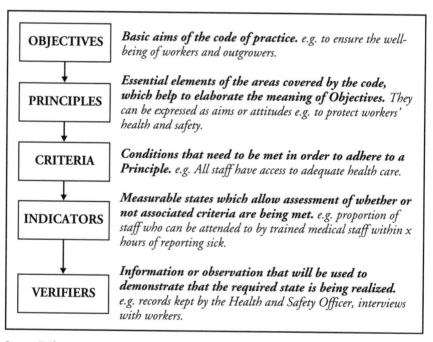

Source: "What Are Criteria, Indicators and Verifiers?," NRET Theme Papers, paper 3 at www.nri.org/NRET/TP3.pdf.

FIGURE 11-1 Definition of Criteria, Indicators and Verifiers (CIVs)

Most standards or codes of conduct will provide guidance in terms of the objectives and principles, and the standards that we have discussed provide the process and performance criteria. The specific indicators of performance and the means of verifying that performance, however, are usually left to the individual company and its supplier community to work out.

As with all performance indicators, numbers will need to be aggregated at supplier factory department levels (i.e., waste disposal, energy usage, number of injuries per month, absenteeism), upward through the operating locations and group and regional functions, so that management and the board (and eventually investors) can get an accurate picture of performance and risk in the supply chain. In any case, the more specific and quantifiable the verifiers and indicators, the better.

What Makes for Good Indicators and Verifiers?

What makes for a good indicator?
A good indicator is one which is:

Relevant and acceptable to all stakeholders (e.g., if it is about worker welfare, workers should agree that the indicator is a good measure and encapsulate the essence of the criterion, and managers should also accept it and be willing for it to be measured).
Clearly defined (unambiguous and easy to understand).
A reliable measure of the criterion—it is clearly linked to the criterion, and will always be a good measure of whether or not the criterion is being met.
Easy to measure and record—the information is easily available and practical to measure (cost-wise and time-wise).

And if possible . . . **integrative,** that is, it measures progress against more than one criterion, therefore saving time and resources (e.g., compliance with the indicator "implementation of a 3-year crop rotation program" demonstrates partial compliance with both sustainable soil management and also integrated pest management criteria.

What makes for a good verifier?
A good verifier is one which is:

Embedded—that is, it uses available records which are already being kept. If records aren't being kept, be creative and make use of visual and verbal verifiers if possible, rather than creating an unnecessary paper trail.
Relevant and acceptable to all stakeholders (e.g., if it is about worker welfare, workers should agree that the verifier provides the critical information necessary to

measure the indicator, and managers should also accept it and be willing for it to be used).

Reliable — it is a reliable source of information. When it comes to choosing verifiers for social indicators, it can be particularly difficult to identify an "objective" source of information. In such a case, you need to make sure you have at least 2 verifiers for each indicator, that is, you need to triangulate. If the two verifiers give you conflicting information, you need to look for a third or even fourth verifier.

Practical — it is not too time-consuming or expensive to use (e.g., on a farm employing 2,000 workers, it will be too time-consuming to ask every single worker what they earn as a means of checking up on weekly earnings. Instead, you may consider checking the payroll records, plus interviewing a sample of workers to cross-check the records).

And if possible . . . **integrative.**

Source: "What Are Criteria, Indicators and Verifiers?," NRET Theme Papers, paper 3 at *www.nri.org/NRET/TP3.pdf.*

SustainAbility suggests that indicators of performance should be SMART: specific, measurable, attainable, relevant, and time-framed.[1] NRET has their own helpful list of characteristics.

Generally speaking, a company should have at least one strong indicator of performance for any key principle, again keeping in mind that pledges such as "we will pay a living wage" or "we will use an environmentally sound recycling program" will vary enormously in terms of indicators of performance, depending on countries and industries. And, of course, to be meaningful to stakeholders reading these figures in a report, they will need to be standardized and normalized to reflect commonly accepted comparisons (i.e., overtime hours worked per week, energy output per month, injuries per employee per year).

Moreover, each stakeholder group — investors, NGOs, customers, trade unions, government agencies — may require its own specific indicators of performance. In short, there will be several layers of increasing detail, even among these performance indicators themselves.

ThirdWave, a sustainability consultancy for the building trade, provides some good examples of high (level 1) performance indicators.

---

1. "Performance Indicators," Sustainable Development Tools, *SustainAbility* at *www. sustainability.com/services/tools-performance-indicators.asp.*

Performance Indicators from ThirdWave

Performance Indicators for Sustainable Organizations

1. **Making sustainability a corporate priority**
   - Does the organization have in place a written corporate sustainability policy statement?
   - Does the organization have a clear statement of corporate sustainability objectives?
   - Has the organization set specific sustainability targets and implemented a sustainability action plan?
   - Has the organization appointed a main board member with specific responsibility for sustainability?
   - Has the organization created an internal employee training and education program for sustainability?
   - Does the organization have an ethical investment policy?

2. **Contributing to stable community building**
   - Is the organization a member of the Investors in People scheme?
   - Does the organization source its supplies and services locally wherever possible?
   - Is the organization a participant in the New Deal Initiative?
   - Has the organization set and published social responsibility standards for its operations?
   - Is the organization actively involved in local community regeneration projects?
   - Does the organization actively support the Ethical Trading Initiative?

3. **Accepting the responsibilities of leadership**
   - Does the organization regularly benchmark its performance against sector best practice?
   - What amount of the organization's research and development budget is directed to improving sustainability performance?
   - What number of sustainable technologies has the organization introduced to improve its performance?
   - Does the organization undertake systematic sustainability assessments of any new product or services?
   - Does the organization practice life cycle stewardship of its products, processes and services?
   - Has the organization introduced a voluntary eco-labelling scheme for its products?

4. **Developing and delivering products and services**
   - Does the organization have in place an environmental management system such as ISO14001?
   - Has the organization set specific targets for waste reduction, energy saving, packaging recovery, etc.?

- What proportion of the organization's energy supply is drawn from renewable sources?
- What investment has the organization made in energy use monitoring equipment?
- Does the organization set sustainability criteria for the awarding of contracts to suppliers?
- Is the organization a member of a green purchasing program or co-operative buying group?

5. **Developing and operating sites, buildings and facilities**
- What investment has the organization made in on-site air quality monitoring equipment?
- Is the organization a member of a waste minimization club or waste exchange scheme?
- Has the organization implemented a green transport plan to reduce staff commuting by car?
- Does the organization specify the use of natural local materials for building and landscaping?
- Does the organization prohibit the using of timber from unsustainable sources?
- Does the organization have a biodiversity policy to protect habitat and enhance site ecology?

6. **Monitoring and reporting on progress towards sustainability**
- Has the organization identified its own key sustainability performance indicators?
- Is there an internal sustainability audit process in place in the organization?
- How does the organization rate on the business-led Index of Corporate Environmental Engagement?
- Does the organization communicate with all stakeholders in accordance with ACBE guidelines?
- Does the organization publish an independently verified annual sustainability report?
- Does the organization have systems in place for sharing good practice between sites or departments?

Source: www.thirdwave.org.uk/resource/indic.html.

Each one of these level one indicators will need to be broken down, often several more times, into ever greater levels of detail and granularity. Origin Energy, an Australian energy company, provides a good example of this multilevel approach to performance indicators for each of its three key categories of sustainability: social, environmental, and economic (see Figure 11-2).

FIGURE 11-2 Origin Energy's Multilevel Approach to Performance Indicators

Categories	Objectives	Strategies	2002/2003 Actions
Environment	To measure and accurately report the company's greenhouse gas emissions.	Improve the company's greenhouse gas measurement methodology, audit and report regularly.	Develop an audited greenhouse gas inventory.
	To reduce the greenhouse gas intensity of our energy production and distribution.	Seek economic avenues for reducing greenhouse gas emissions in our energy production activities.	Identify opportunities to reduce the greenhouse gas emissions intensity of the company's gas production and power generation portfolio.
		Identify and invest in renewable energy technologies that are economically viable.	Assess potential wind farm sites. Continue research and development efforts towards the manufacture of solar PV systems.
		Seek economic avenues to reduce fugitive emissions.	Identify opportunities to reduce losses in the natural gas distribution systems under management.
	To reduce the carbon intensity of customers' energy consumption.	Provide a range of competitively priced clean energy products and services, which allow customers to choose their level of greenhouse gas intensity.	Increase the GreenEarth customer base to 25,000, increasing annual savings to 89,000 tons of CO_2e for 2002/03. Install 125 kW of solar PV systems, saving 5,610 tonnes

(continues)

FIGURE 11-2 (*Continued.*)

Categories	Objectives	Strategies	2002/2003 Actions
		Provide information for our customers so they can measure and reduce the carbon intensity of their energy use.	of CO_2e over the life of these installations. Sell 20,000 kg of hydrocarbon refrigerants, saving 80,000 tons of CO_2e for 2002/03. Expand the provision of education programs on energy efficiency. Reduce customer greenhouse gas emissions by an additional 35,000 tons per annum through energy efficiency consulting services. Include greenhouse gas indicators on mass-market electricity bills by January 2003 and on gas bills by 2004.
	To take all reasonable steps to eliminate or minimize any adverse impact that our activities have on the local environment.	Ensure all environmental impacts are appropriately assessed and all environmental approvals are obtained. Comply with all environmental conditions of approval and promptly report any noncompliance	Obtain environmental approval for the BassGas Project and development of the Thylacine and Geographe gas fields. No material breach of obligations under environmental regulations or licences. No hydrocarbon spills that contaminate land or water.

Categories	Objectives	Strategies	2002/2003 Actions
		to relevant authorities. On completion of use, ensure land is managed and/or rehabilitated to approved environmental standards.	Complete entry of Australian licences, authorizations and permits into RCMS and continually review legislation that may impact on the company's regulatory obligations. Measure and report the volume of water produced from gas fields and water used in generation plants. Compile dossier on endangered regional ecosystems within potential upstream development areas. Reduce noise complaints through improved designs and more effective consultation processes. Before relinquishment, rehabilitate all gas or petroleum exploration sites to State Government standards as a minimum. Ensure the plans for managing contaminated land at owned or leased sites are approved by local EPAs, and where the site is for sale, ensure there is full disclosure of the status of the site to the purchaser, EPA and other relevant parties.

(continues)

FIGURE 11-2 *(Continued.)*

Categories	Objectives	Strategies	2002/2003 Actions
Social	To provide and maintain a satisfying and rewarding working environment for all our employees.	Provide employment conditions consistent with community expectations.	Identify areas in our operations in which more flexible working conditions can be introduced without adversely affecting productivity or customer service and develop procedures for implementing appropriate changes.
		Work toward having Origin's workforce reflecting the diversity expected by the communities in which we operate.	Complete implementation of consistent long service, maternity and paternity leave entitlements across the company.
		Provide access to the necessary job training and assist employees obtaining additional skills to develop their careers.	Benchmark levels of employee turnover by gender, length of service and occupation.
		Encourage and support employee participation in community-based activities that form part of the company's corporate community involvement.	Further analyze workforce composition to better understand how the diversity of Origin's workforce compares to the wider community.
			Clarify criteria for recruitment and promotion to ensure there are no impediments to selecting candidates on the basis of merit.
			Improve process for resolving issues related to equal employment

Categories	Objectives	Strategies	2002/2003 Actions
			opportunity and harassment prevention.
			Continue review of remuneration processes and working conditions to ensure there are no systemic discriminatory practices.
			Ensure information systems are capable of adequately capturing total investment in employee training and ensure the level of investment is appropriate.
			Continue development and implementation of HSE skills and competency measures.
			Develop an employee Community Involvement Program, including matched giving.
	To maintain community support and goodwill for the company's activities.	Maintain an open and constructive approach to gaining access to land and resources.	Improve the timeliness and impact of our community consultations, directly and with government, to ensure agreements with landholders and indigenous communities are reached in a timely fashion.
		Identify and participate in public debates where we can make a relevant and meaningful contribution. Maximize value of	Contribute to energy policy development that encourages

(continues)

FIGURE 11-2 (*Continued.*)

Categories	Objectives	Strategies	2002/2003 Actions
		company sponsorship to recipients by focusing on activities that most leverage Origin's skills and resources. Facilitate improved access to services and support for the disadvantaged in our community so they can also enjoy the comforts of energy use.	investment by the private sector. Revise Origin's sponsorship program based on the external impacts of the company's activities. Incorporate a community support mechanism in our Corporate Community Involvement Program. Fully implement a hardship policy in the retail business by June 2003, incorporating LPG by December 2003. Work with government to improve or provide safety net arrangements for customers with an inability to pay for energy.
	To eliminate or manage hazards and practices in our business that could cause accident, injury or illness to people, damage to property, or unacceptable impacts on the environment.	Continuously improve the Health, Safety and Environment Management System.	Complete review of HSE management plans for all sites and activities. Shift the focus of incident reporting to the Total Reportable Case Frequency Rate so that it becomes the company's prime safety indicator. Achieve an LTIFR target of 2.5.

Categories	Objectives	Strategies	2002/2003 Actions
Economic	To provide sustainable returns to Origin's key economic stakeholders.	Provide shareholder returns in the top third of comparable companies.	Achieve an Operating Cash Flow After Tax Ratio in excess of 9.7%.
		Ensure the reward and remuneration levels for employees are consistent with the market, and will attract the quality of employees required for the business to meet its objectives.	Continue operation of company-wide remuneration benchmark process. Continue to monitor employee turnover and analyse the degree to which it may be affected by remuneration practices.
		Ensure that all payment obligations to government are identified and reported.	Identify and report on payments (royalties, taxes, fees and charges) to all levels of government.
		Identify appropriate levels of investment in community activities.	Identify and report on our investment in community-based activities.

Source: www.originenergy.com.au/sustainability/kpi.html.

CHAPTER TWELVE

Building Awareness and Support for Codes and Standards

*O*ne of the most important steps
necessary when developing an ethical supply chain initiative is to make all
parties — corporate executives, employees, NGOs, suppliers, consumers,
trade unions, investors — aware of the importance of the program, and to
gain acceptance and support among these various stakeholders.

Consider the parties that will typically be interested in a company's supplier monitoring program (see Figure 12-1):

"It is important to find a way of introducing your code," says the Natural Resources Institute, "that is non-threatening, positive, and that makes sense to the audience in question."[1]

The best way to understand who that audience is and what they need from your company's ethical supply chain efforts (as we have learned from countless enterprise change initiatives and business process reengineering projects in the last decade) is to involve all the important stakeholders in the process from the outset. This includes getting stakeholders involved in the early steps of selecting and customizing the codes and standards themselves. There is no more effective technique for communicating the need for a code and creating a sense of shared ownership. (It is surprising how many companies still develop stakeholder expectations without ever actually speaking with the stakeholders themselves.)

This cooperative development process means not only that each party has input to the development of codes and standards selection and the creation of performance indicators—making these more realistic and

FIGURE 12-1 Various Stakeholders in the Modern Enterprise

---

1. "Building Awareness and Support for Codes," *NRET Theme Papers on Codes of Practice in the Fresh Produce Sector,* Natural Resources Institute, p. 4 at *www.nri.org/NRET/TP5.pdf.*

workable—but also it means that each party is given an opportunity to think carefully about what the ethical supply chain program means to them and what their constituency wants to achieve. This, in fact, is where the AA 1000 process standard is invaluable, in that it helps a company identify and involve various stakeholders in the standards development and implementation process.

From a company point of view, there are several important steps in this awareness-building process:

- **Identify Key Stakeholders.** The stakeholder analysis should include those who will benefit both directly and indirectly from implementing the codes, as well as those who will be responsible for the success of the ethical supply chain program itself. "In identifying stakeholder groups," contends Business Strategy for Sustainable Development, "management should consider every business activity and operating location. Some stakeholders, such as shareholders, may be common to all activities or locations. Others, such as local communities, will vary according to business location and activity. Finally, the stakeholder analysis needs to consider the effect of the business's activities on the environment, the public at large, and the needs of future generations."[2]

- **Create a Stakeholder Profile and Statement of Needs and Expectations.** This document will help the CERO and his or her team understand how each shareholder group will be affected by the program. That stakeholder profile, says the Natural Resources Institute, can best be created by addressing several straightforward questions:

  - "What are the likely costs and benefits of compliance to each audience group?
  - Is the audience more likely to find some aspects of the code more sensitive or difficult to implement than others?
  - What are the types of constraints they are likely to face in implementing the code?
  - Do you have the power and interest to help overcome some of those constraints?"[3]

This process of developing a profile for each stakeholder group should help a company understand the three or four major social and environmental issues on which the company will be judged.

---

2. "Business Strategy for Sustainable Development," from *bsdglobal.com/tools/strategies. asp.*

3. "Building Awareness and Support for Codes," ibid.

- **Carefully Choose the Method of Communication.** Each group of stakeholders will require a different, individually customized approach. For example, corporate employees must be given education and training on the company's ethical framework, codes, and standards of conduct. Those employees that will have direct responsibility for conveying or enforcing those ethical standards outside the company—procurement officers, sourcing staff, supplier program team members, quality control or sales staff—will require more in-depth training on standards and expectations.

Moreover, different stakeholder groups may require a different media for explaining the program. Investors, for example, will want to understand how the ethical supply chain program will ensure share price stability and help the company to manage risk, and will probably prefer a detailed, formal report describing the company's ethical framework and standards policies. Factory workers, particularly in developing-world production sites, may speak a variety of local dialects or be illiterate, and therefore may require face-to-face discussions to explain the process, expected standards, and methods for revealing company infringements (a very sensitive issue). They may also feel more comfortable having the standards program explained to them by a local union representative—someone that they trust and who understands more intimately their day-to-day operational realities. Similarly, instead of e-mailing a policy statement or sending company monitors, there may be real advantage, at least initially, to having the CERO approach senior supplier management, establishing a contact and rapport at a higher, more personal level. In short, the communication program should be tailored to each stakeholder group, and should take into account how the group normally receives news or policy information.

The Natural Resources Institute suggests that each stakeholder group should have a dedicated program for providing essential information concerning:

- **Why.** Why a code has been developed in the first place. Who is driving the process. Where does the target audience fit in, why should they be concerned about the code.
- **About the Code Itself.** What's in the code, what issues does it cover.
- **Progress/Stage in Implementing the Code.** What is the current status—is it a pilot stage, or are all suppliers being asked to comply?
- **The Code Process/Cycle.** Induction/period for getting up to speed, first audits, subsequent audits, what happens in between audits, who audits.
- **What You Expect from the Target Audience.** What are their responsibilities in the process, and the time-scale for achieving obligations.

- **What They Can Expect from You.** What obligations/responsibilities you have to them, what support you can offer them, what support they will not be entitled to.
- **Implications of Compliance/Noncompliance.** How do you decide whether a producer is compliant or not, what happens if producers do comply, what happens if they don't comply.
- **Confidentiality of Information Provided.** Reassuring the target audience about the confidentiality of any information provided (e.g., this is important in the case of workers providing information on working conditions for an audit), and the procedures for ensuring confidentiality.
- **Any Other Specific Implications for the Target Audience.**[4]

Whatever approach your company decides to take to stakeholder communication and involvement, obviously one of the most important stakeholder groups will be the company's supplier community itself. Building on the basic principle of strategic sourcing and supplier management from the supply chain revolution of the 1990s, a company's most important task when designing an ethical supply chain framework is ultimately to select, negotiate with, monitor and audit the social and environmental performance of its key suppliers. Known as a "Supplier Program," this is increasingly becoming a required core competency in the modern manufacturing and distribution company, and something we turn to in the next chapters.

---

4. "Building Awareness and Support for Codes," ibid.

CHAPTER THIRTEEN

The Supplier Program

*S*upplier management is the key to a company's ethical supply chain. At its best, good supplier management means working with suppliers collaboratively to design safe products, with high quality standards that do no harm to workers assembling those products, to consumers who buy them, or to the environment in their manufacture or after-use disposal. That means developing a formal program that incorporates much more than just quality, price, and delivery dependability—the standard criteria for judging vendors in the past. As companies become more and more dependent upon suppliers in developing nations, it means a much closer relationship in every way—collaborative design, education, training, and supervision.

A s we have seen, a new level of buyer–supplier cooperation is necessary for several reasons. First, because suppliers in the modern supply chain are much more strategic to success of the company. With JIT concepts and collaborative design, the better a company understands the capabilities of its most important suppliers—and increasingly these will be located in developing countries—the more likely it is to avoid quality and productivity damaging mistakes in the supply chain. Second, as we have seen, just as companies are organizationally closer to third-party vendors, so too is their responsibility in the eyes of investors, consumers, and activists for these suppliers' behavior. Therefore, assurance of high social and environmental standards among suppliers will become increasingly important in terms of protecting a company's reputation.

And given the costs in terms of investment, reputation, and human capital, it makes little sense for companies to simply withdraw their contract as a punishment for suppliers that violate social or environmental standards. The entire process has become too complex for that. In the first place, to cut and run helps none of the parties—the workers, the supplier, or the buying company. In the past two years, most activist organizations have begun to call on companies not to withdraw their contracts when infringements are found, but instead to participate more closely with their suppliers in improving worker health and safety or environmental practices. In fact, in what critics describe as both unfair and ironic, large companies today that choose to immediately withdraw their contracts from factories that are found guilty of violating workers rights, are often criticized for both their failure to enforce compliance, and at the same time, for their insensitivity in withdrawing much needed work from the community.

Accordingly, a supplier program *must go beyond just setting policy and monitoring compliance.* Companies must begin to mentor favored suppliers much in the same way as they would focus improvement efforts on their own operations. This may require education, training, and coaching in management technique, in labor relations, in process efficiencies, health and safety, and environmental quality. Importantly, it may also require investment in schools, housing, or medical care that were initially seen as the responsibility of the supplier itself or the local government—something that, ultimately may be well justified on business as well as humanitarian grounds.

The Supplier Program

The supplier program is quickly becoming a core competency of any manufacturing or distribution company that participates in a global supply chain. It is therefore important to extend the current strategic sourcing efforts made by most companies, using the combined expertise of your sourcing staff and specialists in ethics and standards, to go beyond just price, quality, and performance concerns, and include in supplier selection and monitoring efforts other important social and environmental criteria.

A company needs to take several key steps in developing and implementing its supplier program. First, given the cost and effort involved in these endeavors, because most companies have an extensive supplier base, often stretching around the world, it is important to **rank and prioritize suppliers** according to their importance to the company, their relative potential risk, and the ease or difficulty of replacing them. As the OECD notes, "It is not economically or logistically feasible for all enterprises to monitor and audit all their suppliers."[1] In short, companies need to use their energy wisely, focusing their efforts where they will be used most cost effectively.

As a second step, a company needs to **provide its supplier community with well-accepted, unambiguous codes of labor and environmental practices** and to help them adhere to those codes. As we have seen, even when these codes of conduct do exist, they are often ignored by suppliers, and too often there is little effort made to enforce them by buyers, leaving the buying company vulnerable to accusations of hypocrisy or indifference.

Companies need to make it as easy as possible for their important suppliers to meet these standards. They also need to provide suppliers with incentives to monitor themselves, and to make it clear to suppliers that adherence is in their own self-interest. In keeping with the continued trend toward outsourcing, it makes sense to encourage suppliers—especially in developing economies—to take responsibility for their own improvements in these areas.

There are ways to make it easy on suppliers to adopt higher standards. First, accepting the concept of "harmonization," a company needs to work closely enough with the supplier to understand what other codes they are working toward or being certified for, and collaborate in adapting or accepting those. Reducing the administrative burden of multiple surveys—suppliers today complain of receiving sometimes hundreds of extensive survey questionnaires from each of their buyers, as well as NGOs, activists, and the government—greatly increases the likelihood that the suppliers will understand the requirements of the code and will make efforts to adjust their labor and environmental policies accordingly.

Second, it means that, whenever possible, a company should itself adopt a universally recognized standard—such as the ILO Codes of Labor

---

1. Office for Economic Cooperation and Development (OECD). See Web site at *www.oecd.org*.

Conduct, SA 8000 or ISO 14001 performance standards—so that there is consistency and efficiency in the certification and monitoring process. After all, most suppliers in developing economies will be trading with many major companies, and gaining certification on one universally recognized standard is easier and more cost effective for all parties.

Finally, however close a company's relationship with a supplier, it is important that a company separate the two functions of **monitoring and auditing.** The buying company can and should monitor the progress of its suppliers, but in order to develop an indisputably fair and independent approach to verification, companies will need to enlist independent, third-party auditors to verify compliance.

Step One: Rank and Prioritize Suppliers

How does a company begin to decide what suppliers and business partners fall within the company's span of ethical supply chain responsibility? The general guidelines for strategic sourcing already call for ranking suppliers according to price, dependability of delivery, or quality of product. Added to this list should be criteria that identify suppliers that are likely to be pursuing social or environmental activities that are illegal, in violation of your company's code of conduct, or are likely to cause damage to the company's reputation.

Generally, these suppliers should also then be prioritized according to the product being purchased, the relative amount of money being spent with them, and the type of relationship that your company has with them. For example, a company would be expected to have much less culpability in the actions of a supplier with whom they dealt only through a spot market, or when buying materials that accounted for only relatively small purchases.

The Global Environmental Management Initiative (GEMI) typically classifies suppliers for environmental, health, and safety monitoring into four levels based on the intimacy and mutual dependence of the relationship between customer and supplier:

- **Level 1.** Spot purchasing depends largely on price, and the interdependency between buyer and supplier is minimal.
- **Level 2.** Competitive incumbent relationships are in place for a longer period (typically a year), but involve relatively little substantive cooperation between the companies.
- **Level 3.** Preferred supplier relationships typically last longer than a year, and buyer and supplier collaborate to maximize value.

- **Level 4.** Strategic partnerships involve a mutual investment and sharing of benefits.

"Typically," says GEMI, "buyers have both more dependence upon their level 3 and level 4 suppliers, and more leverage over them. As a result there are more opportunities to cooperate. These suppliers may or may not expose the company to specific EHS legal liabilities, but any improvements in their financial performance or EHS expertise are likely to benefit the buyer company in the long run."[2]

"There are certain profiles," says John Brookes, an auditor and CEO of Manaxis, "that will enable companies to recognize where their risks are. The buying influence that the customer has over the supplier, the country from which the goods are coming from, and the general sense of compliance of the laws in that country, whether there is corruption, whether it is a locally owned company, or whether it is a foreign investment, how old the facility is . . . ."

"There are all sorts of factors," he contends, "that companies have recognized and can actually put figures to—sometimes arbitrary figures—but the types of figures that will help them to work out some kind of risk factor . . . That is the best approach for most companies looking at introducing such initiatives into their supplier base."[3]

Other criteria for ranking suppliers to consider may be:

- Could the supplier directly influence final product quality because of their failure to adhere to environmental standards (by, for instance, using banned components or ingredients)?
- Is the supplier located in a country or an industry known to be guilty of violating environmental or employment standards that may bring either legal penalties or reputation damage to the company?
- Are they acknowledged or obvious tier-one suppliers, that is, are they providing materials or services that make up a good portion of the value of your product?
- Does the public ultimately (for whatever reason) expect your company to have influence over these suppliers because of their dependence on your company?

Gap, Inc. for example, with a compliance monitoring team of 90 employees (responsible for inspecting 2,400 factories), has shifted to what they

---

2. "New Paths to Business Value," the Global Environmental Management Initiative at *www.gemi.org/newpath.pdf*, pp. 14, 35.

3. Interview, August 15, 2003.

call a "variable" monitoring program that focuses verification and improvement efforts on suppliers according to:

- The vendor's and factory's past record on compliance
- How easily [their] VCOs can obtain accurate data from and effectively communicate with the vendor and factory
- [Their] ability to obtain and rely upon information and support from sources outside the factory, including market reports, governmental entities and NGOs[4]

Whatever criteria a company chooses, the goal is to be able to create a short list of the most important suppliers on which to focus efforts for monitoring and audit. To create that final short list, it is possible, again according to GEMI, to categorize suppliers into four levels of relative importance:

- **Unimportant** (not on our radar screen of risks that regulators, courts, or customers care about). Ignore these aspects of performance for now.
- **Relevant** (low liability, low cost, low marketing benefit). An appropriate goal is to have suppliers meet minimum standards, comply with laws.
- **Important** (area of significant risk or potential benefit). An appropriate goal is to optimize performance in the supply chain.
- **Critical** (high risk issue). The appropriate goal is near-zero probability for major disruption, liability, or public relations crisis.[5]

Step Two: Presenting Suppliers with Integrity Guidelines and Expectations

Once a company has identified the critical suppliers that it wishes to include in the certification program, and ranked them according to relative importance, specific requirements need to be communicated to suppliers in a way that helps them understand both what they need to do and why it needs to be done. The way in which a company conveys this message can be all-important, insisting upon cooperation, while at the same time providing information, guidance, and assistance in equal measure.

It is therefore important from the outset that the supplier's organizational leadership understands that the initiative is not simply a cynical

---

4. See *www.gapinc.com/social_resp/sourcing/program.htm.*
5. "New Paths to Business Value," op. cit.

public relations exercise, or that fulfilling the requirements will create an unreasonable administrative burden for them. Too often that has been the case, and it has caused suppliers to be wary.

". . . Many in developing economies perceive codes and monitoring as an 'outside-in' affair," explains Michael Allen, from Global Alliance, "reflecting purchasers' reputational concerns or the political agendas of Northern NGOs and labor unions. Host-country vendors and managers often resent what they see as external intrusions driven by distant interests."[6]

This is another reason to move beyond the all-too-typical survey by mail approach that many companies have turned to when faced with the need to understand a supplier's social and environmental behavior. Introducing the requirements to suppliers usually requires providing supplier management with a written copy of the company's value statement, the code of conduct or specific standards, and a separate list of clearly defined and prioritized actions that they need to take in order to ensure compliance. This written material should include a straightforward explanation of why your company needs this type of certification, as well as:

- A project outline which details key timescales and milestones
- A list of names and contact information for company representatives
- Training materials that are available
- An explanation of company-sponsored funding, guidance, training, or conferences that will be made available to them

Leading practices indicate that there are several important things to consider when introducing standards requirements to suppliers. First, and most important, the initiative should belong as much as possible to the organizational leadership of the supplier. They therefore need to accept not only the value and necessity of the certification exercise, but the importance of achieving genuinely high standards of employment and environmental practices. They need to take responsibility for their actions, but to ensure that this happens, it will be important to be able to make a case for action, not only for your company, but for them as a supplier, as well. That is why, whenever possible, supplier management should be invited to participate in developing the codes and standard program, or at least be invited to attend company-sponsored supplier education workshops.

---

6. Michael Allen, "Analysis: Increasing Standards in the Supply Chain," *Ethical Corporation*, October 2002, pp. 34–36.

Adidas-Salomon: Supply Chain Management

SITUATION

The Adidas sporting goods brand is famous across the world and, like any household name, it could potentially become the target of protests and media pressure if its parent company's policies and practices fail to win public approval.

Using an external supply-chain has allowed Adidas-Salomon to keep its costs down and remain competitive. However, the company's supply chain is long and complex, relying on about 570 factories around the world. In Asia alone, its suppliers operate in 18 different countries. Moreover, its cost-saving use of external suppliers is not without risks: in particular, the company has less control over workplace conditions at its suppliers' factories than it would have at company-owned sites.

Outsourcing therefore raises a broad range of issues and concerns for the company. Employment standards have to be evaluated throughout the supply chain to ensure fairness and legal compliance on such matters as wages and benefits, working hours, freedom of association and disciplinary practices as well as on the even more serious issues such as forced labor, child labor and discrimination. Furthermore, health and safety issues, environmental requirements and community involvement also need to be considered.

TARGETS

Outsourcing supply should not mean outsourcing moral responsibility. Recognizing this, and having regard to the risks and responsibilities associated with managing a global supply chain, Adidas-Salomon has designed and implemented a comprehensive supply-chain management strategy.

That strategy is to source the company's supplies from the cheapest acceptable sources rather than from the cheapest possible. The company has its own so-called "standards of engagement" (SOE) and the level of acceptability is based on the values of the company itself. Contractors, sub-contractors, suppliers and others are therefore expected to conduct themselves in line with Adidas-Salomon's SOE.

The strategy is based on a long-term vision of self-governance for suppliers—adidas does not wish to be forever in the position of looking over the shoulders of its suppliers.

ACTIONS

The company has a 30-strong SOE team, most of whom are based in the countries where suppliers are located (Asia, Europe, and the

United States). They know the labor laws and safety regulations in their countries and are often able to interview workers in their own language.

Before a relationship is formed with any new supplier, an internal audit is carried out to ensure working conditions in that supplier meet Adidas-Salomon's SOE criteria. All business partners sign an agreement committing them to comply with the SOE and to take responsibility for their subcontractors' performance on workplace conditions. The monitoring process is continuous as suppliers are audited at least once a year, and more often if serious problems are detected.

Training forms an even more important part of the process than monitoring because it goes beyond the policing role to one that will have a long-term impact. As of October 2001, some 200 SOE training sessions had been held for business partners during the course of the year, a significant increase on the 150 courses held the year before.

RESULTS

About 800 audits were conducted at different levels in the supply chain during 2000. This involved interviewing managers and workers, reviewing the documentation, and inspecting facilities. Since then, the audit process has continued.

Using the information gained from these audits, presentations are made to the management of the supplier, outlining any problems found and the consequential action points. Clearly defined responsibilities and timelines are then agreed with the site managers. Where serious problems are detected, a follow-up visit may be conducted within one to three months. If the supplier is unwilling to make the necessary improvements, Adidas-Salomon may withdraw its business. This course of action is a last resort; the company prefers to stay in partnership and to work from the inside to help encourage improvements.

In 2000, Adidas-Salomon adopted a system of scoring and reporting on its suppliers' performance. This gave an overview of the supply chain and highlighted the main issues and problem areas on a country-by-country basis, but an improved and extended system is now being developed. This will allow the company to publish even more detailed reports about the progress that it, as a company which manages large and complex supply chains, has been able to make in the important areas of social and environmental performance.

Source: World Business Council for Sustainable Development, January 2, 2002 at *www.wbcsd.org.*

Communication and Training Techniques

Apart from early education and the adoption of clear codes of conduct, effective collaboration between company and supplier is dependent in large part upon a strong, two-way system of communication. That is why it is important that a company dedicate resources such as the CERO and a supplier program staff manned with trained "ambassadors" (or in the case of Adidas-Salomon, their "standards of engagement team;" with Gap Inc., their "vendor compliance group," etc.) that can liaise directly with supplier executives and operational staff. Without making these training efforts or dedicating the right staff, companies only risk alienating their suppliers and undermining cooperation.

"As long as so few brands have local or factory-based compliance staff or provide appropriate training and resources to factories," complains Michael Allen, from the Global Alliance, "compliance will often continue to be seen as a cat-and-mouse affair for getting the approval of clipboard-and-checklist monitors who parachute into factories for snapshot inspections."[7]

Although these "ambassadors" may be from the procurement function, they should not simply be purchasing officers given the part-time duty of handling supplier assessments. A supplier program requires a full-time, professional staff.

There are many examples of innovative supplier training and education programs. Intel, for example offers supplier training days where suppliers gather to understand company policies. General Motors, Ford, and Motorola have company-run universities that provide training to suppliers. Ford has implemented ISO 14001 and required its top 5,000 suppliers to have certified at least one manufacturing site in 2001, and all of their manufacturing sites by 2003. They provide ISO 14001 "awareness training" for their suppliers, which helps to communicate leading practices in the area.[8] Cosmair, a subsidiary of L'Oreal, has initiated a recycling program for its shipping containers, which requires suppliers to make deliveries using only reusable containers, an initiative that saves Cosmair several hundred thousand dollars a year in handling and disposal costs. Their environmental and procurement staff hold group workshops for nearly 100 of their major suppliers each year.[9]

---

7. Michael Allen, ibid.

8. Julian Roche, "Ethical Supply Chain Management—the story so far," *Ethical Corporation*, March 6, 2003.

9. Ibid.

CASE STUDY

Marks & Spencer

Marks & Spencer is helping to spread best practice in factories run by its suppliers in Morocco by supporting an educational program for garment workers. The UK retailer's suppliers set up the training themselves using teachers provided by the Moroccan government.

Like many other companies grappling with the complexities of supply-chain monitoring, Marks & Spencer knows that publishing an ethical code of conduct is actually the easy bit. Getting suppliers to comply with it takes significant commitment in time and effort and what is even more difficult is encouraging factory owners and managers to go that extra mile and introduce wider social programs in their workplaces.

That's why a small-scale but successful educational program among the UK retailer's suppliers in Morocco has been a source of particular satisfaction back at the company's headquarters in London. The program, which began in 2000, involves all six Marks & Spencer garment suppliers in the country, who run 25 factories, offering their workforces free literacy and numeracy classes.

The schooling is provided by the Moroccan government's training board, but the factories have rearranged their work schedules to allow employees to take the three-hour classes on the premises, or to provide transport to local training centers if no suitable classroom is available.

Already several hundred workers, most of them women, have completed courses. In one factory, 200 women have taken their first exams in Arabic, while another has put 60 people through classes. Even factory managers who were at first cool about the concept have warmed to it — not least because they report the classes have improved productivity.

Most of the suppliers say that a literate workforce is easier to manage. Training literature can replace time-consuming meetings with supervisors, while workers who have completed the course more easily understand safety instructions and health warning notices. From Marks & Spencer's point of view, the key strength of the program is that the company has not imposed it from the center. The suppliers set up the training themselves and tailor it to their requirements. Marks & Spencer's crucial role has been as an enabler.

The idea sprang from "local benchmarking groups" set up by the company, at which suppliers share local problems and discuss Marks & Spencer's Global Sourcing Principles, a set of workplace standards adopted in 1999. When Marks & Spencer convened the Moroccan benchmarking group, the participants found that two of the suppliers had already set up an educational program. Marks & Spencer discreetly made other suppliers aware it thought this a good idea, and when they found the costs were low and the benefits high, the suppliers became enthusiastic.

"We've been careful to ensure there's no competitive edge in these benchmarking groups because it's important all suppliers achieve compliance and beyond," says Muriel Johnson, who has supervised the program from within Marks & Spencer's quality management department. "That was important in getting this idea to grow. It was also important to stress to our suppliers we are in a long-term partnership. That way it is easier to develop a social compliance program."

Marks & Spencer encourages suppliers to introduce their own social programs because it says this is the simplest and most dynamic way of effecting change. "Letting the suppliers take the initiative works best," says Johnson.

The Moroccan program shows how a light touch can deliver improvements. "We are a broker," she adds. "We have not had to put money into this because the government finances the training. But we've enabled best practice to spread from two businesses to all our suppliers. The credit for that goes to the suppliers."

Source: www.ethicalperformance.com/best_practice/0602/case_studies/mands.html.

"Improving EHS performance is a topic well suited for communication within supplier networks and between supplier and customers," says GEMI. "Like quality, it is relevant to virtually all players, and can be discussed in useful detail without forcing potential competitors to reveal proprietary information. Thus EHS issues are easily integrated with the varied communications and relationship management tools companies use to cultivate continuous improvement in their supply chain."[10]

Step Three: Monitoring Supplier Performance

Standards such as SA 8000 or ISO 14001 will provide the requirements for companies wishing to assess their suppliers, and usually also provide (to a limited extent) coaching and consultancy suggestions. When combined with process standards such as AA 1000, the complete package should provide any company with enough process and performance guidance (critics would argue too much) to create a strong supplier monitoring process. There has been a good deal of experience and labor put into these standards, and there is little point in a company creating supplier monitoring strategies—that is, reinventing the wheel—independently.

---

10. "New Paths to Business Value," op. cit., p. 51.

Typically, monitoring procedures will involve a combination of surveys, "desk-based" research assessments, site visits, and full-blown code inspections. Obviously, in a company with many hundreds of suppliers, prioritizing and ranking suppliers and then choosing the most effective monitoring approach becomes an important exercise. In a recent survey of monitoring techniques used by member companies in the Ethical Trading Initiative, roughly one-third of monitoring was desk-based, using survey responses, public domain information, and the Internet. A third of monitoring activities involved site visits, and a third involved more formal "whole code inspection visits" (17 percent) and full external audits (10 percent).[11]

The Integrated Social and Environmental approach (ISE), for example, was developed by the Natural Resource and Ethical Trade Program (NRET), and draws on the experience of extensive agricultural auditing that has taken place in Africa. The approach combines many of the best practices found in the Ethical Trading Initiative, SA 8000, and EMAS guidelines and standards.

Characteristics of the ISE Audit Approach

The following text is directly quoted with permission, from "Integrated Social and Environmental Auditing." See source note below.

Involves Consultation with All Stakeholders. All stakeholders are consulted, i.e. managers, smallholders and workers. It is particularly important to consult with different types of workers, since they may face differing conditions and treatment by managers and supervisors.

Encourages Bridge-Building. One of the indirect benefits of such consultation is that you get better communication between management and workers. Through the exit interview and the audit report, the audit team feeds back the concerns and priorities of the workforce to the management. In this way, the management can increase their understanding of worker concerns and priorities, and can also find out which farm policies are followed, misunderstood or ignored by workers. Improved communication can by itself help to improve worker morale.

Integrated Social and Environmental Auditing — A Team Approach. Social and technical (i.e. environmental and food safety) aspects of the code are audited together. Within the audit team, different members may have specific expertise in the

---

11. The Ethical Trading Initiative's *2000–2001 Annual Report* at *www.eti.org.uk/pub/ publications/ann-rep/2000_en/page04.shtml.*

social or technical aspects. However, each audit activity is a team activity involving both the social and technical "experts". The advantage of . . . combining the two aspects is that many indicators and verifiers measure a combination of social, environmental, and/or food safety criteria. For example, assessing the knowledge of the pesticide spraying team regarding selection and safe application of pesticides will tell you something about worker health and safety, as well as environmental and food safety risks, at one and the same time. Integrated auditing therefore avoids unnecessary duplication of effort, and therefore saves money.

Triangulation — Reliance on Nonwritten Information Sources (Verifiers). ISE auditing relies just as much on non-written verifiers (i.e. information gathered from interviewing people, or from direct observation) as it does on written records. This characteristic is important because, in Africa, most small and medium-sized farms keep very few written records. While these farmers would undoubtedly benefit from better record-keeping, the audit approach used in such circumstances also needs to be effective despite the current paucity of written records. Moreover, the audit team responsible for piloting the audit protocol found that, even where written records do exist, information revealed through interviews and direct observation often turn out to be more accurate than the written records. The combined use of written, verbal and visual verifiers is also important because it provides a means of cross-checking — or triangulation — of data collected.

Flexible and Informal Nature of Data Collection. Flexible and informal data collection methods — as opposed to formal questionnaires — are used because it helps to relax both workers and managers. This encourages them to talk freely and openly about the different aspects of the code, and makes it more likely for auditors to identify unexpected problems. Both social and environmental issues are often complex, and linked to each other in ways that are difficult for an outsider to see. Open, flexible interviews and discussions give interviewees a greater opportunity to highlight complexities and linkages (see examples in section below on interview techniques).

Use of Local Auditors. A number of characteristics of the auditing approach — in particular the reliance on non-written verifiers — demands the use of local, rather than foreign, auditors. It is essential that the audit team can speak the same language(s) as the workers (and farmers), and that they understand local farming systems and social conditions. Moreover, it is important that auditors are resident in the country. Otherwise, it will be difficult to maintain frequency and continuity of auditing, and to ensure that capacity-building aspects of the auditing approach are upheld (see below).

Frequent Visits. The ISE auditing approach — unlike many other auditing approaches — is based on a schedule of short, frequent visits, rather than intensive annual audits. Frequent visits help to build trust between the farmer, workers and the audit team, which in turn increases the chance of getting reliable information. Frequent visits also help to keep the code alive. Regular discussion about the code means that the issues will stay in the minds of farmers and workers, so that they are more likely to take it seriously and do more work on it. Shorter visits are also less disruptive to the operations of export farms. There will not be time to audit against all aspects of the code within one visit. A list of non-audited areas is made at the end of the audit, which serve as a focus for the next audit visit, perhaps three months down the line.

Continuity of Auditors. Experience of researching labour and other social issues on commercial farms shows that reliable information can only be ensured if trust is built up between the workers/farmer and the researcher (or auditor) through repeated visits. It is therefore important to ensure that there is continuity of auditors i.e. the same auditors go back to a particular farm over a period of time. However, the benefits of continuity need to be balanced against the increased risk of favouritism and/or bribery . . .

Advise, Support and Inspect — A Capacity-building Approach to Auditing. In the ISE auditing approach, the auditor is not just an "inspector". He/she also plays a supportive and advisory role to the farmer, in particular in the early stages of setting up a code and/or when the farmer in question is new to the code. Recent experience of implementing codes of practice in Africa shows that many farmers are willing to implement code requirements, but don't know how to go about it. That is, they need basic advice, training and encouragement on understanding different elements of the code and how to translate them into practice. The advantage of integrating the advisory and inspection roles is that farmers come to see auditors as a friend or "adviser" rather than a "spy". With this type of relationship, auditors are much more likely to get a reliable and complete picture of the social and environmental performance of a farm."

Source: "Integrated Social and Environmental Auditing," NRET Theme Papers on Codes of Practice in the Fresh Produce Sector, Number 7 at *www.nri.org/NRET/TP7.pdf.*

Training Company Monitors

It is important to remember that monitoring is not the same thing as auditing. Monitoring includes an element of guidance, cooperation, and improvement. An audit comes later, and is a formal process for determining compliance that should usually be conducted by an independent third-party.

Again, all of the major emerging standards—SA 8000, ISO 14001, AA 1000, the ETI—will provide training for member company's staff, which will include discussions on the codes themselves, along with other important background information on labor and environmental policies for different regions and countries, and best practice techniques for monitoring and dealing with noncompliance issues. Social Accountability International, for example, provide the Corporate Involvement Program, which helps companies evaluate the SA 8000 platform, implement the standard, and then create an SAI-verified public report for stakeholders. The program includes training for managers, suppliers, and workers, and provides implementation assistance and access to a best practice supplier database.

Survey Techniques and Questionnaires

As we have seen, there is no substitute for on-site visits, but in order to begin the formal documentation process, nearly every supplier will still need to be sent a self-assessment survey as part of the supplier monitoring program. Some standards provide those questionnaires as part of membership, although there is some concern about the value of a "one-size-fits-all" type of survey, particularly as specific questions may be needed in particular vertical industries to really understand a supplier's social and environmental performance.

"There may be little procurement value," contends GEMI, "in conducting a one-size-fits-all comprehensive supplier survey asking many suppliers questions about many aspects of EHS performance. Such a survey is not adequate to minimize legal liability, is overkill for purposes of protecting reputation, and is not particularly effective as a means to stimulate supplier commitment to continuous improvement."[12]

> ## Inspector Workshops at H&M
>
> Twice yearly, H&M is organizing workshops for the inspectors and other key people in the production offices. These workshops are further education for our inspectors with the purpose of exchanging best practices in different areas. Supplychain topics such as worker interviews, overtime, network building, piece-rate systems, migrant workers, work methodology, and statistics are addressed. In 2002, the workshops were held in Phnom Penh, Cambodia for our East and South-East Asian inspectors and in Istanbul, Turkey for our European inspectors.
>
> Source: www.hm.com/corporate/pdf/social/csr_report_social.pdf.

Over the past several years, many companies have chosen to develop their own supplier questionnaires, both as part of the prequalification process, and increasingly, as a part of ongoing supply chain monitoring. For example, AMD, the electronics manufacturer, has developed both a general questionnaire for all suppliers, and a second, more commodity-focused questionnaire for their chemical suppliers. These questionnaires focus on environmental health and safety issues, and request information on reporting, staffing, and document retention policies and procedures.

"We really use our surveys," says Rich Weigand, director of Environmental Health and Safety at Advanced Micro Devices. "We don't just file

---

12. "New Paths to Business Value," op. cit., p. 38.

them." The company carefully reviews supplier responses, with a dedicated team evaluating each supplier for strengths and weaknesses, then ranks them according to their responses. Suppliers that fall below a strict numerical threshold are then put on probation or removed from the supplier list. AMD now has extended the survey program to both European and Asian suppliers.[13]

HP provides a good, straightforward example of a first-level supplier questionnaire (see Figure 13-1).

The problem with questionnaires and surveys, of course, is that as companies have become aware of the need to better understand supplier policies, suppliers throughout the world have found themselves suddenly inundated with questionnaires from sometimes hundreds or even thousands of buying companies—or potential buying companies—none of whom have attempted to coordinate their efforts in any way. Moreover, suppliers complain of company surveys written by legal counsel with hundreds of questions, many of which are redundant or ask for information

invent

Supply Chain Operations
Social and Environmental Responsibility Program
January 21, 2004

HP Supplier Code of Conduct Questionnaire

Suppliers are requested to provide candid answers to the following questions. HP encourages its suppliers to accurately identify any areas in which their operations do not conform to the requirements of the *HP Supplier Code of Conduct*. As indicated in *HP's Supplier Code of Conduct*, HP expects to work collaboratively with its suppliers to achieve these standards.

Date:	HP Contract Number(s), if applicable:
Company Name:	Contact Name:
Address:	Position:
	Telephone Number:
	Fax:
	Email:

Purpose of the Questionnaire
This questionnaire is part of the annual performance report for HP suppliers under ***HP's Supplier Code of Conduct*** and ***Supplier Social and Environmental Responsibility Agreement***. It provides a mechanism for HP to gather information about the environmental, occupational health and safety, and labor and employment practices and performance of its suppliers.

Note: The *HP Supplier Code of Conduct* and *Supplier Social and Environmental Responsibility Agreement* are located on HP's web site at: http://www.hp.com/go/supplierE

Scope of Questionnaire
Questions that ask for information about the "company" should be answered for the company as a whole.

Questions that ask for information about the "facility" should be answered for each company facility at which products supplied to HP are manufactured.

1. Does your company have a company representative for Corporate Social and Environmental Responsibility, or someone who otherwise has responsibility for addressing in your company the requirements set out in *HP's Supplier Code of Conduct*?
☐ Yes ☐ No If "yes", please provide contact information below.

Name:	Position:
Address:	Telephone Number:
	Fax:
	Email:

2. Does your company have procedures in place designed to ensure that the requirements set out in *HP's Supplier Code of Conduct* are met in your company?
☐ Yes ☐ No

2.1 If yes, please attach copy of procedures or provide URL.	☐ Attachment Title: ☐ URL:

3. Does your company have procedures for internal reporting of any non-conformances with these requirements that may occur within your company? For correcting any non-conformances as they are identified by your company?
☐ Yes ☐ No

3.1 If yes, please attach copy of procedures or provide URL.	☐ Attachment Title: ☐ URL:

4. Does your company have a code of conduct or similar standards to which you expect your suppliers (including temporary labor agencies) to adhere?
☐ Yes ☐ No

4.1 If yes, please attach copy or provide URL.	☐ Attachment Title: ☐ URL:

Page 1 of 2

invent

Supply Chain Operations
Social and Environmental Responsibility Program
January 21, 2004

5. Is your company currently subject to any enforcement action by any governmental authority for non-compliance with environmental, safety or labor requirements at any facility at which products supplied to HP are manufactured?
☐ Yes ☐ No

5.1 If yes, please describe briefly the nature of the action and what steps your company is taking to resolve it.

Thank you for completing this questionnaire. Please email your completed questionnaire and attachments to Lindsey.ridgeway@hp.com with a copy to your assigned HP Commodity Manager.

Page 2 of 2

FIGURE 13-1 Sample Code of Conduct Questionnaire

Source: www.hp.com/hpinfo/globalcitizenship/environment/pdf/supcodequest.pdf.

13. AMD Case Study at *www.usaep.org/scem/case1.html* (still under construction).

that has no obvious use. This new workload, and the fact that self-certification does not ensure that a supplier has the policies in place that it contends it has, has meant that companies need to begin to approach supplier surveys in a more coordinated and systematic way.

"There can be twenty auditors coming into an individual factory," says John Brookes, "which, apart from everything else, [can be] very disruptive . . . Therefore they [suppliers] are quite keen to get the single, internationally recognized certification from an independent body in lieu of these multiple customer audits—different standards, different requirements, different expectations . . ."[14]

Moreover, as many suppliers and industry analysts have warned, questionnaires should not be sent out as if they were the monitoring process itself. It is important to remember that surveys and questionnaires are most valuable not as an absolute assessment tool, but as a way of initially identifying potential supply chain problems and better understanding a supplier's basic profile in terms of social and environmental policies. Therefore, they should not necessarily be designed to gather huge amounts of information or to serve as part of a compliance assurance policy. A good questionnaire is most helpful if it provides the type of information your company needs in order to prioritize suppliers, and to highlight the need for site visits and a higher level of monitoring of potentially risky, but important, suppliers.

This is one of the more important reasons, of course, why companies are driving toward a standardized process, both in terms of questionnaires and surveys, and also in terms of certification. Standardization allows suppliers to move through a single certification process, or to use a common response to survey questions, reducing its workload and ensuring consistency among questions and answers. Moreover, once a buying company has committed to an international standard, suppliers have a much greater incentive to take self-certification, and self-improvement of their processes, more seriously, since inspections and audits are much more likely.

There are several "leading practice" techniques to consider when developing a survey:

- The level of detail and complexity of questions should reflect a supplier's importance and risk ranking. There is no point sending out comprehensive surveys to spot market vendors. For suppliers of low or medium priority it is often best to simply ask broad, revealing questions such as, "Do you employ workers under the age of 16?," or "Have you received certification by any major social or environmental certification group?"

---

14. Interview, August 15, 2003.

- Included in the survey should be permission to inspect the supplier's site for verification.
- Phrase questions, whenever possible, so that the supplier can provide a short qualitative response, or a simple "yes" or "no" answer. If a question requires a more lengthy answer, it is often better asked in an interview.
- Questions should be as straightforward as possible in order to avoid misinterpretation.[15]

Site Visits

Unlike an impersonal survey or questionnaire, the value of site visit monitoring is that a company's team has person-to-person access to management and workers at a factory or farm. But effective interviews require good training, sensitivity, and a willingness to look beyond management assurances—to interview workers at different levels, gain their trust, and be able to understand the reality of day-to-day working conditions and environmental procedures on days when the inspection team are not on site. This is particularly important in developing world operations where the difficulties of managing against widely varying norms for working conditions, wage rates, and working hours is compounded by broad differences in cultural norms and languages.

"Monitoring must take account of local culture and language including the nuances of words and body language," says Jane Tate of HomeNet, an NGO concerned with improving working conditions of laborers who receive work—stitching footballs, sewing soft toys—at home, in developing countries. "In many cultures women workers will not speak openly to male auditors, or they will speak in groups but not individually. For that reason, our inspections are conducted wherever possible by teams comprising both women and men. In some cultures, respect for age is such that young auditors will make little progress, while elsewhere, younger workers feel best able to talk to people of their own age."[16]

Finally, as with the CERO in the buying company, it can be helpful to have the supplier's management team appoint a "point person" that will be responsible for assisting with all aspects of the code implementation and audit process. This single supplier contact will help provide the CERO

---

15. "New Paths to Business Value," op. cit.
16. The Ethical Trading Initiative's *2000–2001 Annual Report,* op. cit.

and his or her team with a responsible, single point of contact for coordinating all logistics, scheduling, and data gathering activities.

"Monitoring compliance with labour codes demands the right team, the right methodology, skill and sensitivity," says the Ethical Trading Initiative in its Annual Report. "Interviewing skills are vital. Interviewers must be able to select a cross-section of the workers, not least the ones who look intimidated, and get to the heart of workers' everyday reality. Our experience shows that commercial audit firms are good at identifying health and safety issues, but sensitive interview techniques of the kind used in community development can reveal more about everyday abuse of workers' rights."[17]

But selecting and monitoring suppliers is only half of the battle. A good ethical supply chain program also requires a company to ensure proper verification of supplier performance—something best accomplished through a well-organized and professional audit process.

---

17. Ibid.

CHAPTER FOURTEEN

The Audit Process

As with most other inspections — OSHA, health and safety, EOE — the audit process almost always begins with a preaudit visit where any major problem areas are identified and recommendations for action are given, followed after a period of time by the official audit visit, where the facility is formally audited for compliance. Third-party audit teams usually document their findings to both the hiring company and to the supplier's management team, providing them with the written results marked against the required codes and scores. Good audit firms also go further, providing recommendations for action that can help a supplier make important improvements.

As we have seen, the two processes—monitoring and auditing—are not the same, and should be dealt with in separate, differently constructed programs. Supporters of an independent audit contend that just as no company would expect to have its financial statements unchallenged, a company's social and environmental performance also merits some level of verification. And also just like financial audits, a strong verification program can not only identify areas for improvement, but can also provide independent and certified evidence of accomplishments.

Auditing Tools and Techniques

Whether a company chooses to use its own auditor or bring in a third party, there are still a number of items that the audit team will need before the official audit process begins.

• **The results of all the surveys and questionnaires that have been sent to the supplier.** Although in many cases the information will need to be verified by the audit team, the supplier's response to a questionnaire can go a long way toward speeding up the process, and will often provide valuable information on areas of potential concern. As suppliers become more familiar with the audit process, and the results of audits and survey responses can be compared, repeat audits often can be prioritized and customized, allowing the company to focus on high-priority or suspect suppliers, while reducing the frequency of audits to occasional spot-checks on suppliers that have proven their adherence to standards in the past.

• A detailed **supplier description** that provides the audit team with all relevant information on the supplier: products manufactured, volume of purchases, number of employees, previous violations, etc. (see Appendix B).

• All required **standards and performance indicators** that apply to the supplier.

• An **audit checklist** that provides the audit team with a structured, step-by-step guide through the entire interview and inspection process. These checklists need to be comprehensive enough to guide the team quickly from issue to issue, and should include all areas to be addressed, including relevant performance indicators, a grid for indicating compliance/noncompliance, and space for comments—all in a compact and easily followed format (see Appendix C).

• A **violation guideline,** detailing specific procedural guidelines for supplier management when the audit reveals violations, so that the issues can be addressed immediately and constructively as part of the audit itself.

Providing the supplier's management with a "leave behind" guideline can help them make improvements quickly and effectively.

The Audit Process

Preaudit visits are usually the most productive (and often the most time consuming) part of the audit process, and as with monitoring visits, can be used to help explain to the supplier's management team the importance of compliance. During these introductory visits, audit teams should explain the code or standard against which the supplier is being audited, the approach, who will need to participate, how long it will take, how employee confidentiality will be maintained, and how concerns and non-compliance findings will be dealt with.

It is also important at this early stage to explain the key performance indicators that the audit team will be using to judge compliance (indicators which, if best practice techniques were used, the supplier may have helped to develop), and to modify these as necessary to reflect legitimate operational differences between suppliers (there is no point, for example, assessing them on their success at managing pesticides if they are only involved in packaging, rather than growing, etc.). The relevance of these performance indicators will become obvious if the audit team uses the preaudit visit as an opportunity to collaboratively complete the supplier description document with supplier management and employees.

At this point the audit team can develop a timetable for the actual audit, making certain that the scheduling of interviews and walk-arounds disrupts the supplier's activities as little as possible. Demonstrating sensitivity to the supplier's production process—break times, work shifts, avoiding peak hours—can make the audit more effective and will go a long way toward building support for the process.

The **audit** itself usually involves a quick meeting with the supplier's management team before the audit begins, where audit activities are reviewed, and timetables and interviews are confirmed. Most audits will involve a combination of at least four elements:

- Collecting and verifying data and objective, quantifiable records.
- A tour of the factory or farm during which the audit team sees for themselves the working conditions, waste disposal methods, hygiene and safety standards of the site.
- Key individual employee (and often trade union representative) interviews.

- Group discussions with employees without management being present.

Obviously, each verification method has its merits and drawbacks: activities can be staged during visual inspections, records may not reflect reality, and workers may be afraid to divulge exploitation or abuse for fear of reprisal. By combining these four methods, however, the audit team has a much greater likelihood of making a balanced and well-informed appraisal of the supplier's practices.[1]

NRET Audit Structure Based on Ghana Pilot Audits

The following list is directly quoted with permission from "Integrated Social and Environmental Auditing." See source below.

- "Interview with farm manager(s), accountants, or code manager, combined with document checks
- Group discussion with non-permanent workers
- Group discussion with permanent workers
- Key informant interviews with pesticide sprayer, farm manager, supervisor
- Farm tour/transect walk: with farm manager, ad hoc chats with workers along the way
- In-promptu chats with individuals or groups during "dead time" e.g. when waiting for farm manager to turn up for interview"

Source: "Integrated Social and Environmental Auditing," NRET Theme Papers on Codes of Practice in the Fresh Produce Sector, National Resources Institute, Number 7, at *www.nri.org/NRET/TP7.pdf.*

Audit Management Review Meeting

Once the initial audit (or in some cases the preaudit) is complete, the team will need to summarize their findings, listing any areas of concern or noncompliance. These issues should be discussed with the supplier's management as soon as possible, and agreement should be reached on how

---

1. "Integrated Social and Environmental Auditing," NRET Theme Papers on Codes of Practice in the Fresh Produce Sector, National Resources Institute, No. 7 at *www.nri.org/NRET.TP7.pdf.*

and when improvements will be made. Any areas that were not audited should also be noted and a follow-up visit should be scheduled.

H&M, the European clothes retailers, provides a good example of the sequence and activities of this audit process.

CASE STUDY

> ### H&M's Supplier Compliance and Inspection Procedures

PRIOR TO INSPECTION

Compliance Commitment—Supplier has to sign the Code of Conduct commitment before the first inspection. This commitment includes all subcontractors who are also inspected.

THE INSPECTION

The following text is directly quoted from H&M's Social Responsibility Report. See source note below.

- **Management Interview**—The management is interviewed about relevant management practices, about salaries, working hours, freedom of association etc. according to a fixed list of questions.
- **Factory Inspection**—The factory is inspected to evaluate working environment, safety, child labour, etc. in accordance with a questionnaire.
- **Interviews with Workers**—Information sometimes needs to be validated through interviews to ensure that the suppliers are observing our requirements.
- **Inspection of Residential Area**—The residential facilities are inspected for cleanliness and safety according to a fixed list of items to check.
- **Document Review**—Documentation to verify working hours, wages and overtime compensation is checked. Staff records and age certificates are checked.
- **Closing Meeting**—The inspection results are discussed with the supplier, as well as realistic time limits for improvements.
- **Pre-Inspection Questionnaire**—If an inspection cannot be made immediately due to geographical distance, the supplier should fill in a pre-inspection self-assessment questionnaire.

AFTER THE INSPECTION

- **Corrective Action Plan**—The supplier signs the corrective action plan.

We also, due to other severe violations such as minimum wage not paid, unsafe premises, denied access to premises etc., grade the suppliers or their subcontractors as Unacceptable. If a supplier's production unit is graded Unacceptable, our purchase order system obstructs the buyer from placing an order with that particular supplier. This obstruction will not be taken away until the supplier's production unit has made the necessary improvements.

Source: H&M's Social Responsibility Report, pp. 8 – 9 at *www.hm.com/ corporate/pdf/social/csr_report_social.pdf.*

The Pros and Cons of Third-Party Audits

A debate concerning the relative benefits of third-party versus company (sometimes known as first-party) auditing continues to rage among the several interested groups. Obviously, if the entire process is conducted as part of a company-to-supplier exercise, it can be much more nuanced, flexible, and certainly less expensive, both for companies and their suppliers. This type of company-to-supplier approach tends to be focused more on correction than on testing, and many would argue that improvement is the ultimate goal (i.e., not certification), and therefore these types of activities should be limited to the supplier monitoring process.

Yet, companies have so often been found guilty of ignoring or underreporting infractions today, that, as we have seen, company-run audits (especially if done in a perfunctory way), carry little credibility with NGOs and investment analysts.

Moreover, there are ways to focus on improvement while still maintaining third-party independence. In this regard it is important, again, to remember that the two processes—monitoring and auditing—are not the same thing and should be treated as separate initiatives. Supplier monitoring should be seen as an ongoing initiative that helps suppliers improve their social and environmental policies. The auditing process is a formal verification of those policies used to assure the board, senior executives, investors, and consumers that the suppliers that the company is dealing with meet those agreed standards.

There seems to be a growing acceptance among those experienced in this area, however, that setting requirements and monitoring suppliers requires a closer and more ongoing approach—something better suited to the type of close and long-term relationships that companies often need with suppliers in an age of greater dependency and collaboration. Auditing, on the other hand, favors autonomy, if only because the policing and whistle blowing aspect of inspections is hardly conducive to a close and trusting business relationship.

That is not to say that the audit process cannot also contribute to the improvement process. Again, as with most health- or safety-related enterprise audits, the suppliers are almost always given a period of time, even after failing the audit, to make improvements. This time period, depending on the severity and the complexity of the failure, can be from six months to a year. And, as we saw with Apparel Avenue in Thailand and its attempts to cut overtime in order to comply with SA 8000 requirements, the certification process itself can often provide the necessary impetus for a supplier to rethink long outdated and unproductive processes and policies.

Moreover, company employees with audit training, language skills, and a knowledge of the local culture can be difficult to find and expensive to employ on a full-time basis. Leading practice indicates that an audit team should be composed of two to three auditors with the following skills and experience:

- Training or certification in the company code of conduct or international standard
- Specialist training in either social or environmental issues, including local and national legislation
- Knowledge of local languages and culture
- Experience in audit interviewing and building rapport with both management and employees at all levels

In addition to all of these skills, team members will need to be able to put in long, often strenuous days, viewing factories, walking through fields, talking with and cajoling employees and management. It is also often sensible to ensure that teams include both men and women, particularly if there is a likelihood of sexual harassment or intimidation of women workers or if the culture is one where female workers would be hesitant to talk openly of these types of issues with a male auditor.[2]

Consultants

A growing number of consultancies are emerging to provide advice on issues ranging from CSR strategy development to environmental health or safety monitoring of suppliers. Some advise on data retention policies or supporting software, and others will help a company to collect disparate

---

2. Ibid.

information from various corporate departments and suppliers. Many consultancies and standards groups will also advise a company on how to compile and write a sustainability report. These advisors fall into a variety of groups: the traditional large accountancy firms, smaller specialized CSR or software consultants, independent auditions, or CSR-campaign-related organizations.

As might be expected, the large, traditional accounting firms such as PriceWaterhouseCoopers and KPMG have been active in this area for some time. In fact, according to a recent survey, 65 percent of company sustainability reports reviewed were audited by the major accounting firms.[3] KPMG has its well-established Sustainability Advisory Services as well as their Supply Chain Integrity service that has been operating since the late 1990s. PricewaterhouseCoopers has a similar Assurance/Business Advisory practice with more than 400 consultants in 32 countries worldwide. In April 2002, PricewaterhouseCoopers also announced that it had become a charter sponsor of the Global Reporting Initiative (with which it has been actively working since 1998 in an advisory capacity). Globally, PwC provides clients with a variety of services, from traditional compliance reviews and factory audits, to strategy development, metrics definition, data collection, product life-cycle analysis, environmental policy assessments, or responsible supply chain impact studies.

"We help companies understand all the things that they are doing around being responsible or not," says Martin Ogilvie Brown, from PwC's, Sustainable Business Solutions group. "This includes helping multinational corporations to sort through the often disparate and difficult-to-collect information concerning their social and environmental performance from various departments and functions around the world."

"We look at the whole sea of information that is relevant and important to stakeholders," he says, "and then help them to collect and assess information that addresses their specific reporting requirements. Then we help them sort through what they are doing well, or not so well, and point out where they may need to develop a new policy, metric, or initiative."[4]

On the international supplier audit side, a good example of a more specialized service is Bureau Veritas, which provides independent monitoring and auditing services of suppliers for companies worldwide. Bureau Veritas covers many industries, including apparel, foods, and other consumer goods, and will provide audits against a company's own code of conduct, or against recognized standards such as the Fair Labour Association (FLA) or the World

---

3. "Beyond Numbers," *KPMG Assurance and Advisory Services Booklet,* p. 17.
4. Interview, November 6, 2003.

Responsible Apparel Production (WRAP). They also provide site certification for SA 8000.

Finally, there have emerged in recent years a number of smaller CSR and sustainability specialist consultancies that help companies devise their social and environmental strategies, or develop their nonfinancial reporting process. They can advise on most of the key features of an ethical supply chain—creating a strategy, program management, change management, developing performance indicators, supplier monitoring, coaching and auditing—that we have been examining. Stratos, for example, a sustainability consultancy and research group based in Ottawa, Canada, provides clients with strategic planning, benchmarking, and standards implementation, audit, and reporting advice. "We have a specialization in sustainability and CSR type issues," says Stephanie Meyer, a Principal with Stratos, "so we are all very conversant in all of the different disciplines—and that really is our core focus."

"When I look at various assurance statements and look at what I think really does add value," she says, "it is when you do see the assurance providers recommendations in there—where [assurance auditors] are providing some recommendations on how the company can improve, included within the assurance scope. Typically an audit assignment does not include recommendations, but you can come to some agreement to use those. We're not scared to go down that path, and that can be part of what can differentiate us from some of the "big Four.""[5]

Similarly, London-based Impactt Limited provides companies with services such as vision and strategy development, troubleshooting assistance, and factory assessments. They also help companies construct tools and methodologies. "We work by opening people's eyes to the impacts and the risks of how the company works now," says Louise Jamison, Director at Impactt, "and opening their minds to the possibility of change. We create a safe environment for people to question what they do and how they do it and then work with them to develop creative, pragmatic solutions and strategies and robust tools and systems which deliver measurable and demonstrable results."

Impactt has developed its own in-house approach to evaluating labor conditions in production sites known as the "Impactt Diagnosis," which combines "rigorous data-gathering with common sense and an open and cooperative approach to working with factory managers."

"This enables us regularly to uncover issues which other auditors miss," she concludes, "and to reinforce the business case for improvement with production site managers."[6]

---

5. Interview, September 2, 2003.

6. See *www.impacttlimited.com*.

CASE STUDY

Impactt

The following text is taken as a direct quote from the Impactt Web site. See source note below.

The Pentland group owns a number of international sports & leisure brands, including Ellesse, Speedo, Kickers, Berghaus and Red or Dead. In addition, Pentland supplies own label footwear and clothing to high street retailers, mainly in the UK. Pentland commissioned Impactt to work intensively with management, union and workers at one of its supplier factories in Vietnam to:

- Understand the factors driving excessive overtime.
- Build a shared understanding of the need for change.
- Develop verifiable management systems for recording overtime.
- Ensure that information is available to workers, union, management, and Pentland on hours worked.

Impactt worked with MRSC, a Vietnamese NGO specialising in working with migrant workers, to ensure that workers' views were properly represented in the negotiation. This approach has brought about real change in the factory through:

- Enabling workers to choose whether they work overtime or not
- Enabling workers to choose how much overtime they work
- Developing verifiable record keeping systems for overtime
- Ensuring that workers have information about hours and pay

The lessons learnt at the factory will be rolled out to Pentland's other suppliers around the world.

Source: Impactt Web site at *www.impacttlimited.com*.

Statistically among these various consultancies and auditors, the larger accounting firms are favored by most large corporations, but in a recent reporting analysis performed by SustainAbility, companies that used the smaller audit groups or CSR-specialist consultancies, (especially if those CSR organizations were teamed with an audit firm or specialist consultancy) tended to produce better CSR reports, actually scoring significantly higher in terms of accuracy, verification, and customer satisfaction. The formal accountancy approach, of course, focuses more on validation of facts and figures, whereas CSR groups often feel free to comment more broadly on performance, even providing recommendations that are useful both to the reader of the report and to the company itself.[7]

As with financial auditors, if your company does decide to hire a third-party to verify compliance, the Global Reporting Initiative has some useful advice about selecting auditors. This includes:

- Make certain of the auditor's degree of independence and freedom from bias, influence, and conflicts of interest.
- Understand their ability to balance consideration of the interests of different stakeholders.
- Be certain that the auditor was not involved in the design, development, or implementation of the organization's sustainability monitoring and reporting systems and did not assist in compiling the sustainability report.
- Allocate enough time to enable the process to be carried out effectively.
- Be certain that the auditing company, and the individual auditors assigned, are competent and experienced enough to meet the objectives.[8]

---

7. Allison Maitland, "How to Prove Good Intent," *The Financial Times,* November 18, 2002.

8. "Sustainability Reporting Guidelines," *The Global Reporting Initiative,* p. 78.

CHAPTER FIFTEEN

Compliance Issues

It is socially responsible to have kids at work in some of these communities . . . because if they are not in the workplace, they are on the streets . . .

—John Brookes, CEO of Manaxis

As the application of standards and this type of supplier monitoring process have become more widespread during the past two years, one of the central questions to arise has been what exactly should a company do when they find that one of their "critical" suppliers is in serious breach—employing child labor, requiring excess working hours, dumping toxic wastes—of key elements of the performance standards? There are several issues to consider.

First, companies need to realize that many developing-economy operations will in fact not meet the minimum requirements of these common performance standards, therefore leaving them in something of a difficult position. A recent ETI survey reveals the extent of the problem. Of the 6,763 suppliers monitored, nearly one-third were "noncompliant," with health and safety issues leading the list of concerns, but there were also union restrictions, low wage, and long hour issues. Ten countries—seven of which were in Asia—accounted for 90 percent of these violations.[1]

A similar study by the Ethical Trading Initiative found that member companies found noncompliance in almost every area covered by the ETI code. The good news is that nearly half of the 2,472 compliance failures (1,144) were actually successfully resolved. Again health and safety issues topped the list of noncompliance failures (62 percent), with 15 percent of failures related to wage levels, and 10 percent reflecting excessive working hours. What is interesting to note is that, despite the tremendous amount of media attention that this issue attracts, fewer than 1 percent of all violations were for employing child labor.

The ETI found that health and safety violations were the most difficult problems to overcome (nearly half of the 599 "unresolved" noncompliance violations), with only 5 cases of child labor still unresolved on the second audit (after all, employing children is quickly remedied, whereas fundamentally dangerous operations and policies are often difficult to alter).[2]

Gap Inc. provides a good example of what companies are up against. In December 2002, Gap employed 90 people on their vendor compliance team, responsible for covering 2,400 factories in 50 countries. Each of these vendors is subjected to an initial evaluation, where they are introduced to Gap's code of conduct and standards policies and assessed against those. Most suppliers fail initially, but are often given an opportunity to correct noncompliance issues before a second site visit by Gap inspectors. Even so, 20 percent of factories that were reviewed in 2002 failed to gain approval for contracts.[3]

For many companies, their first reaction to discovering that a key supplier is in breach of ethical codes is simply to break off the contract, make an announcement to the press, and flee. But as we have seen, though this may remove the immediate threat to a company's reputation, withdrawal doesn't really help any of the parties—the company, the supplier, or the employees.

"It is extremely challenging in terms of cost and culture," says John Brook, CEO of Manaxis and veteran assurance auditor. "There are people knocking on the doors of facilities looking to get work and dying on the street because they don't get work. They would be happy to work for a sub-minimum wage just to give themselves some bread. There are children

1. The Ethical Trading Initiative's *2000–2001 Annual Report* at *www.eti.org.uk/pub/publications/ann-rep/2000_en/page04.shtml.*

2. Ibid.

3. See GAP Inc.'s Social Responsibility Ethical Sourcing Program at *www.gapinc.com/social_resp/sourcing/program_body.shtm.*

of 10 years old that would work just to keep their brothers and sisters fed—so the noble morals of 'no child labor' and 'a fair living wage' are laudable in a strategic and global sense, and in setting a goal for an overarching target to aim for, but they are not going to be resolved by a code of conduct—they are not going to be resolved by passing a law in the Guatemalan parliament tomorrow."[4]

Again, H&M's policies in this area are worth citing. "At H&M [we] wish to work together with our suppliers, on a long-term basis, to improve the conditions in the factories," they insist. "We are sometimes asked why we do not immediately terminate our cooperation with suppliers who do not comply with our Code of Conduct. Obviously, that would be a simple solution for us, but H&M also feels a responsibility towards the people working in the factories. If H&M leaves a factory due to poor management, the ones that are truly affected are the workers. Another buyer indifferent to workers' rights might then replace H&M. However, when we encounter serious violations a strong statement must be made. If the factory management is faking documents or if a supplier has subcontracted production to a production site that is not known to us or in other ways refuses to cooperate, we are forced to cease the cooperation."

"In our monitoring effort there is a strong element of consultation/education to really make our suppliers understand the importance and the advantages of complying with our code."[5]

As we have seen, increasingly, rather than simply withdrawing from the contract, companies are focusing their efforts on improving the supplier's performance. Companies have been able to bring suppliers into standards compliance in many cases simply by explaining expectations clearly and helping finance improvements and reforms—timecard systems, strict overtime reporting—that are simple improvements but can be very effective (when applied appropriately) in countering labor and environmental abuse. And this type of policy seems usually to be met with strong support by NGOs, themselves, for the most part, very much aware of the dilemma of supplier noncompliance.

"The objective we're working for is not to divide factories into those that are acceptable and not acceptable so that companies only do business with the companies that are doing well," says Alice Tepper Marlin, President of Social Accountability International, creators of the SA 8000 standard. "The objective is to provide incentives and assistance to build

---

4. Interview, August 15, 2003.

5. H&M Social Responsibility Report, p. 7 at *www.hm.com/corporate/pdf/social/ csr_report_social.pdf.*

capacity, to have good human relations and good working conditions in all factories and farms."[6]

David Croft, of CoOp agrees. "We start with a postal questionnaire to help with risk planning," he says, "then we can organize a site visit where we need to investigate further. This might be through our own team or with commercial auditors. We have been carrying out detailed assessments with up to three or four auditors over a two- to three-day period, and we have also been developing a shorter one-day assessment that highlights areas of risk."

"Where we find breaches of the code," he explains, "we aim to establish an action plan with the supplier. If we get no cooperation, then we would reconsider our relationship with the supplier, but we prefer to work with suppliers to improve conditions."[7]

Moreover, the ETI has found that working with suppliers to improve weak areas often pays off. "Companies were able to rectify much of what they found," says the ETI. "Successes included raising wages to the legal minimum, the installation of fire prevention measures, recognition of trade unions, and enrolling under-age employees in education. These are real advances which can have a significant impact on the everyday lives of the workers . . ."[8]

GEMI lists candidate EHS performance indicators. For most of these indicators, five different questions could be used to assess supplier performance:

- Is the supplier aware of this impact/issue?
- Does the supplier have goals or policies regarding this impact?
- Does the supplier have detailed plans in place to measure, manage, and improve this impact?
- What is the supplier's performance regarding this impact during the most recent year?
- Is the supplier's performance improving over time, and by how much?

"Focusing solely on question 4 [the supplier's performance in the most recent year]," warns GEMI, "can be ill advised. Infrequent accidents can seriously depress performance statistics in the year they occur. It is wiser to augment the evaluation of single-year performance measures with an assessment of performance trends over several years, and/or management systems."[9]

---

6. David Drickhamer, "SA 8000 Sets a Standard," *Industry Week.com,* June 1, 2002 at *www.iwvaluechain.com/Features/articles.asp?ArticleId=1263.*

7. The Ethical Trading Initiative's *2000–2001 Annual Report,* op. cit.

8. Ibid.

9. "New Paths to Business Value," the Global Environmental Management Initiative at *www.gemi.org/newpath.pdf,* p. 42.

Moving Beyond Compliance to Self-Sustaining Continuous Improvement

Compliance, of course, is simply the first step, and many would argue, only fleeting if more fundamental issues are not addressed. It is one thing not to employ child labor, or to provide on-site washing facilities, but it is only when the labor force is well-trained, safe, and adequately compensated that any sustainable improvements can be assured. But to truly move from minimum compliance to higher levels of productivity and continuous improvement requires something more than just imposing international codes of conduct. This level of productivity improvement is most likely, not when it is imposed by an outside code, but when the management and employees of the supplier themselves take responsibility for continuously improving working conditions, environmental policies, and productivity methods. This is just as true for a manufacturing site in Indonesia, India, or China as it is in Toledo, Birmingham, or Lille. This usually means helping the supplier to develop other, more advanced management techniques, such as creating a program for worker training and development or providing incentives for productivity improvement.

Both H&M and Chiquita have gone even further.

CASE STUDY

Chiquita

The following text is directly quoted from "Ethical Performance," Autumn 2001. See source note below.

Chiquita, which produces a quarter of Latin American bananas, has spent eight years working to ensure all its banana farms in Latin America meet labour and environmental standards that are independently verified by an international non-governmental organization.

In the often-troubled Latin American banana industry, where labour unions have been seeking change for more than a decade, one company has made a bold—and so far lone—move to become a model of best practice on workplace conditions and environmental management.

Last autumn, after eight years of hard work, the fresh food group Chiquita met an independently verified social and environmental standard for the 127 banana farms it owns in Latin America. The standard is run by the Rainforest Alliance, an international non-profit organization responsible for certifying farms under its Better Banana Project (BBP).

Chiquita is the only global banana company to have undertaken and met the BBP's standards, which are the centrepiece of a rapidly expanding corporate social responsibility programme. Chiquita outlined many of its initiatives in its first Corporate Responsibility Report published in September 2001.

The publication of this report sets a high standard for the whole industry. The same can be said for the groundbreaking recent agreement with unions in Latin America that commits Chiquita to respect the core labour conventions of the International Labour Organization and establishes mechanisms for regular consultation, and for oversight of compliance.

The Rainforest Alliance began the BBP in 1991, around the same time that Chiquita, which produces roughly 25 per cent of the world's bananas, began looking for just such an authoritative environmental standard to improve life for its employees and safeguard the environment.

Jeff Zalla, corporate responsibility officer at Chiquita, says senior management at the company had reached the conclusion — through "education and increased awareness" rather than any reputational catastrophe — that things needed to change. "We wanted to improve our social and environmental performance in an authentic way and BBP was the most rigorous standard," he says.

"We felt we had a particular responsibility as an agricultural producer in developing countries to do something — and as a brand to lead our industry." As a result, Chiquita and the Rainforest Alliance began talks, that, in 1992, led the company to test out the idea of trying to meet the BBP standards.

The standards, which are detailed in a 19-page document, cover a wide range of topics, from workers' rights to the storage of packaging material on plantations. When two pilot farms in Costa Rica achieved certification, senior management decided to extend the work. The first batch of Chiquita farms was certified in 1994, and the long haul to 100 per cent certification began.

Since then Chiquita has, among other things, made efforts to reduce pesticide use, reforested more than 1000 hectares with native trees and put 525ha of land under protection. On workers' welfare, certification has helped Chiquita employees attain a much higher standard of living than other agricultural workers in the countries where the company operates.

Employees in Costa Rica, for instance, now earn more than one-and-a-half times the standard minimum wage. They also have improved training, housing, health benefits, education, and transport. All company workers have the right to associate freely, and Chiquita has almost as many union workers as all other banana companies in Latin America combined.

The Chiquita farms are certified only after frequent visits by trained independent inspectors, who are brought in from a network of conservation organizations affiliated to the Rainforest Alliance. They verify that the changes needed to meet the standards are being made, and that farms have introduced measures to improve the quality of life of workers, reduce agrochemical use and increase water quality and wildlife habitat.

All farms owned by the company in Colombia, Costa Rica, Guatemala, Honduras and Panama, cultivating more than 28,400ha, have now been certified. A further 30 per cent of independent farms selling bananas to the company have also been certified, and the company is keen to encourage the remaining 70 per cent of independent producers to follow suit. Together, according to the Rainforest Alliance, total production from Chiquita's certified owned and independent producer farms, amounts to almost 15 per cent of banana exports from Latin America.

Complying with the BBP has cost the group more than $20 million in capital expenditure, along with millions of dollars in annual operating costs, but Tensie Whelan, executive director of the Rainforest Alliance, says the company's "extraordinary efforts" to reach compliance are "leading the way for the rest of the industry." George Jaksch, Chiquita's quality director in Europe also judges the money has been well-spent.

"What we have done in our tropical division is hugely important for our European business," Jaksch says. "Many of our retail customers would not be doing business with us unless we had a really thorough and deeply rooted programme like this."

Zalla says the BBP "has helped align the whole organization behind a clear performance standard." He adds: "We see a lot more discipline throughout the company as a result of what we have done under the BBP. It's hard to put a cost figure on the improvements, but they are very real in terms of workplace conduct and productivity. There have also been real cost savings through measures such as reducing the use of pesticides."

Even without those benefits, Zalla says Chiquita would have done what it did because "we are committed to doing the right thing." He adds: "In a country such as Colombia there are huge social problems in the areas where we produce bananas. It makes a real difference that the company has a programme of this kind. It creates a workplace where people can feel valued and work safely."

Source: Ethical Performance, Autumn 2001 at *www.ethicalperformance.com/ best_practice/archive/1001/ case_studies/chiquita.html.*

H&M, the European clothing retailers provide another good example of an innovative program that helps to deal with the issue of child labor. Rather than severing contact with a supplier that is found guilty of employing child labor, H&M require the supplier to pay for the child's education costs until he or she is old enough to begin to work legally.

"When a child is found, H&M executes an action plan together with the child's family and the supplier in order to get the child back in school," says H&M. "When seeking a solution for the child, H&M makes sure that the measures taken are in the child's best interest. This is our primary focus. H&M demands the supplier pays both for school and retained salary. H&M stays in contact with the supplier, the family, and the school to make sure that the child continues his education. If this is not cared for, the children often are off to another job, trying to earn double incomes."[10] (See Figure 15-1.)

"It is a truism of business strategy that sustainable change does not result from adapting systems, procedures and processes," says Michael Allen from the Global Alliance, "but requires a shift in an organization's culture—in the ethos, attitudes and behavior of its people. This may seem abstract in relation to improving workplace conditions in an Asian apparel factory or a Central American plantation."

"Our experience," says Allen, "based on confidentially consulting over 10,000 workers and managers in several Asian countries, suggests that investing in employee training, services and development—including critical health, workplace and life skills—can be a catalyst for changing workplace culture and cultivating local ownership of workplace improvement."[11]

One method for deciding the level of effort and strategic importance of the company's efforts in this area is simply to define how the company wishes to be perceived by stakeholders by using the following scale:

1. Minimum effort: Indifferent to ethical or legal issues.
2. Below the industry average, or unable to accurately judge ethical or environmental standards.
3. Complies with all laws.
4. Has made the decision to create an ethical framework and to actively promote social and environmental policies.
5. Industry leadership.

One of the most innovative companies in the area of CSR and supplier management is British Telecom, which, with 28 million fixed phone lines and another 7.5 million mobile phone customers, already has in place a

10. H&M Social Responsibility Report, op. cit., p. 10.
11. Michael Allen, "Analysis: Increasing Standards in the Supply Chain," *Ethical Corporation,* October 2002, pp. 34–36.

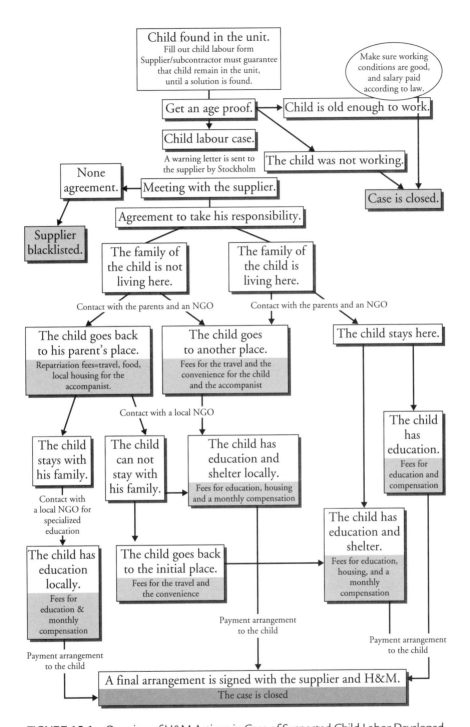

FIGURE 15-1 Overview of H&M Actions in Case of Suspected Child Labor Developed by Our CSR-Team in India (similar procedures are followed in other countries)

Source: H&M's Social Responsibility Report, p. 11 at *www.hm.com/corporate/pdf/social/csr_report_social.pdf.*

strong set of environmental programs governing their emissions, energy usage, and disposal of waste and used materials. As part of a comprehensive environmental management system they have implemented ISO 14001 in all of their UK operations. Their recycling program now recycles nearly 1/3 of the company's total waste, reducing waste to landfill by 5.6 percent. This focus on waste recycling saves them more than $4 million each year on landfill tax alone. At the same time they have focused on improving their fleet size and efficiency, and in the last decade have reduced company energy usage by 23 percent, saving them more than $6 million during the same period.[12]

Equally important, BT have put together a broad program for implementing high standards within its extended supply chain, and have issued a set of guiding principles that can be valuable for any company contemplating adopting standards and developing a supplier program. These guiding principles provide a strong framework for their ethical supply chain program.

Principle 1: Working Together

BT will:

- Work collaboratively with suppliers in pursuit of these standards.
- Guide relationships by the principle of continuous improvement.
- Welcome rather than penalise suppliers identifying activities that fall below these standards (undertaken by themselves or sub-contractors) and who agree to pursue our aspirations.
- Review and, where appropriate, revise these principles in the light of experience.
- Consider a similar ethical trading standard as a reasonable alternative where suppliers are already working towards this alternative.
- Not hold a supplier to a higher standard than BT's own policy on these issues.

Principle 2: Making a Difference

BT and it suppliers should:

- Use a risk-based approach to the implementation of these standards.
- Focus attention on those parts of the supply chain where the risk of not meeting these standards is highest and where the maximum difference can be made with resources available.

---

12. Conference discussion with Chris Tuppen, November 2002; also "Case Studies, BT: Staying online with ISO 14001," 2001 Business in the Environment, Ernst & Young.

BT's suppliers should:

- Be prepared to share with BT the basis of their approach with regard to the above.

Principle 3: Public Reporting

BT will:

- Report publicly our performance and practices with regard to the implementation of GS18 Sourcing with Human Dignity.

Principle 4: Awareness Raising and Training

BT and its suppliers should:

- Ensure that all relevant people are provided with appropriate training and guidelines to implement the standards.

Principle 5: Monitoring and Independent Verification

BT will:

- Recognise that the implementation of these standards may be assessed through monitoring and independent verification, and that these methods will be developed as our understanding grows.

BT's suppliers should:

- Provide BT or its representatives with reasonable access to all relevant information and premises and cooperate in any GS18 Sourcing with Human Dignity assessment—using reasonable endeavors to ensure that subcontractors do the same.
- Use reasonable endeavours to provide workers covered by the standards with a confidential means to report to the supplier failure to observe the standards.

Principle 6: Continuous Improvement

BT and its suppliers should:

- Apply a continuous improvement approach in agreeing schedules for improvement plans with suppliers not meeting these standards.
- Base improvement plans on individual case circumstances.
- Not use this project to prevent suppliers from exceeding these standards.

BT will:

- Following an escalation to BT's Chief Procurement Officer, consider terminating any business relationship with the supplier concerned where serious shortfalls of these standards persist.[13]

Whatever level of supplier engagement a company ultimately chooses, the SEAAR movement continues to push companies toward creating reports for their investors that reflect what policies and procedures a company has put in place in order to manage risks that might come from the workplace and environmental policies of its suppliers. Creating those sustainability reports is the final feature of an ethical supply chain framework.

13. "GS18 Sourcing With Human Dignity: A Supply Chain Initiative," *British Telecom,* Issue 3, September 13, 2002, pp. 4–5 at *http://216.239.51.100/search?q=cache: Y2QOEfgf8nQC:www.selling2bt.com/data/working/humandignity/gs18.pdf+ethical+ supply+chain&hl=en&ie=UTF-8.*

CHAPTER SIXTEEN

Reporting Your Good Work — Moving Toward Triple- Bottom-Line Accounting

T ransparency is at the core of the ethical supply chain. Reporting on a company's activities and its perform- ance with regard to supplier behavior is therefore central to creating an ethical supply chain framework. In fact, the way in which a company's social and environmental activities are reported is in many ways as important to a company as adopting the performance standards themselves, in that it is through a believable (and readable) sustainability report that a company can best explain its efforts and its accomplishments.

As we have seen, hoping to capitalize on the upbeat press garnered by the original group of companies—such as the Body Shop—that produced social reports in the late 1990s, and bowing to growing pressure from NGOs, investors, consumers, and governments, the number of companies producing some form of social and environmental reports has ballooned to more than 2,500. Nearly half of the world's largest companies (those in the Global Fortune 100 and the FTSE100) now produce some type of social and environmental or sustainability reports, with the number in Britain alone jumping from 18 of these large corporations in 2001, to 50 in 2002.[1]

"What I am seeing is steady growth, if not explosive growth, in companies reporting," says Allen White, cofounder of the Global Reporting Initiative.[2]

Ironically, however, as we have also seen, this uncontrolled rush toward reporting has gone a long way toward undermining both the reporting process and the standards themselves. Just as with the lack of early agreement on a common standard, the lack of a single, agreed reporting process has hampered early reporting attempts. As companies scrambled to produce some sort of social and environmental report, corporations have for the most part simply written up their activities, cherry picking and creating a publicity document, or worse, compiled massive volumes of information, particularly on the environmental side, that can only be read by specialists.

"The quality of [CSR] reports is still deemed to be very poor," says Deborah Doane, head of the corporate accountability program at the New Economics Foundation.[3] With the average sustainability report jumping from 59 pages to 86 pages in the past two years (as companies compile ever greater amounts of data under the illusion that more is better), readers are now subject to what SustainAbility calls "carpet bombing"—enormous amounts of often irrelevant or inconclusive information.[4]

"The increase in reporting is good news," says Peter Knight, director of Context, a CSR consultancy. "But there's still too much fluff about."[5]

To be fair, many companies have taken their reporting process very seriously, and have made legitimate efforts to monitor their suppliers'

---

1. Alison Maitland, "Social Reporting: Pressures Mount for Greater Disclosure," *FT.com*, December 10, 2002.

2. Interview, August 12, 2003.

3. Sarah Murray, "Benchmarks for Good Behaviour," *FT.com site*, December 4, 2002.

4. Alison Maitland, "Truants, Nerds and Supersonics," *The Financial Times*, November 18, 2002.

5. "KPMG International Survey of Corporate Sustainability Reporting 2002" at *www.global reporting.org* as cited by Alison Maitland, "Survey of Sustainable Business: Companies Start to Detail What on Earth Is Going On," *The Financial Times*, August 23, 2002.

activities and report on conditions in a balanced and transparent way. That is why many of the more progressive corporations in the world are leading the crusade to recognize the GRI as a standard, global reporting framework. For them, without a consistent reporting process, their good efforts are undermined by inconsistent, overweight, or misleading reports from their competition. After all, why should a company be rigorous in applying standards and honest in reporting its failures if its competition can simply write up a public relations document that only describes broad, positive results and omits any negative issues?

In fact, many would argue that the lack of a single recognized reporting framework is what contributed to the *Kasky* v. *Nike* lawsuit. Although the case has taken on new concerns over corporate free speech, the dispute had its origins in accusations that Nike was misreporting the employment policies of its suppliers. Although some would contend that being bound legally to claims made in these reports will drive companies away from reporting, the more logical evolution of the conflict would be for companies not to avoid making any claims at all, but instead to move toward independent, third-party audits that bring consistency and legitimacy to the whole process. After all, in the world of financial reporting auditors are expected to present a legitimate certification of a company's financial performance, ostensibly, at least, free from company pressure.

For all of these reasons, companies, NGOs, and increasingly governments, and agencies such as the UN's Global Compact, have begun to recommend a reporting regime which has become known as the Global Reporting Initiative. The purpose of the GRI is to provide a single, consistent, universally recognized reporting process—just as financial reporting has the Generally Accepted Accounting Principles framework—that will form the basis for consistent and comparable company social and environmental reporting.

The **Global Reporting Initiative** was initiated in 1997 by a U.S.-based group known as the Coalition for Environmentally Responsible Economies (CERES), and is probably the leading reporting initiative today. Working in partnership with the United Nations Environment Program, and a broad group that includes corporations, universities, NGOs, major consultancies, and accountancy firms, GRI's mission is to create universally applicable guidelines for social and environmental reporting. This means making sustainability reporting, according to Allen White, the GRI's former CEO, "as routine as financial reporting."[6]

Dr. Judy Henderson, Chair of GRI's Board, thinks that things are moving in that direction. "Reporting will become as routine as financial reporting," she

---

6. Tim Dickson, "The Financial Case for Behaving Responsibly," *The Financial Times,* August 19, 2002.

agrees. "And that will happen through various routes whether it happens through the legislative route or through other incentives—probably a combination of both—or down the track it becomes a regulatory issue the same way that financial reporting has."[7]

To do this, the GRI guidelines provide a framework that explains the principles and procedures that companies need to adopt in order to prepare a balanced and easily comparable report on environmental, social, and economic performance.

Endorsed by NGOs, the UN's Global Compact, and integral to many of the process and performance standards, the GRI is very much at the center of the European move toward requiring triple-bottom-line accounting, in that it (and other methods) provides guidance to companies on how to develop consistent and easily compared reports that reflect their activities (and the activities of their suppliers) in these areas. When combined with leading codes of conduct and performance and process standards, the GRI provides the final key feature of the ethical supply chain framework—audited, consistent, and verifiable social and environmental reports.

More than 140 companies—including such household names as Proctor & Gamble, BASF, Volvo, Electrolux, ICI, and Johnson & Johnson—have already adopted the GRI guidelines, including most of the 50 companies that made SustainAbility's "best global reporters" list in 2002. The initiative has been recommended by the European Commission, and was the basis for France's new mandatory reporting legislation that requires first-tier listed companies to produce social and environmental reports. It is also endorsed by the UN's Global Compact, has been adopted by government departments in Australia, the United States, Japan, South Africa, and the United Kingdom, is compatible with SA 8000, and is integrated into the AA 1000S assurance principles. The GRI was even one of the principal recipients of Ted Turner's largesse, receiving a grant for $3 million to help in its development. In short, the Global Reporting Initiative is quickly emerging as the *de facto* global reporting standard.[8]

Core Features of the GRI

Unlike SA 8000, AA 1000, or ISO 14001, the Global Reporting Initiative is not a code of conduct (explaining what a company should or should not do), a performance standard (providing measurements by which a company

---

7. Interview, July 29, 2003.

8. Alison Maitland, "Social Reporting: Pressures Mount for Greater Disclosure," *FT.com*, December 10, 2002.

can judge how well it is performing), or a management system (mandating the necessary management processes and policies that should be in place to ensure compliance). What the GRI framework does do is provide the principles and content guidelines that allow an organization to prepare social and environmental "sustainability" reports in a competent, consistent way.

The framework addresses three areas of company performance: social, environmental, and economic. Within these three areas there are 110 "indicators" of performance (of which 57 are mandatory and 53 are voluntary) covering employment policies, disciplinary practices, bribery and corruption, political contributions, product safety, emissions and waste polices, supplier activities, and various supply chain issues such as the safety and disposal of manufacturing materials, and safe and environmentally sound transportation and logistics policies.[9]

Moreover, in response to criticism that a "one-size-fits-all" model means that many of these indicators are inappropriate for differing industry sectors, the GRI has now developed sector-specific supplements that provide more appropriate indicators for sectors such as mining, car manufacturing, financial services, and tour operators.

The structure of the framework incorporates several important principles:

- First, it provides a standard reporting process (ensuring **transparency** and **auditability**).
- Second, it helps companies decide what to include in their reports (**completeness, relevance,** and **context**).
- Third, the framework is designed to ensure quality and reliability (**accuracy, neutrality,** and **comparability**).
- Finally, it helps to ensure that the reporting is relevant and readable (**clarity** and **timeliness** of information).

Pros and Cons of the GRI Framework

Adhering to these principles, claims GRI, ensures that reports present a "balanced and reasonable account of economic, environmental, and social performance, and the resulting contribution of the organization to sustainable development." The framework also helps readers compare performance between companies, and eliminates the credibility concerns that many NGOs and investors have about accuracy and reliability.[10]

---

9. "Sustainability Reporting Guidelines," the *Global Reporting Initiative*, 2002, p. 36.

10. Ibid., p. 22.

"Reporting should be the end result of a year's worth of management activity," says Nicholas Eisenberger, CEO of Ecos Technologies. "If you are doing a good job of managing your performance on an ongoing basis, creating a report is a simple activity—it is simply gathering what you already know and distilling it, taking away proprietary information, adding any explanatory information, taking away material that doesn't matter to anybody, and reporting it."

"That is not what is actually happening," he warns. "Because they have all these disparate systems, most companies don't know until 9, 12, even 16 months later what they actually did."[11]

Aside from the obvious benefits that come from consistent and standardized reporting, a single, universally recognized reporting framework also would relieve companies of having to respond to sometimes hundreds of different questionnaires in various reporting formats from various stakeholders.

"All sorts of people—ethical investors, NGOs, and governments—are asking companies for information and they all want it in their own format," says Mark Moody-Stuart, the former Shell chairman, now on the GRI board of directors. "If companies can say: 'We'll give you the information but in the GRI's standard format,' hopefully everyone will accept [that]."[12]

The Ford Motor Company agrees, contending that if the GRI became the "one-stop source" for reporting efforts, a single framework "could save companies the huge workload involved in responding to myriad requests for information from other bodies."[13]

"The GRI gives companies a benchmark, and it gives assurance providers a specific framework against which to assure," says Allen White. "The problem until now has been a 'wild west' of assurance—no standards, no norms, no protocols, in terms of what is being assured. So outside of reliance on the existing financial assurance procedures . . . there has been no development, no institution, no specialized procedures for sustainability reports. This is now changing, thanks to organizations like AccountAbility and its AA 1000S Assurance standard."

"As the GRI moves toward a higher level of general acceptance," he concludes, "analogous to GAAP for financial reporting, it will provide the 'concreteness' that assurers need in order to provide consistent assurance statements."[14]

---

11. Interview, August 25, 2003.

12. Alison Maitland, "Businesses Called to Account," *FT.com*, July 24, 2002.

13. Alison Maitland, "Social Reporting: Pressures Mount for Greater Disclosure," *FT.com*, December 10, 2002.

14. Interview, August 25, 2003.

There are still problems to be resolved, however. For one thing, the GRI framework is principally intended to help companies complete audits on their own operations, and although it assumes some level of extended responsibility throughout the supply chain, where an organization decides to erect the boundary to that responsibility is largely left up to the individual company. Although they recommend that a company work closely with stakeholders to determine "appropriate" reporting boundaries for their company's broader "footprint" (i.e., their extended supply chain), there is less focus on noncompany operations. Given so many of the serious social and environmental violations occur in a company's extended global supply chain, it is an issue that needs to be clearly addressed.

Moreover, though the GRI is becoming better recognized and supported, the initiative still remains just short of the economy of scale necessary to gain universal support. Critics point out that to coax investors and analysts away from their favorite, self-composed reporting format, the GRI has to become comprehensive enough (and accepted enough), to satisfy all parties that certification really does mean that a company is truly protecting its reputation as much as possible from unexpected social and environmental violations. Until then, they argue, the GRI will be seen by many companies as "just another" reporting option.

Moreover, as thorough and balanced as the reporting process is, the level of detail and standardized approach means that the reports that are produced make for extraordinarily dry reading—nothing like the often colorful and emotional corporate social responsibility reports that companies so often produce through their public relations office. The output from the GRI is said by critics to be of little value except to experts familiar with social and environmental standards. It is not an easy issue to remedy, because it is just that sort of public relations "spin" that the GRI is hoping to eliminate. After all, the GRI is trying to push companies toward putting social and environmental reporting on par with normal financial reporting—and financial reports, even when furnished with company-friendly photos and an upbeat style, are still judged on content and make for pretty dry reading themselves.

Moreover, the GRI allows companies to implement the framework incrementally, with the option of omitting many of the core indicators altogether. Several companies have chosen to avoid the phrase "in accordance with the GRI," choosing instead to simply contend that the GRI "informed development" of their report. It is an uncomfortable, but probably necessary concession to the practical issue of attracting companies that are still not, for whatever reasons, prepared to fully disclose their activities.

"The potential drawback is that this is a voluntary code," says Alison Maitland, in the *Financial Times*, "allowing companies to continue to use reporting as an opportunity for public relations spin rather than a serious effort at measuring and improving performance. Some companies use the guidelines loosely, while others are more rigorous about telling their story 'warts and all'."[15]

Independent Verification

As we have observed, although no company would imagine that it would be trusted to perform its own financial audits or to certify itself for a quality standard such as ISO 9000 without independent, third-party auditing, many companies are still determined to provide verification of compliance to these internationally recognized standards for social and environmental performance themselves. Few shareholders, however, and certainly no pressure groups, are willing to accept a company at its word—issuing a statement of commitment to worthy principles without providing some sort of verifiable evidence of real performance. The dangers of this unvalidated approach are obvious, as companies will have an incentive to write social and environmental reports that emphasize the areas in which they excel, and ignore the areas where they perform badly. Even if they don't do this, skeptics will suspect that they have.

All of this means that some form of external verification is necessary in order to bring credibility to the social and environmental reporting movement. The GRI provides both a consistent approach to gathering information and a consistent format for reporting that information—providing a level of standardization to the nonfinancial reporting process that up until recently has been plagued with widely varying report formats, and enormous differences in emphasis and quality.

"You don't even have to be a good corporate citizen," says Allen White. "All you have to be is a smart businessman to recognize that full disclosure is essential to business credibility; is important to business reputation. Emerging research demonstrates that transparency pays in terms of lower cost of capital, longer-term investors, and less share price volatility."

"Whether you are reporting on an environmental risk, a social issue or a nonfinancial economic issue," he concludes, "all of these can be bundled up into nonfinancial information that has real value added to companies. And whether you prepare a separate GRI report, integrate it into your financial statement, or weave it into your 10K filings, it doesn't fundamentally matter. What matters is that the information is available, and that it is credible."[16]

---

15. Alison Maitland, "Survey of Sustainable Business: Companies Start to Detail What on Earth Is Going On," *The Financial Times,* August 23, 2002.
16. Interview, August 12, 2003.

Although initially resisted by many companies, the concept of independent auditing is becoming more broadly accepted as important and necessary. In fact, third-party scrutiny using independent auditors to verify what a company has claimed in its sustainability report is considered the "leading practice," and independent verification is already done by most of the Top 50 companies that appear on SustainAbility's "Global Reporters 2002 Survey." Some 68 percent of the reports benchmarked in 2003 by SustainAbility, for example, had been independently verified, a total up from 50 percent in 2000 and a frail 28 percent in 1997.[17] Again, perhaps reflecting the different levels of acceptance and dedication to this type of reporting, the Global Fortune 250 (mostly American-owned companies) independently verified only a quarter of all its sustainability and CSR reports.[18]

In order not to frighten potential participants away, the GRI has purposely left the question of third-party validation to the discretion of the individual company. All that is necessary to affirm compliance with the framework is a signed statement by the board or the CEO certifying that the report was prepared "in accordance with GRI guidelines, and that the result represents a balanced and reasonable presentation of our organization's economic, environmental, and social performance." And although in order to be "in accordance" a company must note the reasons for any omission of core indicators, an organization is still free to take that course.

The Way Forward

Reporting on these, or very similar, process and performance standards will almost certainly become routine for companies during this decade. Acceptance and recognition of this new social and environmental reporting framework, however, is very much dependent upon making the process both effective and affordable.

SustainAbility, the research and consultancy group, provides some worthwhile advice to companies contemplating a reporting program:

- **Bust Silos.** CSR requires thinking trans-functionally: breaking down those walls created to compartmentalise the daily tasks of the corporation. Start with a reporting kick-off meeting which includes all of those who are contributing perspective, stories or data to the CSR report. Then converse constantly, most often with those with whom you are most likely to disagree.

---

17. "Beyond Numbers," *KPMG Assurance and Advisory Services Booklet,* p. 17.

18. Alison Maitland, ibid.

- **Define What Is Relevant.** Determine early on what issues really matter—to the corporation and to its stakeholders—and focus efforts on them. Then advise your readers why you chose not to go into detail on the rest.
- **Go Beyond Reporting Results or Lauding Company Achievements.** It's not just about past results. Readers want confidence that your company (a) knows where it is going, (b) has systems and processes in place to get there, and (c) understands the full impacts of its processes and products.
- **Build Processes to Link Reporting to Business Decision-Making.** Inevitably the process of creating a CSR report will uncover unforeseen risks and hidden opportunities. Don't let them go unaddressed. Use the report as a springboard to improvement, not as a final resting place for valuable information.[19]

Will this type of nonfinancial reporting truly become the norm in American companies? The GRI is not alone in believing that it will.

"Yes, I do believe that it will soon be standardized," concludes John Brookes. "I believe it will increasingly become normal for publicly held companies to at least make declarations and reports and have some sort of independent attestation of the validity of the data presented . . ."[20]

Finally, if nonfinancial reporting and the GRI are not yet universally accepted, it is worth considering just how rapidly the triple-bottom-line rise to prominence has been.

"I believe that GRI and CERES and a lot of the other efforts going on out there to focus companies on reporting . . . have been a fantastic effort, and very successful," says Nicholas Eisenberger, CEO of Ecos Technologies. "If you were to use as a benchmark 'What has been the increase in reporting over time?,' we have gone from 3 public companies [reporting] in 1992, to 3000 in 2003. I say that is a success."[21]

Allen White agrees. "This is very new stuff," he says. "If you rewind the tape of history and ask how, beginning in the 1930s and 1940s, the business world received financial accounting standards—the balance sheet, the profit and loss, the income statement, the concepts of depreciation and amortization—you would have witnessed the same type of confusion that one sees today in CSR standards. And because most CSR standards are so young—in the range of 5 years old—it points to the need to proceed with both care and optimism."

"All of us in the CSR community—the standards creators, standards users and their stakeholders—must be patient and take the long view of this new and critically important dimension of accountability," he concludes.[22]

---

19. "The CSR Reporting Process—Critical Success Factors," SustainAbility Web site at *www.sustainability.com/services/tools-CSR-reporting-process.asp*.
20. Interview, August 15, 2003.
21. Interview, August 25, 2003.
22. Interview, August 12, 2003.

CHAPTER SEVENTEEN

Systems to Monitor and Audit Social and Environmental Performance Within the Supply Chain

*A*s with any new supply chain
*development, as the SEAAR movement has grown, a variety of software
tools and consultancies have emerged that perform various functions for
companies that are interested in monitoring and reporting on the activities
within their supply chain. These include data collection and management,
decision support, risk analysis, and reputation scanning capabilities.*

Many of these systems already exist, in whole or in part, within companies, although at this point they are seldom focused on the monitoring or certification of overseas suppliers. Environmental Health and Safety systems (EHS), for example, are commonly used in manufacturing companies to help manage company compliance with U.S. law. Enterprise Resource Planning (ERP) systems, now the backbone and nerve center of the modern company, have strong procurement, sourcing, and supplier management offerings. Supply Chain Management systems are also integrating with ERP and EHS programs to help companies track hazardous materials and domestic supplier performance, and to automatically update the system with changing regulatory requirements.

Beyond refocusing these traditional supply chain systems, however, as standards such as ISO 14001 and SA 8000 have become more accepted, other supporting software has emerged to help a company assess its readiness and implement and manage these standards among their suppliers on a global basis.

This is a promising sign, because as we have seen with important productivity initiatives in the past—business process reengineering, ERP, advanced planning and scheduling, customer resource management—new ideas often really only take off in the United States when the combined effect of new IT productivity tools (and the drive by software companies to sell them) begins to gather pace and to capture the interest of consultancies, the business press, and ultimately, company managers.

There are four principal areas where information technology is making global supplier management easier and more efficient. The first, **Supply Chain Environmental Management Systems (SCEM),** have traditionally provided applications for managing environmental compliance issues—EHS—for companies and suppliers in domestic operations. Increasingly, these SCEM and EHS systems are evolving to take on greater emphasis in several important areas. First, they are beginning to shift their focus away from simple compliance and toward quality improvement—providing applications that help companies achieve greater cost savings through better monitoring and improving environmental waste management and energy efficiency. Second, reflecting the global trend toward outsourcing, instead of a singular focus on local operations, these systems are beginning to evolve toward a greater focus on overseas supplier management. Accordingly, they are also beginning to add on to their existing human resource and safety modules specialized labor modules that can help a company monitor more basic labor issues, such as working conditions, child labor, and living wage.

A second important IT growth area is **Supplier Relationship Management software (SRM).** Usually Internet based, these programs allow suppliers around the world to log on to a company portal and provide required social and environmental performance information. These SRM tools promise to facilitate "total global sourcing" of materials, and help companies to manage their entire supply chain by monitoring criteria such as social and environmental performance, standards certification, and quality and delivery performance of suppliers worldwide.

Third, there have recently emerged a number of more sophisticated **Risk and Incident Management Systems** that help a company to continuously "scan" its supply chain for potential risks, and then to deal with those risks in a focused and coordinated way using knowledge management techniques and incident management software.

Finally, new **Standards-specific implementation software** has been developed specifically for implementing, managing, and assessing compliance with standards such as SA 8000 or ISO 14001.

These systems provide companies with a means for moving away from collecting all supplier-related information manually, which means that information concerning working hours, wages, underage employment, safety records, incident or accident reports, environmental damage, fines, or audit results can all be collected electronically, integrated according to logical relationships, and pro-vided to any party that needs the information, worldwide and simultaneously. This information itself can often be used to create collaborative improvement programs that can help a supplier not only comply with legal and ethical requirements, but actually improve its productivity and efficiency. It also can be used to sense and respond to risks within the supply chain—ethical violations, use of dangerous materials, poor environmental policy—before those risks become full-blown incidents. Finally, information collected on social and environmental policies can be used for the formal audit and reporting process that so many companies are now adopting as part of the SEAAR movement.

Supply Chain Environmental Management Systems and Environmental Health and Safety Systems

Supply Chain Environmental Management systems have become popular among companies over the past decade as a means for monitoring, improving, and reporting on the environmental performance of their supply chain operations, including those of its (usually domestic) suppliers. Often based on the same reporting requirements as company-wide EHS systems (except that they focus specifically on the supply chain), most of these systems have gone well beyond being just a tool for gauging and recording environmental performance. Moreover, responding to the need for companies to provide social as well as environmental performance information, these systems have recently begun to build in a broader range of features encompassing other economic and social criteria.

"SCEM is gaining attention for a number of reasons," says BSR (Business for Social Responsibility), the U.S. consultancy and research group. "A growing number of companies realize that to achieve their environmental goals and satisfy stakeholders' expectations, they need to look beyond their own facilities and to involve their suppliers in environmental initiatives. Leading companies also understand that customers and other stakeholders do not always differentiate between a company and its suppliers and may hold companies accountable for suppliers' environmental and labor practices. In addition, many companies are working to streamline their supply base and develop more cooperative, long-term relationships with key suppliers, a practice that has fostered greater opportunities to work together on environmental issues."[1]

"It is fundamentally irresponsible," says Nicholas Eisenberger, CEO of Ecos Technologies, a sustainability software and consulting company, ". . . for a company to talk about how important [corporate social responsibility and sustainability] is, and then when you lift the covers you see that they are managing sustainability by Powerpoint and spreadsheet."

"That is not acceptable." he says. "Not acceptable from a shareholder perspective. . . . From a shareholder's point of view, it [what an organization is doing with regard to sustainability] matters to a company's reputation, it matters to cost structure, and it matters to efficiency. I want to know what [a company] is doing in this area and how they compare with their competitors. And they can't give me an effective answer to the question if they only know the answer to that question 15 months later, and are managing [the process] through a spreadsheet."[2]

In fact, there is more and more software for managing sustainability available to companies. Multifunction software platforms are rapidly overtaking the manual, paper-based survey and strategic sourcing process, with systems that allow data submitted from suppliers to be compared relationally, so that a company can complete searches based on criteria for high levels of employee health and safety or strong environmental policies, or compare social and environmental performance among potential suppliers. In fact, as with most SCM and procurement systems, the entire contract procedure, from submitting an RFI (Request for Information)

---

1. "Supplier Environmental Management," *BSR White Papers* at *www.bsr.org/BSR Resources/WhitePaperDetail.cfm?DocumentID=527.*
2. Interview, August 25, 2003.

through completion and payment, can be done electronically. And, of course, the information can be accessed by organizational leaders, the CERO, or supplier management team members, whenever needed, and additional information from third-parties and the media can be entered as accompanying notes.

Typically, SCEM and EHS platforms provide a wide variety of support functions, including guidance for companies on how to develop a supplier certification program, how to educate and train suppliers on pollution control polices such as the safe handling and disposal of materials, and how to monitor and audit compliance. These platforms also usually include:

- **Environmental Information Management.** These systems provide information concerning regulations and safety requirements for materials and chemicals, including information on government regulations and safety requirements. They also provide electronic access to continuously updated data sheets on toxicity, safe handling, labeling, and disposal of dangerous materials and chemicals.

- **Materials Management.** Apart from providing information, SCEM systems also help to actively track, maintain, and report on the use of regulated or dangerous materials and chemicals as they move through the supply chain. The software provides information on materials origin and groups that have been in contact with the materials, and provides names of responsible persons for hand-offs at each stage of the supply chain. The software also provides electronic alerts for storing or handling hazardous materials.

- **Waste Management.** These systems also provide information on waste production and disposal, including all information necessary for documentation for U.S. government compliance and reporting. As with the materials management systems, waste management modules usually provide information on waste material handling and storage safety and regulatory requirements for shipping and disposal. This type of information can be used to manage recycling and reuse of materials as well as the disposal of waste. The waste management modules also help a company track costs and savings associated with the process, and alert the company to infringements or regulatory violations.

- **Energy Efficiency.** Most systems will also help a company track energy usage by plant or location, help management create energy-saving plans, and monitor the results in terms of costs and savings.

- **Employee Safety.** These systems also help a company manage all the information associated with employee health and safety, including incident and accident information, environmental spills, and the materials or chemicals involved in any injury or exposure. Most platforms have a report generator that automatically provides accident and incident reporting as required by OSHA and other regulatory agencies. These systems also help management provide employees—and supplier employees—with safety training and certification requirements.

• **Report Generation.** These systems also usually provide easy report generation tools so that companies can extract relevant information for annual reports or government or NGO requests for information or compliance reporting. They also tie directly into ERP, SCM, or Procurement systems, and often provide a direct link into supplier and vendor EMS (Environmental Management Systems) or other performance reporting systems.

• **Situation and Risk Analysis.** Increasingly, these systems also direct a company through an environmental impact analysis, which involves examining potential risks concerning materials being used, supplier behavior, or other supply chain activities that may have environmental risks. This type of environmental "risk scanning" helps a company anticipate potential areas of risk or exposure.

• **Policy Development.** Many of these systems today also provide tools for policy development, including assistance with creating policy statements and specific standards, targets and objectives that reflect the organization's environmental goals concerning monitoring and enforcement, supplier certification requirements, and employee health and safety standards.

• **Implementation Planning.** These systems not only provide a process for communicating, training, and educating employees and suppliers, but also provide a management review process, flagging calendars and providing company leaders with access to relevant documents and updates.

• **Communication Tools.** SCEM software can also provide an effective tool for communicating company ethical policy and environmental and safety standards to suppliers and to stakeholders via the Internet. With suppliers, this communication can be ongoing, both as part of the qualification process and as part of the RFP process, automatically building into tender documents the necessary guidelines and requirements. The software can develop standardized contract documents and compliance questionnaires for suppliers, based on local laws or standards, and prompt managers to ask for specific safety or environmental performance statistics, recording the response for audit purposes.

• **Document Retention.** These systems also provide document retention capabilities for capturing and storing supplier documents, governmental requirements, e-mails and correspondence, certification documents, and survey results. The system automatically flags missing, invalid, or overdue items, and makes certain the necessary documents are secure and accessible and are kept for the right period of time.

Equally important, from an operational point of view, these systems provide broader management guidance by systematically leading the company through management processes and procedures, such as risk identification, resource allocation, assignment of responsibilities, and periodic verification of compliance. And there is good evidence that the combination of international standards and this formal "management system" approach is starting to be adopted by companies.

"EHS performance management systems . . . help a company convert its strategy into effective execution at every level of the company," says Nicholas Eisenberger. "What you need in order to be able to do that is to have tight coordination between the strategy and measures that are being looked at, and the processes that are operating and managing the business. So we help companies collect the data for the KPIs and safety incidents—or if you are at the facility level focused on energy consumption, or at the division level focused on greenhouse gasses. Whatever level that you are in the company, [you need to know] 'what are the key indicators that effect whether you are supporting the company's strategy?'"

"Because all metrics ultimately are the result of business processes," he explains, "we also help to automate business processes, so we can help automate greenhouse gas tracking and management processes, we can automate a GRI process for reporting, automate an incident management process . . . [we] make [the process] as flexible as possible, yet repeatable enough that companies can link up the things that they are doing every day with the strategies they are trying to achieve."[3]

Those that implement global standards such as SA 8000 or the Ethical Trading Initiative code "are seeing substantial improvements in productivity, substantial reductions in turnover, substantial improvements in motivation and skill levels in the workforce," says Alice Tepper Marlin from Social Accountability International. "Some because of the labor standards specifically, and some because SA 8000 has a management system, and you get these results from any management system. An operation that has a good management system is going to be more productive, more efficient, and is likely to have lower turnover than one without a management system. On top of that, because it is focused on your workforce, you get other benefits as well."[4]

A good example of this evolution beyond domestic environmental operations and toward a combined social and environmental "management system" approach to the company's global supply chain can be seen with the Entropy System suite of software from Entropy International.

"The Entropy System is moving into total risk management," says Entropy International's Chief Executive, Hewitt Roberts. "Although the

---

3. Interview with Nicholas Eisenberger, August 25, 2003.
4. Interview with Hewitt Roberts, February 13, 2003.

foothold is environmental health and safety monitoring, there is a natural, built-in transition into any of the other risk disciplines—whether it be ethical sourcing and SA 8000 or information security and 7799 or beyond and down the chain that would be covered by the umbrella of corporate governance and risk management."

The Entropy System platform, like other SCEM and EHS systems, is not a monitoring system itself; it does not attach to output pipes or chimneys. Instead, the system provides a framework for a corporate-wide environmental, health and safety management system, based on any of the "Deming-like" standards: ISO 14000 on the environmental side, for example, or SA 8000 for social compliance monitoring. The software provides for processing and capturing all documents necessary to improve policies and procedures, and using an executive-level risk management "dashboard," helps companies set objective targets and build action plans, as well as audit performance and rectify nonconformity problems once they are identified. The system can be used by individual factory sites as an operational compliance tool, or more broadly by the corporation to monitor performance across various sites.

"All these disciplines [health, employment standards, and environmental] do cross," explains Hewitt Roberts, "and in the future it is going to have to be a one-stop-shop for the corporate risk manager."[5]

Nicholas Eisenberger agrees. "Whatever your performance is that you are trying to manage, our system can help you to do that by giving you greater clarity about what is actually happening, and by helping to automate [and optimize] the processes involving all these people, systems and databases."[6]

Supplier Management Software

Understanding that monitoring suppliers in the extended global supply chain is becoming more and more important to companies, the major ERP vendors have also attempted to incorporate supplier relationship management tools in their "one-stop-shop" approach to supply chain management. Leading platforms such as SAP and PeopleSoft already provide supplier performance monitoring capabilities in their supplier relationship management modules, including scorecards that can help analyze a supplier's safety, environmental, and labor performance. Other companies have moved quickly to provide dedicated software suites for supplier relationship management (SRM).

---

5. Interview with Hewitt Roberts, February 13, 2003.

6. Interview with Nicholas Eisenberger, August 25, 2003.

In its SI Solution, for example, SupplierInsight provides a set of supplier management tools that are designed specifically to help companies work with suppliers in developing economies. The company has completed supplier evaluations in 46 countries worldwide and also offers a service for conducting supplier reviews and audits. The SI Solution allows suppliers to enter their own compliance data, and then provides analysis and reporting tools. Using this software and SupplierInsight services, Whirlpool claims to have reduced the time required to evaluate its suppliers from 2–6 months to 3–6 weeks, with each of the company's 400 buyers saving two hours per week just on better management of supplier information.[7]

Similarly, Strategic Environmental Consulting (SEC) offers supplier management software that provides a consolidated view of supplier performance, including:

- Supplier ratings for performance and reliability
- Suppliers' own internal management or control systems
- Product information
- Manufacturing location information
- Environmental performance data
- Packaging data
- Raw material data
- Forestry products auditing information
- Corporate social responsibility standards

This type of software focuses on specific emerging areas such as corporate social responsibility and the sustainability policies and certification status of suppliers in fields such as the paper and raw wood materials industry.[8]

Other firms, such as DataSavvy, now provide a social compliance database system that schedules social audits, tracks compliance issues and recommended corrective actions, and captures negotiation-related documents. It also has operational and executive report generators and an audit management suite that provides agent scheduling information, guidance standards, compliance tracking worksheets, and audit reports.[9]

---

7. "Falling Short of Global Sourcing Goals?" *SupplierInsight.com* at *www.supplierinsight.com/examples03_china.cfm.*

8. See Strategic Environmental Consulting's Web site at *www.strategic-environmental.co.uk/SEC%20Resources.htm#Supplier%20Manager.*

9. See *www.datasavvy.com.*

Risk and Incident Management Systems

A third category of systems that are now available to help companies to manage, monitor, and report on supply chain activities are risk-, knowledge-, and information-gathering programs. There are various IT related services, ranging from specific risk and incident management systems to everyday corporate e-mail, information search facilities, hotlines, skills databases, and specialist networks. Many of these systems already exist in the modern company, but hitherto have seldom been focused specifically on providing information and management guidance for supplier sourcing and risk management. Good examples include:

- **Portals, Groupware, and E-Mail.** Probably one of the most important applications available for ensuring an ethical supply chain is simply extending the existing company portal, as well as its groupware and e-mail services, to help to communicate standards, codes of conduct, and corporate news and expectations to employees and suppliers around the world. Developing a database of Frequently Asked Questions for suppliers, as well as providing original documentation for standards, codes, policies, and procedures online, can be used almost universally to communicate real-time with supplier management (if not employees) in factories worldwide.
- **Hotlines and Confidential Reporting Systems.** In keeping with new requirements for confidential hotlines now required in the United States, a worldwide confidential hotline can be a valuable tool for supplier (or company) employees who discover unethical or illegal activities happening at supplier sites.
- **Business Research and Analysis and Reputation Scanning Tools.** One of the great advantages of the Internet is that, just as corporate misbehavior can instantly be transmitted globally, companies can monitor their own reputation in the online and printed press worldwide. There are many new packages that provide this "reputation scanning" service, which can help a company understand at all times potential "hot" issues, including how their company's or suppliers' names are featured in the press, political or economic changes in their operating territories, potential supplier infractions, or new legislation or litigation that could have an effect on supply chain operations.
- **Risk and Incident Management Systems.** One of the most important advancements in this area are systems which provide analytical tools for identifying potential risks within the company or the supply chain, and converting those risks into easy-to-understand reports for the various parties involved in managing risk within an organization—the board, the CEO, the CERO, and the supplier program team members.

The Entegra Corporation, for example, has an enterprise risk management system known as Ki4, which includes more than 220 preconfigured reports, and 70 query functions so that managers can view risk data in ways that are most meaningful to them. The system also provides an interface to other applications, including all the standard spreadsheets and data processing packages.

"Ki4 Risk and Reputation System is an enterprise technology solution," explains Jim Kartalia, Entegra's CEO, "that provides executives and managers with an 'early warning system' to organize all data associated with corporate incidents and issues."

"These risk reports that are produced by Ki4 go to the ethics committee of companies and can literally be reviewed in ten minutes a day, keeping the company informed about any issues that have come up over the last 24 hours."[10]

Standards-Specific Implementation Software

Finally, a variety of standards-specific implementation software has recently emerged, specifically designed to implement, manage, and assess compliance with standards such as SA 8000, or ISO 14001.

The Entropy System, the software platform developed by Entropy International (mentioned above), for example, supports SA 8000 implementations. GreenWare, used by companies such as Delta Airlines and British Petroleum to help implement or assess their ISO 14000 readiness, has developed a software suite based on the ISO 14000 standard for environmental management that includes ISO 14000 series assessment, implementation, procedures, and audit modules.[11]

Similarly, Global Resource Management has a set of software tools that specifically focuses on helping companies manage their suppliers based on requirements set down in performance standards such as ISO 14001 or the ISO 9001:2000 quality standard. Designed as both an assessment and a management tool, their software measures supplier performance in terms of quality, environment, health, safety, and ethics against these international standards, providing both a "snapshot" of current practice as well as a "toolkit" that guides users through a step-by-step approach to "manage risks more effectively, ensure legal compliance, im-prove efficiency and implement robust systems," all according to ISO 14001 and other standards.[12]

---

10. Interview with Jim Kartalia, January 23, 2003.

11. See *http://greenware.ca/index.html.*

12. See *www.grm-uk.co.uk/index.htm.*

Applying Technology to the Ethical Supply Chain

There are many other companies that provide software in these areas, and many more just beginning to expand their traditional procurement, supply chain, ERP, and EHS platforms to incorporate this type of functionality in their suites. The combination of complex standards and reporting requirements, the importance of keeping auditable, easily available records, and the need to engage potentially thousands of suppliers from all over the world makes an Internet-accessed, integrated software suite very attractive to companies that are implementing standards, monitoring overseas suppliers, or are beginning to produce sustainability reports. There are several obvious benefits:

• **Better Risk Management.** As we have seen, over the past decade, as part of the supply chain revolution, companies have shifted responsibilities for materials management and production, whenever possible, to their supplier community. The early development of SCEM platforms reflected that shift in responsibility. Moreover, as companies continue to require suppliers to provide greater proof of performance—fair employment, recycling, waste disposal, or materials sourcing policies—company Environmental Health and Safety, supply chain, and risk management processes all begin to overlap. And, of course, supplier risk is not limited to only reputation or legal liability for poor social or environmental performance. These types of SCEM, EHS, and risk management platforms also help companies anticipate production and delivery interruptions or avoid surprise contract cancellations.

• **Productivity Improvements.** At the heart of any IT-based management system, of course, is quality assurance and productivity improvement. Much of the information that is channeled from supplier to buyer through these types of SCEM or EHS systems—information concerning hours, wages, underage employment, safety records, incident or accident reports, environmental damage, fines, audit results—can all help contribute to productivity improvements, reduce waste, or avoid costly fines. Recycling policies, cleaner production methods, prebanning of toxic or dangerous chemicals or materials used in the production process, improved energy usage, and efficiency by plant operations will all contribute directly to bottom-line savings.

• **An Enhanced Reputation.** Finally, given the pressures for better social and environmental performance that companies now face, making a conscientious and well-organized attempt to manage environmental issues within the supply chain can only help an organization's reputation in today's environment. These types of systems not only make the process of supplier monitoring and social and environmental reporting easier for a company, but they also demonstrate genuine commitment, in that they provide the overall monitoring and certification framework and data collection capacity that can only really be achieved with a consolidated software platform.

Ultimately, of course, the success of these systems will depend on their capacity to absorb the various emerging standards, including ISO 14000 and SA 8000. They must also provide data integration and support for reporting initiatives such as the GRI, and will need to support companies of different sizes from many different industries. Possibly most important, as we have seen, these types of systems, and a supplier-focused program of social and environmental monitoring and reporting, will be most effective if the entire process is built into a company's strategic and everyday processes—led by senior management, supported strongly by a CERO, and serving as a supporting structure for a company's ethical framework.

"EMS software will move front and center once sustainability starts being integrated into the broader suite of business performance metrics," concludes Carl Frankel, a consultant specializing in business and sustainability. "That may seem a long way off, but it's on the way."[13]

---

13. Carl Frankel, "The Future of EMS Software Depends on Two Types of Integration," *EccoNet.com* at *www.ecconet.com/ecconet/CommunityChat/spotlights/Archive/archive_emssoftwareCF.htm*.

CHAPTER EIGHTEEN

Pulling It All Together: The Switcher/Prem Case Study

C*reating an ethical supply chain, as we have seen, is a complex task, and as many companies have discovered over the past several years, even the best of intentions may fall short of achieving stated corporate ethical goals. The many activities that we have just explored — the development of a corporate ethical framework, the adoption of performance and process standards and codes of conduct, an active supplier management program, reporting the results of these efforts via a comprehensive reporting regime such as the GRI, and the adoption of new software tools — can all help make the task of overseeing the activities of overseas suppliers much easier and more productive.*

So what does this type of ethical framework look like in practice? The Switcher Company, a casual clothes retailer based in Switzerland, provides one of the best examples of the type of comprehensive approach to ethical supply chain management that we have been exploring. Combining all of the best elements of the ethical supply chain—strong leadership, good project and change management, aspirational codes, SA 8000 and ISO 14000 and other horizontal and vertical standards, independent and thorough audits, and a strong collaborative supplier–buyer relationship—the case study is an extraordinary example of how a company and its key suppliers can implement a cost-effective and humane sustainability program.

CASE STUDY

The Switcher/Prem Group Case Study

The following case study is reprinted with permission from the ILO, from "Building Reputation Through Social Accountability—The Switcher/Prem Group Experience in India," presented by Professor Ghislaine Cestre at the 6th International Conference on Corporate Reputation, Identity and Competitiveness, the Reputation Institute, Boston, 23–25 May 2002.

Headquartered in Mont-sur-Lausanne (Switzerland), Mabrouc's offices and warehousing facilities are spread over 10,000 square meters. The company counts 100 employees in Switzerland and generates annual revenues of over 60 million CHF. . . . The company's two main brands are Switcher and Whale. Switcher has become the better known brand and now represents a full line of basic clothes: T-shirts, sweat-shirts, tracksuits, shirts, polos, pants, jackets and accessories for adults and children . . . In 1999, over 5 million Switcher and Whale items were sold in Switzerland and the rest of Europe (mainly Germany).

. . . A CLEAR PHILOSOPHY

The Mabrouc/Switcher (called Switcher below) philosophy is one of sustainable development, preserving the environment, acting in a socially responsible manner and making the work environment as enjoyable as possible, under economic constraints. Owner Robin Cornelius strongly believes that "although economic pragmatism is a must—we are in business to make money—it should not prevent a company from being an active contributor to social development and environmental protection."

R. Cornelius sees Switcher as a service company specialized in clothes: "Switcher is at the service of customers, resellers, manufacturers and their families," he says, "but also the public in general and future generations." Concretely, it means granting partners special warehousing arrangements, recycling packagings, developing anti-pollution manufacturing processes, implementing energy conservation measures, improving working conditions, developing social programs for workers and their families, contributing to health and education programs, etc. The company's web site (www.switcher.ch) describes the Switcher philosophy in detail.

Many Swiss consumers are aware of Switcher's involvement in social issues. This is not due to advertising: Switcher does not advertise its social-related activities. Awareness undoubtedly comes from the numerous press articles portraying the company as a vivid example of good social/economic coexistence and revealing Switcher's owner particular charisma. The "citizen brand" image is well developed, but still essentially limited to Switzerland, due to Switcher's geographical market concentration.

INTERNATIONAL STANDARDS

In the 90's, Switcher aimed at ensuring product quality at all production/distribution stages and at complying with international environmental and social standards: the company gained ISO 9001 certification in 1997 and Switcher and Whale products are Oeko-Tex 100 certified (absence of harmful chemicals in production process). More recently, the company engaged in ISO 14001 (environmental protection) and SA 8000 (social accountability) certification. Switcher requires from all its business partners that they engage in the same process.

Switcher's Code of conduct is in line with the Clean Clothes Campaign (CCC) principles (www.cleanclothes.ch). Started in the Netherlands in 1990, the CCC was launched in Switzerland in 1999. Its Code of Labour Practices for the Apparel Industry including Sportswear, common to all European CCCs, is inspired from ILO labour standards, the Universal Declaration of Human Rights and the International Children Rights Convention.

In 2000, along with two other Swiss companies (Migros and Charles Veillon), Switcher agreed to be part of a pilot project for the independent monitoring of its own Code of conduct: "Switcher has nothing to hide," says Daniel Rufenacht, Head of Environment and Social Relations since 1999. "We have set high environment and social standards for ourselves and work hard to implement them; we remain open to any suggestion that could help us improve." Rufenacht adds "Social accountability and environmental protection are serious matters. When we realize a potential partner is not committed to our Code's requirements, we stop talking and look elsewhere." Switcher's policy is to apply the same standards everywhere, in Asia as well as in Europe. It recognizes however that cultural differences may require adaptations, for example in the management of wages.

AUDITING PARTNERS

Implementing these rules is done through a systematic audit of Switcher suppliers. Several points of the company's Code of conduct are particularly scrutinized, on a regular basis:

- work is freely chosen (ILO conv. 29 and 105),
- no discriminatory practices (ILO conv. 100 and 111),
- no child labour (ILO conv. 138),
- labour unions and collective bargaining are allowed (ILO conv. 87 and 98),
- salaries are satisfactory,
- working hours are not excessive,
- working conditions are satisfactory (hygiene, health, safety),
- formal labour contracts are established for all workers,
- the company accepts to be audited by an independent body trusted by the workers.

The audit takes place through observation, checking company records and legal documents, talking to labour union representatives, individual workers and their families. The audit procedure leads to the grading of the partner-company on a four-level scale:

1. working conditions are excellent,
2. working conditions need some adjustments but are fair; the company accepts to improve conditions,
3. working conditions are bad, however the company is ready to launch necessary efforts over medium term to upgrade and finally meet requirements,
4. working conditions are bad and the company is not willing to undertake corrective actions.

In cases 2 and 3, Switcher is ready to provide support to help the supplier move up the ladder, establishing a step-by-step procedure over an adjustable time horizon. In case 4, Switcher refuses to consider business relationships any longer. A possible deterioration of work conditions follows the same rules: Switcher's Environment and Social Relations Department keeps an open eye on each supplier's social performance, through frequent factory visits, discussions with labour unions and individual workers, checks of performance indicators (absenteeism, overtime hours, defective pieces, customer complaints, . . .), etc.

SWITCHER/PREM PARTNERSHIP IN INDIA

In the early 80's, Mabrouc SA developed a unique partnership with Indian manufacturer-exporter Prem Durai Exports, today a part of the Prem Group of Companies. The Prem Group started in 1984 as a 100% cotton garment stitching factory located in Tirupur (Tamil Nadu), with a production capacity of 0.5 million units per year and a workforce of 100 employees. Both Robin Cornelius, owner of Mabrouc/Switcher, and S. Duraiswamy, Managing Director of Prem Group, were early believers in a long-term partnership and personally committed to make it a success. They signed an exclusivity contract by which Prem Group's full production was destined to Switcher, Prem Group being in return Switcher's unique supplier in India.

Stimulated by Switcher and eager to respond to growing concerns about quality, environmental protection and social accountability, Prem Group went for ISO 9000, ISO 14000 and SA 8000 certification. In the process, the company realized that the standards required for certification could only be met through greater control of upstream activities, which led to vertical integration. Today, Prem Group is composed of companies specialized in cotton churning and spinning, knitting, dyeing, cutting and stitching, embroidery and printing. It is thus fully integrated at the production level, with the exception of raw material since it does not own the cotton fields. Production was first intended solely for export to the Swiss and German markets. Since 1999, Prem Group also supplies Switcher with products for the Indian market which is growing steadily.

Production has increased 1.5 fold in one year, from 3.6 million units in 1999 to 5.1 million units in 2000, moving from 60% to 84% capacity utilization, with a workforce of 1,250 and an annual turnover of 10 million US $. Higher productivity has been matched with a significant improvement in quality, with an average rework level decreasing from 20.4% in 1998–99 to 8.3% in 2000–01 and average rejection level decreasing from 10.6% to 4.8%.

Major improvements can be traced to both equipment/technology upgrading (new machinery in spinning, dyeing, knitting, and cutting departments), and new management practices (systems based approach, moving from batch to line production, standardizing processes, online monitoring, improving internal and external communication, focusing on customer satisfaction, and human resource development).

SOCIAL MANAGEMENT

In complying with SA-8000 standards, Prem Group put into place in early 2001, a complete set of social accountability procedures. The Group's management structure reflects this new focus, as shown in one of its companies' (Vikram Knitwear) organogram, with a Social Accountability Representative, in direct line to the Managing Director, supervising Safety, Health & Environment, Grievance handling, Human Resource Management, and a Unit Manager in charge of the company's different functional activities.

The company's Social Accountability Systems Policy is well known and widely spread: the policy statement is distributed to workers in their native language (Tamil), to active NGOs and to local and regional political authorities. Several recent press articles have contributed to its diffusion to the public. Social management factors are reviewed below, with some of the operational specifications thought to have a direct impact on the company's competitive standing.

WORK ENVIRONMENT

A visit of Prem Group factories shows the importance the Switcher/Prem Group partnership gives to work environment factors: workplaces are well spaced, light is abundant, high ceilings control for heat from neon lighting; good ventilation in all sections is provided by regularly spaced fans (regular maintenance ensures proper ventilation); different noise-generating activities (spinning, dyeing) are isolated from the more labour-intensive downstream activities; air quality is optimized by blocking out fibers (churning and spinning) and odors (dyeing) by isolating the related activities or by installing exhaust fans to suck micro dust; outdoor embellishment (plants and flowers around the factory buildings) is also part of the environment improvement program.

Switcher/Prem also provide complementary services such as a free canteen. As any other aspect of the work environment, it needs to be monitored and workers' feedback is solicited for improvement . . . in addition to ensuring that each worker gets sufficient nutrition for the day, the canteen is a socializing space that may contribute to workers' sense of belongingness. It can also contribute to decreasing absenteeism by allowing a better control of work hours.

HUMAN DEVELOPMENT

Ongoing training takes place at all levels to help workers develop multiple skills and competences and thus provide career progression opportunities. With the exception of handling fabric lots and controlling machines, upstream operations (spinning, dyeing, cutting) have been progressively automated. These are the more dangerous operations (due to fumes, burns, cuts) for which human intervention represents less added value. Workers are trained for more downstream operations (stitching, embroidery, printing, ironing, packing) and for machine monitoring and quality & task checking.

Identifying a particular need for training usually comes from unit managers who arrange with training officers for specific training sessions to take place. For example, competent people are sought from machinery manufacturers and suppliers to help Prem Group workers acquire the appropriate skills in machinery handling and maintenance. The training process contributes to motivating workers to develop their abilities, helps in identifying higher-potential personnel for future promotion and is considered to be a major factor of general performance improvement.

Training is also provided to all incoming workers on the following issues:

- Background of the company, products and customer (Switcher);
- SA-8000 and its importance;
- Company's procedures on accidents, disciplinary actions, complaints, working hours, overtime, etc.;
- Committees in the factory and their activities.

All workers are thus well informed of the importance of social management issues and the company's philosophy in that respect.

Building workers' self-esteem and sense of responsibility is achieved by developing awareness of each task's importance in ensuring customer satisfaction, and setting objectives for decreasing complaint levels. Feedback from Switcher helps in measuring results. It is often provided live to Prem management and workers, frequent trips (every 2–3 months) taking place between Switzerland and India.

Switcher/Prem Group believe in employee empowerment. "For some workers," says D. Rufenacht, "it means a revolution. We encourage workers to take initiatives, make suggestions, which many are not used [to] doing." "Empowerment comes with skills and education," adds B.K. Prakash. "As a worker becomes more mature and skilled through training, the company can transfer authority. Prem Group has developed programs in that direction which focus on conflict resolution, problem solving, quality principles, safety principles, etc."

WORK ORGANISATION AND GENERAL CONDITIONS OF WORK

Working conditions (task definition, workload, rest periods, wages, . . .) are set in collaboration with the labour unions. Inter-departmental communication and inter-personal relationships have been enhanced to strengthen a collective approach to solving problems and improving processes.

Working hours are clearly defined and communicated on a notice board in the canteen. Regular working hours do not exceed 48 hours for a six-day week, including rest periods. Overtime, on a voluntary basis, does not exceed 12 hours in a week, in accordance with Indian law.

With improved productivity, proper planning, and a better work organisation, overtime work has significantly decreased. Average monthly overtime in 2000 was 46 hours, decreasing to 22 hours in the first semester of 2001, representing a 52% decrease. In conjunction with a more sensible management of rest periods during the day, such a change has contributed to reducing work stress and fatigue. "It is not easy to find the optimal balance between work and rest periods during the day," says D. Rufenacht. "If employees finish work early enough in the afternoon, some are tempted to take up a second job elsewhere and come back the next day too tired to work properly. Extending rest periods helps to prevent this practice but we have to strike the right balance if we want to avoid the negative impact that prolonged rest periods have on the company's performance."

The company is vigilant against possible mental and physical abuse. It condemns any such actions. The Factory Standing Orders specifically define which behaviours may lead to disciplinary action. In that respect, managers and supervisors are trained to deal with workers, who are entitled to an enquiry. Standing orders are displayed in the canteen in native language (Tamil).

A bottom-up approach was initiated to relay employee complaints and suggestions. Thus, the grievance handling procedure provides for the worker to express his grievance to his supervisor, if necessary to move up to the Section in charge, then to the Unit manager, the Personnel manager, the General manager and finally the Managing director. The procedure provides for discretion, efficiency and effectiveness.

In addition, grievance and suggestion boxes are provided in all working areas. "Unfortunately," says D. Rufenacht, "these boxes are often empty. Indian workers don't express complaints easily, nor do they easily admit having problems. It is often better to talk to a worker individually, spend some time asking questions to get to the root of eventual difficulties."

Better working conditions, human development policy and improved work environment, and a general Switcher/Prem philosophy to re-inject benefits in social programs and work-related improvement measures, are believed to have had a direct impact on absenteeism and workforce turnover rate:

- Absenteeism — % of work days not worked — dropped from an average 20% in 2000, all workers combined (tailors, helpers, checkers, cutters, iron masters, finishers) to an average 9% in first six months of 2001;
- Turnover was also reduced by close to half, from 8.5% to 4.7%.

Overall, significant improvements in performance (output, quality, employee turnover, cost of extra hours, . . .) coincide with better working conditions being implemented to comply with SA-8000 standards.

One of Switcher/Prem's most significant initiatives was to establish work contracts for all employees, a guarantee of year-long employment, contributing to the development of a sense of security and belongingness. All workers also have the benefit of health and retirement plans, which remains an exception in the Indian textile industry.

This has yet to be fully appreciated: "Getting workers to understand the advantages of putting money aside for the future is not always an easy task," says D. Rufenacht. "Many workers still have a one-day-at-a-time mindset. It takes time to get them to appreciate a longer-term perspective of work." However, putting more emphasis on wages (which are above legal minimum wages in all cases) would likely have an adverse effect by contributing to absenteeism: "From experience, a number of workers tend to stop working once they reach the minimum revenue they need to live. Extra wages only drive them to miss out on work."

OCCUPATIONAL HEALTH AND SAFETY

In accordance with Indian legislation (among which the Dangerous Machine Act, 1983 and Personal Injuries Act, 1963), monitored by both Switcher and itself, Prem Group has put into place a series of health and safety measures. H&S functions are both decentralised and centralized: Each Department is responsible for its own employees. In addition, a Health and Safety Manager is appointed to coordinate the H&S functions and monitor their implementation. Safety and fire fighting training is conducted regularly by trained personnel/outside agencies. First aid, health and hygiene training are conducted by visiting doctors. All employees are trained both in safety & fire fighting and in first aid, health & hygiene. Specific safety precautions for daily work include, for example, requiring the use of masks and finger guards for some of the tasks that remain dangerous.

LABOUR RELATIONS

All workers are unionized. The company has two trade unions, the Central Indian Trade Union (CITU) and the Marumalarchi Labour Federation (MLF). Management–labour relationships have developed on a cooperative mode, as reflected in the composition of the company's Corrective Action Committee which brings management and union representatives together to solve problems. Management and Union leaders also meet on other occasions. "When Robin (Cornelius) or I meet with

Prem management," says D. Rufenacht, "Union representatives often come by and we discuss issues together. This is quite an open management system, it helps build confidence."

NON-DISCRIMINATION

Prem Group follows a non-discrimination policy: The company hires, trains, compensates, and promotes employees on the basis of performance and competence irrespective of race, caste, natural origin, religion, disability, gender or political affiliation. With respect to gender, the company employs 43% women and 57% men, with equal pay for equal work, in accordance with the Equal Remuneration Act, 1976.

CHILD LABOUR

ILO standards specify children under 15 (13, under special circumstances) should not be hired for work. Prem Group has set the minimum age for recruitment at 18, for all tasks. To implement such standards, systematic checking of young workers' age is necessary. It is done by asking for birth certificates, local school records, passports, and by conducting medical and past events memorization checks. Upon hiring, identity cards are issued and checked afterwards by security personnel. Contractors/suppliers are requested to implement the same principles and to provide a written commitment to that effect.

Prem Group has always implemented these standards. It has no experience of child labour and therefore no story to tell about how to go from child labour to non-child labour. However, it has set rules to be followed in case a young worker was found to be working in the factory, despite the checks mentioned above: it would be reported immediately to the Personnel Manager. For young workers over 15 years old, the company may try to maintain a light work load for a few hours a day (no overtime), combined with school enrollment. For a child under 15, the company will provide free schooling and may pay a stipend to the child to replace lost income to the family.

B.K. Prakash, Prem Group's General Manager and Social Accountability Representative (SAR), insists that "child labour is not only illegal, it spoils the working conditions of a company: although it may seem to make good economic sense in the short term by cutting production costs," he adds, "it has pernicious effects: it discourages education, which hinders human resource development; by way of consequence, it prevents the development of the company due to a lack of mature and educated workers." "From a market point of view," adds D. Rufenacht, "child labour is a time bomb. Recent widely publicized reports on "children sweatshops" in Pakistan and Bengladesh were highly detrimental to the involved firms' reputation. Companies must come to realize that beyond morality, it makes good economic sense not to take that risk."

FORCED LABOUR

In compliance with the Indian Bonded Labour System Act of 1976, Prem Group does not engage in practices which lead to forced labour: it does not retain personal identification documents, qualification certificates, money deposits and does not support long-term loans, which could prevent workers from leaving the company. Workers are not forced to do overtime, as specified in the labour union agreement. "It is important that workers understand their rights," says B.K. Prakash, "and this can be achieved through good communication: disclosing terms and conditions of work prior to recruitment, making sure that all contracts are fully communicated and fully understood, conducting education programs to make workers fully aware of their rights and obligations."

MANAGEMENT REVIEW MEETINGS

Management review meetings take place twice a year to evaluate the effectiveness of the company's Social Accountability Systems. The meetings are chaired by the Managing Director S. Duraiswamy, and bring together the General Manager B.K. Prakash, as Social Accountability Representative (SAR), and all managers. . . . Management reviews include:

- Review of adequacy, suitability, and effectiveness of the company's SA policy;
- Review of the effectiveness of the systems and procedures;
- Review of the training and awareness programmes;
- Review of supplier conformance;
- Review of concerns expressed by workers, customers and other stakeholders;
- Review of internal/external audit reports.

INTERNAL AUDIT

As mentioned earlier, a Corrective Action Committee has been established to suggest corrective and preventive actions. Members include four Prem Group managers and workforce representatives elected by the workers. As SAR, B.K. Prakash has authority to implement the suggested actions.

He is also responsible for conducting comprehensive internal audits, which take place twice a year. The timing of the audit being announced in advance, the units can prepare for it, showing improved performance when it most counts. However, ongoing monitoring allows for management to check out possible fluctuations in performance and link them to specific events.

SUPPLIER AUDIT

As for suppliers, they are required, once a year, to complete a questionnaire about their commitment to SA 8000 standards, leading to eventual corrective actions when needed. Visits to suppliers' premises allows for checking the authenticity of the data provided in the questionnaire. The company maintains records of suppliers' and sub-contractors' degree of compliance with SA [Social Accountability] standards over the years, providing some sense of progress being made and helping to point out most appropriate remedial action. Ability to reach and maintain SA-8000 standards is an important criterion in selecting and retaining a supplier. This practice is well in line with Switcher's own auditing procedure resulting in a 4-level grading scheme of its business partners.

This backward process consists in vertically "integrating" partners along SA standards. "Our business partners understand the growing importance of complying with SA-8000 standards," says B.K. Prakash, "not only to remain our partners, but because such requirements are quickly spreading and becoming a widely accepted standard globally. SA-8000 will likely follow a development comparable to ISO-9000, which in many cases is no longer a competitive advantage, but rather a 'must.'"

IMAGE BUILDING

The Switcher/Prem partnership has become a benchmark in the Indian garment industry: "We have set an example which is being followed," says B.K. Prakash, "the fact of complying strictly with statutory and regulatory requirements and of reinvesting a share of profits in social programs contribute to Prem Group's exceptional image." Among recent visitors to Tirupur, Neil Kearney, General Secretary of Belgium-based International Textile, Garment & Leather Workers' Federation, praised the company's accomplishments with respect to wages (above the minimum wage for all workers) and working hours, health, and safety.

EXTENDING SOCIAL ACCOUNTABILITY

A charitable trust was initiated by Switcher and Prem Group to provide free health, safety and education services to the workers, their families and to the public in general. "The idea," says R. Cornelius, "was to use some of our benefits to make a social contribution through better health, safety and education." "We pollute water through dyeing," adds D. Rufenacht. "Despite efforts to limit pollution (better management of dyeing sequences, more efficient use of water), we cannot eliminate it. We think we have to give something in return." The "social contribution" philosophy spreads out to a number of activities. Today, the Durai Charitable Trust, named after Prem Group's Managing Director, funds the following activities/services:

- 7 schools are running (12 are planned by end 2002), fully funded by the trust, free of charge, for workers' children and those from poorer families of Tirupur and nearby villages. Over 1,200 children are now registered; In addition to employees' children, who are automatically accepted, other children are selected among the poorer families of Tirupur and nearby villages. A criterion of selection is the family's motivation to see their children through school. Representatives of Prem Group meet with the families to determine their motivation. Through schooling, the company sees that children who do not work due to their age are not left on the streets.
- 4 dispensaries were opened in the factories and schools for free medical service and hygiene advice. Safety awareness and first-aid training is provided on a regular basis in the factory. An AIDS awareness and prevention campaign was launched in 2001, including the distribution of free preservatives [condoms] on the workplace and information sessions regarding their use; Family planning issues are also regularly addressed;
- 12,000 liters of drinking water are distributed daily to remote places which have no access to clean water;
- Living quarters and recreation areas are provided to workers at no cost, with safe separate quarters for single women;
- A daycare center was opened to help working mothers;

After more than ten years, R. Cornelius remains excited about the partnership: "It extends far beyond a typical business deal," he says, "we share the same values and we finance the (social and environmental) projects together."

Source: www.cepaa.org/Document%20Center/The%20Switcher%20-Prem%20 Group%20Experience%20in%20India%202002.doc and also "Corporate Success Through People. Making International Labour Standards Work For You," International Labour Organization, 2002.

Final Thoughts

With that excellent case study in mind, and given all that we have explored throughout the book, there are a few concluding recommendations that are worth considering:

- First, as with the quality movement, implementing a common standard has many advantages over creating a program from scratch. A great deal of consultation and thought has gone into SA 8000, AA 1000, ISO 14001, the ETI, and the GRI, and although some of these initiatives still need to be streamlined and made applicable to individual industries, they are, nonetheless, a valuable set of tools for developing a company ethical supply chain framework. Designed to be flexible and interactive with each other, these standards and guidelines are invariably more thorough, and easier to implement, than reinventing the wheel by designing a code or standard independently.

- Second, it is important, once a business case is made, that the corporate leadership decide on a policy of genuine transparency for the company, both for the monitoring of suppliers and for reporting overall efforts and activities in the social and environmental arena. As with financial reporting, accuracy, dependability and transparency are key attributes of a good report, and any attempt to misstate or hide issues (as has so often been the case with recent accounting scandals) invariably undermines the company's credibility among shareholders once the real information is made known. For that reason, a policy of full transparency of supplier monitoring and reporting on social and environmental activities—supported by independent, third-party auditing—is ultimately the most legitimate course of action and a crucial element of a company's ethical framework.

- Third, given the likelihood that the SEAAR movement will be well established within the next several years, it is in the best interest of companies to support the development of indices and ratings groups such as AA 1000's Gradient Index. These groups provide a forum for competition and open comparison among high-performing companies, and the publicity and objectivity that they bring to the markets is something that companies should welcome, not resist.

- Companies (particularly U.S. companies) should clearly separate their philanthropic "corporate social responsibility" activities from a broader program for ensuring an ethical supply chain. Philanthropy can be overseen by the corporate affairs department; supplier behavior cannot be. And however genuine and however helpful, philanthropy is still optional; maintaining an ethical supply chain, increasingly, is not. Maintaining an ethical supply chain is simply how business must operate in the modern global economy.

- Monitoring the social and environmental activities of suppliers has become too important, too critical to a company's reputation, simply to leave in the hands of procurement department alone. However competent purchasing officers may be in their sourcing efforts, the criteria and methods for selecting, monitoring, and reporting on suppliers needs to be seen as a strategic corporate process, with all of the leadership and resource issues that then implies.

- Finally, it is probably also worth saying that however burdensome or unfair these new responsibilities may seem to be, they should be seen for what they are—an inescapable fact of the modern business environment.

As we have seen, as the legal and ethical separation between buyer and supplier—once so straightforward—has been called into question, companies have been struggling to find an approach to supplier management that can reconcile the need for continued company profitability and market stability with the broader concerns for workers and the environment in developing economies. Until that ambiguity concerning the boundaries of ethical responsibility between buyers and suppliers is reconciled, investors will continue to feel vulnerable, corporate leaders will be chided for making empty pronouncements about "caring companies," and the public will be left with a feeling of unease and mistrust of business.

And however valid arguments calling for local government oversight may be, the reality is that, at least in this phase of the supply chain revolution, governments in developing nations are still some years away from the level of control or supervision necessary to effectively prevent social and environmental exploitation. In the end, therefore, the issue is a practical, rather than legal, matter of obligation. The fact is, buying companies are being forced to take on the burden for controlling the misbehavior of suppliers in part simply because, given the current lack of government regulation or enforcement in developing economies, corporations remain the only party at this point that have the capacity to influence supplier behavior. It may not be fair, but it is reality.

And despite early reticence, U.S.-based companies are in many ways even more susceptible to pressures to accept this new level of responsibility for supplier behavior—and for reporting on efforts in this area—than their European counterparts. Not only does the investor community have greater influence on U.S. corporate behavior, but new legislation and litigation, including revised SEC transparency and reporting rules, state and federal antisweatshop laws, the Alien Claims Tort Act, the potential fallout from the *Nike* v. *Kasky* case, and the growing number of class-action suits filed on behalf of overseas workers, combine to create a volatile and dangerous situation for U.S. companies that remain ignorant or indifferent to social and environmental violations that are occurring in their extended supply chain.

Finally, and possibly most important, all of the above combined mean that progressive companies already see the writing on the wall and are beginning to accept the need to adhere to international standards and to report on social and environmental performance, both within their own operations, and more importantly, within their supplier community. This will lead inevitably to a bandwagon effect. Progressive companies will be able to boast of their advanced policies in these areas—in advertising, in product comparisons, with their inclusion in ethical indices—using their progressive social and environmental policies as a strong differentiator among their competition.

On the other hand, those companies that resist or are indifferent to the movement will find their lack of participation increasingly difficult to justify, leaving themselves open to accusations that they are laggards, are indifferent, or are hiding something, for refusing to do what other companies have done. Ultimately, competition, not humanitarian motives or government-sponsored regulation, may prove to be the strongest incentive for companies to establish an ethical supply chain.

It is likely, therefore, that in the next five years, as triple-bottom-line accounting and better supplier management become the norm, these types of policies will become a prerequisite for inclusion on the "100

Best"-type lists that are so important for company reputations. As the economy improves and the labor market strengthens, these types of ratings will begin to affect a company's ability to hire and retain good employees—because the best employees will want to work at a company that is concerned about supplier employment and environmental issues.

"Put aside all the publicity aspects and the greenwash," contends Nicholas Eisenberger, CEO of Ecos Technologies, "and there is a very large bank of real effort and interest, because people who work for these companies are human beings, and . . . they belong to a generation where they grew up with this as an issue. If you have been taught for 30 years that [corporate social responsibility] is an issue, . . . you don't want to come home to your kid at night and respond to the question, 'Daddy, what did you do today?' by saying 'I destroyed the planet.'"[1]

Moreover, from all evidence, compliance to standards and independently audited social and environmental performance reporting will soon become *de rigueur* for operating, as analysts and institutional investors increasingly see potential supply chain instability—poor operations and opportunities for fines, lawsuits, or reputation damage—as reasons not to invest in companies.

Of course, the reality is that this type of CSR—in the form of standards implementation for environmental and social reporting—is already becoming the status quo in Europe. It follows that with U.S. companies in active competition and operating in the same markets—abetted by new litigation and legislative pressures—U.S. corporations will soon be adopting these same standards and reporting regimes. As support for the SEAAR movement continues to grow among multinationals, and as European, Japanese, and Australian organizations continue to adopt strong ethical supply chain and reporting transparency policies worldwide, the combined effect of new European laws and straightforward competition may force U.S. companies to adopt similar policies whether they want to or not. After all, nonparticipation will be a difficult case to argue in any WTO conflict between the United States and the EU or Japan, once these standards and requirements are agreed upon (particularly if it appears that U.S. companies are refusing to accept levels of responsibility and transparency that other global companies are readily agreeing to). Refusing to adopt SEAAR against all the moral arguments of activists, the examples being set by foreign-owned corporations, and the demands of investors and consumers will put U.S. companies in the unenviable position of appearing—with all of their enormous wealth and influence—to choose profits over the good of overseas employees or the environment. It is not an easy position to defend, and more broadly, such a position could potentially

---

1. Interview with Nicholas Eisenberger, August 25, 2003.

cause a much greater uproar than has been caused by stepping back from the Kyoto treaty.

In this sense, the issue of an ethical supply chain and the SEAAR movement begins to overlap with concerns of globalization and anticapitalism that, at least these days, are too often focused on the behavior and attitudes of U.S. companies anyway. Accordingly, many would argue that it is much better for U.S. companies to help influence the sensible development of these standards during these formative years than to refuse to participate once the SEAAR movement has become fully implemented in other countries.

In short, these are complex and important issues, and companies ignore them at their own peril. For all these reasons, the most sensible way forward for companies is to adopt a formal ethical supply chain program using an approach such as the one we have been exploring in this book; a framework that combines a strong corporate ethics program, stringent codes of conduct, international process and performance standards, a viable supplier management program, and transparent, independently audited social and environmental reporting. Such a program is important for the company's reputation, for bottom-line efficiencies, and ultimately for the good of the environment and workers in developing countries.

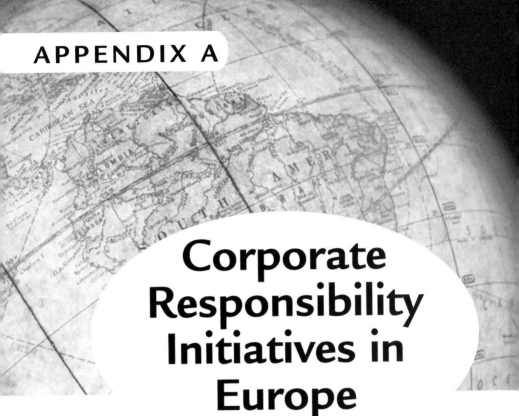

Corporate Responsibility Initiatives in Europe

The following chart outlines legislation and initiatives by the European Commission, European Parliament and EU member governments to promote corporate responsibility and social investing. It is not a comprehensive list and does not include initiatives sponsored by European companies, business associations, nongovernmental organizations or trade unions.

Country	Date	Initiative
European Commission	July 2001	Commission issues Green Paper on "Promoting a European Framework for Corporate Social Responsibility."
	January 2002	Commission posts comments from stakeholders on the Web site of the Employment and Social Affairs Directorate.

Country	Date	Initiative
	January 2002	Commission launches consultations with EU-level employers' and trade union organizations about how to manage and anticipate the social effects of corporate restructuring.
	April 2002	Employment and Social Affairs Directorate launches European Multi-Stakeholder Forum on CSR.
	July 2002	Commission issues communication concerning "Corporate social responsibility: A business contribution to sustainable development," which establishes a permanent EU Multi-stakeholder Forum on CSR with its first meeting in October 2002.
	July 2002	UNICE signs a joint letter with the ETUC to the European Commission to announce the organization of a seminar on socially responsible restructuring in October 2002. This event seeks to identify best practice examples of socially responsible restructuring.
European Parliament	January 2000	Parliament adopts resolution on a "Code of conduct for European enterprises operating in developing countries," which calls for a model European code of conduct. combining environmental, social and economic standards.
	May 2002	Parliament passes resolution with recommendations to the Commission on corporate social responsibility.
Belgium	November 2001	Belgian Parliament adopts law to promote development of a voluntary social label. The label requires enterprises to observe labor standards drawn from five ILO fundamental conventions. It will be available to all enterprises, Belgian and foreign, that sell products in Belgium. The law provides for technical assistance to allow enterprises from developing countries to respect the criteria for the label.
	November 2001	Belgium government organizes "Conference of the Belgian Presidency: Corporate Social Responsibility on the European Social Policy Agenda," which was held in Brussels on November 27–28, 2001, to showcase European efforts to promote corporate

Country	Date	Initiative
		responsibility and ascertain how governments at the national and international level could encourage global adoption of CSR strategies.
	2001	Belgian Council of Ministers approves pension fund disclosure regulation requiring pension funds to report how and whether they weigh the ethical, environmental and social performance of the stocks in which they invest.
France	February 2002	French Parliament publishes the requirements of their "new economic regulations" law, which passed in 2001. It mandates all French corporations to report on the sustainability of their social and environmental performance. The new law divides social reporting into human resources, community, labor standards and environmental issues.
	May 2002	Roselyne Bachelot appointed as France's first Minister on Sustainable Development in the new government. Ms. Bachelot had previously been in charge of equal employment initiatives in the French National Assembly.
Germany	May 2001	German government passes legislation requiring pension plans to declare whether and how they integrate social and environmental factors into their investment decisions.
	February 2002	German government publishes a set of voluntary guidelines for publicly traded companies on the management and transparency of their business. The Guidelines contain no sanctions for noncompliance, but a new law that entered into force in July 2002 requires all companies to declare whether or not they abide by the code.
	May 2002	German government, together with the Confederation of German Employers' Associations (BDA), the Federation of German Industries (BDI), the German Trade Union Federation (DGB) and NGOs, sign a Joint Declaration on International Protection of Human Rights and Economic Activity. Reference is made to the *Universal Declaration of Human Rights*, UN Global Compact, *OECD Guidelines for Multinational Enterprises*, and ILO *Declaration on Fundamental Principles and Rights at Work*.

Country	Date	Initiative
	2002	German government is considering a statutory code of conduct for German companies operating in China.
Norway	1999	Under the 1999 Accounting Act, all companies must include environmental information in their annual financial reports from 1999 onward. The Norwegian Environmental Department develops a standard for environmental reporting.
Netherlands	1998	Over 300 companies are covered by legislation on mandatory environmental reporting beginning in 1999.
	March 2001	Dutch government issues a position paper on CSR. In addition to CSR In the national context, the paper outlines CSR in the international context. It underlines the importance that the Dutch government attaches to the proper behavior of Dutch firms abroad. The *OECD Guidelines for Multinational Enterprises* are seen as the proper framework within which firms are expected to operate. Particular importance is attached to respect for the ILO fundamental labor rights.
	June 2001	Dutch Parliament proposes corporate responsibility conditionalities for companies receiving Dutch export credits, subsidies and insurance. The conditionalities include companies signing a declaration of intent to observe the *OECD Guidelines for Multinational Enterprises.*
	April 2002	The Global Reporting Initiative (GRI), the international sustainability reporting institution that was formally inaugurated at a United Nations ceremony on April 4, 2002, announces that its permanent Secretariat headquarters will be opened later this year in Amsterdam.
Sweden	1998	Swedish Annual Accounts Act of 1999 requires mandatory environmental reporting in annual financial reports starting in 1999.
	March 2002	Three Swedish Cabinet Ministers send a letter to Swedish companies, which calls for a *Swedish Partnership for Global Responsibility.* The letter states that the Government's basic expectations of Swedish companies' action in

Country	Date	Initiative
		the global market particularly in developing countries, are expressed in the OECD Guidelines and the UN Global Compact. It asks companies to express public support for the Guidelines and proposes that companies report once a year on measures they have taken or lessons they have learned relating to the OECD Guidelines and the UN Global Compact.
	June 2002	Swedish government pension fund, AP7, awards mandates to two hedge funds on the condition that they not invest in companies that have broken certain United Nations conventions.
United Kingdom	September 1998	British government develops Ethical Trading Initiative, a corporate partnership between government, business, labor and NGOs to improve labor standards in factories in the developing world.
	March 2000	British government creates a new ministerial post for corporate social responsibility to help make the business case for CSR and coordinate CSR policies across the government.
	July 2000	British Parliament became the first legislative body in the world to require reporting on socially responsible investing. The Pension Disclosure Regulation amended the 1995 Pensions Act to require all U.K. occupational pension funds to disclose the degree to which they take into account ethical, social and environmental considerations.
	November 2000	U.K. Minister for CSR forms intergovernmental network with counterparts in Ireland, Netherlands and Denmark on CSR issues and best practices.
	December 2000	British government, together with the U.S. government. launch *Voluntary Principles on Security and Human Rights,* which serve as a voluntary guide for companies in the extractive and energy sectors to maintain the safety and security of their operations within an operating framework that ensures respect for human rights and fundamental freedoms.

March 2001	U.K. Minister for CSR publishes first government report on CSR, "Business and society: Developing corporate social responsibility in the UK" It sets out the business case and outlines government plans, including work to develop the business case for CSR and encourage good practice; promoting CSR internationally; and improving coordination across government.
October 2001	British government issues guidelines on corporate environmental reporting, following Prime Minister Tony Blair's call for all top firms to start issuing environmental reports.
2002	British government establishes interdepartmental group to examine how labeling schemes might be made more consistent and coherent.

Source: With permission from the United States Council for International Business October 2002 at *www.uscib.org/docs/EUCSRMatrix.pdf.*

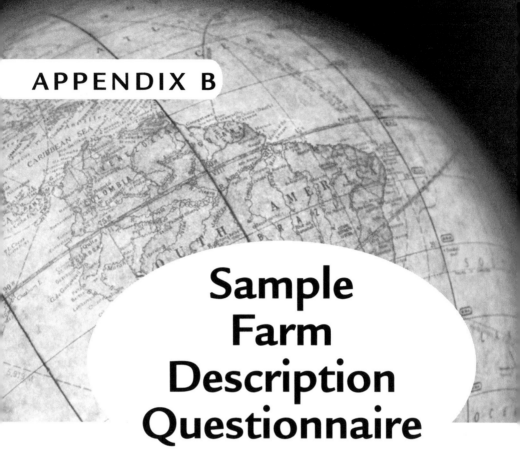

APPENDIX B

Sample Farm Description Questionnaire

Farm Description Questionnaire

Date:

1. Name of farm
2. Name(s) of owner:
3. Management:
   Director/Gen. Manager:
   Other Managers:
4. Contact Person:
   Postal Address:
   Telephone: *Mobile*   *Fax*

From "Integrated Social and Environmental Auditing," Natural Resource and Ethical Trade Programme (NRET), Theme Papers on Codes of Practice in the Fresh Produce Sector at *www.nri.org/NRET/TP7.pdf.*

5. Location of farm:
6. Office location:

Labor

Total workforce including management:
Breakdown of current labor force:

		Permanent		Casuals	
Worker Status	Total Number	Male	Female	Male	Female
Director(s)					
Managers					
[1]General workers					
Drivers					
Security					

Note: [1]Workers' status is not well defined. They are supposed to be permanent but have not been afforded full permanent rights.

Assets

7. Farm history (period of establishment):
8. Total farm size (acres):
9. Active farm size (acres):
10. Farm size under fallow (if any):
11. Farm machinery and equipment:
12. Farm map (check):
13. Soil Analysis (check):

Farming System

Crops Grown	When Started	Cropping System (Mono or Mixed)	Current Stage(s)
1. ....(for export)			
For subsistence			
2.			
3.			
4.			

14. Outline of major farm specific operations/activities from land preparation through to the sale (local and exports) of produce

Pineapple

Activity 1	Activity 5
Activity 2	Activity 6
Activity 3	Activity 7
Activity 4	Activity 8

APPENDIX C

Sample Audit Checklist

Principle		To promote the well-being of workers						
Criterion 4		Protection of workers' health and safety						
Indicators	Process	Suggested verifiers	Name of document/ alternative verifiers	Confirmed by interview with management?	Have relevant documents been checked?	Confirmed by worker interviews or observation?	Results (compliance C, noncompliance NC, partial compliance PC)	Comments
Outcome								
Access to potable water at all reasonable times		(1) Maps (2) Water tanks and/or wells observed (3) Worker interviews confirm access	Farm map	✓	✓	✓	Partially comply	Only one well – workers have to walk far if they are on the other side of the farm

From "Integrated Social and Environmental Auditing," Natural Resource and Ethical Trade Programme (NRET), Theme Papers on Codes of Practice in the Fresh Produce Sector at *www.nri.org/NRET/TP7.pdf*.

APPENDIX D

The Sustainable Development Commission's Sector Strategy Self-Assessment

Reprinted with permission from the Sustainable Development Commission.

The following list of assessment questions can be used to judge the quality of a strategy. To be adequate, a strategy should answer each question either fully or satisfactorily. Additional weight should be given to fully answering questions which are of most significance to the sector. Many of these factors may and should interact. For example, it will not be enough to list principles of sustainable development, if it is clear that these have not been reflected throughout the document. Where best practice is

Source: The Sustainable Development Commission at *www.sd-commission.gov.uk/ pubs/sag/index.htm.*

identified, the strategy should set out proposals for dissemination and adoption of this practice. Where targets are established, the strategy should identify how they are to be achieved and where responsibility for this lies.

Appraisal Questions

General Principles

To what extent does the strategy:

1. Show a recognition and understanding of the meaning and objectives of sustainable development in general and as they relate to that sector?
2. Acknowledge the costs and limits of unsustainable activity and the benefits of action to achieve sustainability?
3. Acknowledge the need for a precautionary approach?
4. Place people at the centre of the strategy and involve stakeholders including supply chain partners, customers, and disposers?
5. Demonstrate a high level of commitment to the implementation of the strategy among participants?

Assessment of Current Performance of the Sector and Recent Change

To what extent does the strategy:

6. Identify clearly and openly the general economic, social, and environmental impacts, both good and bad, of the sector and take responsibility for those impacts? Does this include:
   - Consideration of the supply chain?
   - Source of raw materials and energy impacts from manufacture and processing?
   - Impacts from transport?
   - Impacts on employees and communities?
   - Use of products and final destination?
   - Overseas impacts as appropriate?
7. Identify threats to the sector from unsustainable practices and identify opportunities for the sector to benefit from more sustainable practices?
8. Assess the past performance of the sector (clearly defined) against appropriate indicators (see Table D-1) and assess the move toward (or away from) sustainable development over time? Does this assessment reflect the concerns of stakeholders and the wider public? Can additional or more appropriate indicators be added? Can these indicators be applied to future performance for consistent reporting?

TABLE D-1. Objectives and possible indicators for sectoral strategies for sustainable development.

Ref. No.	Objective	Suggested Indicators	Relevance	Objectives Check List	Your Indicators and Desirable Outcomes
	Maintaining high and stable levels of economic growth and employment				
1	Contribute to economic growth.	Net profit/earnings/income. Return on capital employed. Trade balance with other countries. Economic impact of products. Develop new markets.	A strong economy provides good conditions for business, including strong markets. High profits enable expansion and innovation in business activity.		
2	Invest in modern plant and machinery as well as research and development to achieve prosperity.	Levels of investment in plant, machinery, buildings, research, and development.	Investment is recognized as vital to increased efficiency, profitability and competitiveness.		
3	Maintain high and stable levels of employment.	Numbers of people employed in sector. Productivity of workforce.	High levels of employment create larger markets. Productivity of the workforce is crucial to profitability.		
	Social progress which recognizes the needs of everyone				
4	Help build sustainable communities.	Company involvement in community projects. Support for local economy (local sourcing schemes). Support for training,	Supports positive business reputation. Community involvement activities can help to raise understanding of diverse		

(continues)

Ref. No.	Objective	Suggested Indicators	Relevance	Your Indicators and Desirable Outcomes
		(access to company facilities, etc.).	customer segments and identify opportunities for new products.	
5	Equip people with the skills to fulfill their potential	Level of investment in training Ratio of training budget to operating costs Businesses recognized as *Investors in People*	All industries need to invest in training to be efficient, innovative and competitive.	
6	Achieve fairness at work.	People working long hours. People on low pay. Employment of women and ethnic minorities (including numbers in middle and senior positions). Employee retention. Job satisfaction. Human rights violations.	A diverse, respected, and well-managed workforce is likely to be committed, productive, and support positive business reputation. Cost savings can be made by improved recruitment and retention rates as well as productivity. Significant legal costs and loss of reputation can result from poor performance against these indicators.	
7	Maintain safe and healthy environment at work.	Work fatalities (including those not at the workplace but work related, e.g. asbestosis).	Preventing illness and injuries can avoid loss of productivity and increased	

Ref. No.	Objective	Suggested Indicators	Relevance	Objectives Check List	Your Indicators and Desirable Outcomes
		Working days lost through injury and illness. Levels of absenteeism.	overall labor costs (as replacements need to be paid.) It can improve business reputation and avoid costs in insurance premiums, medical and legal costs.		
8	Tackle poverty and social exclusion.	Corporate giving and community projects. Social impact of products. Number of companies involved in volunteering/mentoring schemes. Number of companies involved in New Deal or other government initiatives.	Corporate engagement in local communities can improve reputation and trust. Supporting initiatives in inner cities and developing countries can open up new markets.		
9	Raise quality of life of workers in global supply chains.	Companies implementing ethical trading codes of conduct.	Unethical treatment of workers abroad can be severely damaging to business reputation and market position.		
	Effective protection of the environment				
10	Reduce emissions of greenhouse gases now and plan for	CO_2 output and output of other greenhouse gases (include output from not just	Reduction in output CO_2 and other gases is a measure of resource productivity and can		

(continues)

TABLE D-1. *(Continued.)*

Ref. No.	Objective	Suggested Indicators	Relevance	Your Indicators and Desirable Outcomes
	further reductions in future.	manufacture or extraction). Use of energy from renewable sources. Depletion of fossil fuels.	lead to cost reduction. Effective management of emissions suggests good business management.	
11	Reduce air pollution and ensure air quality continues to improve.	Outputs of pollutants covered by national air quality objectives. Include emissions from transport, supply-chain users and disposers as well as core business.	Reducing emissions can be very beneficial to business reputation, indicate more efficient and controlled processes, and can result in a healthier workforce.	
12	Improve water quality in rivers, estuaries, and the sea.	Emissions of substances into watercourses and the sea. Use of extracted water. Water efficiency of products.	Reduced use of water can save costs. Water pollution can cause negative profile.	
13	Maintain and enhance biodiversity.	Amount of land owned, leased, or otherwise affected by organization by habitat type and status (degraded, pristine, etc.). Habitat changes due to operations. Amount of habitat protected or restored. Impacts on protected areas.	Enhanced biodiversity will improve the quality and amenity value of the local environment. Damaging such habitats can have severe and long term effect on reputation.	

Ref. No.	Objective	Suggested Indicators	Relevance	Objectives Check List	Your Indicators and Desirable Outcomes
14	Reduce noise.	Level of noise from processes and transport. Noise from suppliers. Noise from product or use of product. Impact on noise sensitive environments, e.g., national parks, residential areas.	Noise can be damaging to reputation of the organization and the health and safety of the workforce. Can suggest inefficient or outdated process. Can result in claims and legal costs.		
15	Reusing previously developed land, in order to protect the countryside and encourage urban regeneration.	Reuse of previously developed land compared to take of greenfield sites. Creation of derelict land. Amount of permeable surface as % of land owned.	Urban sites may benefit from local suppliers and availability of labor. Grant support/rate holidays may be available for brown-field sites. Planning permission may be easier to obtain.		
16	Improve choices in transport and reduce need for travel.	Kilometers travelled by mode (air, rail, road, water), by freight, and business travellers. Active policies on fleets, business travel, workforce commuting (green travel plans), and visitor transport. HGV mileage intensity.	Careful management of transport of employees and goods across a range of modes can result in significant cost savings. For example, lorries run full each way and by the best routes, vehicle are efficient and suitable.		

(continues)

TABLE D-1. *(Continued.)*

Ref. No.	Objective	Suggested Indicators	Relevance	Objectives Check List	Your Indicators and Desirable Outcomes
17	Assess environmental impacts, set targets, and produce reports.	Adoption of environmental management systems (ISO 14001) and EU Eco-management Audit Scheme (EMAS). Companies setting organizational and performance environmental targets. Companies reporting on their environmental performance to government standard. Number of companies signed up to *Making a Corporate Commitment* or other schemes of this kind.	Reputation enhanced by being seen as leader in environmental management, may provide marketing advantage and reduce risks and costs in insurance, capital, etc.		

Prudent use of natural resources

Ref. No.	Objective	Suggested Indicators	Relevance	Objectives Check List	Your Indicators and Desirable Outcomes
18	Greater energy efficiency.	Energy use in the sector. Efficiency of transport used in sector. Energy efficiency of products. Energy efficiency of supply chain.	Energy efficiency reduces costs.		
19	Greater resource efficiency.	Use of key resources and materials in sector. Resource efficiency of supply chain.	Considerable savings can be achieved if use of resources can be minimized.		

Ref. No.	Objective	Suggested Indicators	Relevance	Objectives Check List	Your Indicators and Desirable Outcomes
20	Move away from disposal of waste toward waste minimization recycling and recovery.	Total waste by sector. Waste to landfill. Waste arising from use of products. Proportion of product recyclable. Levels of materials recycled. Levels of hazardous (special) waste produced. Levels of radioactive waste.	Disposal of waste is costly. Reduced waste is an indicator of efficient process.		
21	Avoid storing up pollutant problems for the future.	Emissions of persistent organic compounds, radioactive discharges.	Reduces potential liabilities and improve business reputation.		
22	Use consumer information to encouraging movement in the market toward sustainability.	Amount and accuracy of information provided (accreditation to ISO 14021).	Good marketing of sustainable practices and products can increase market share and take up of products as well as sector reputation.		

Specific Sectoral Performance, Indicators, and Targets

To what extent does the strategy:

9. Identify opportunities for the sector to contribute to improvements and breakthroughs (such as technological innovations) which might help achieve sustainable development? Does the strategy include proposals for their implementation, including the costs of such work?

10. Identify opportunities for sectors to work together to achieve greater progress or any constraints which exist if sectors are forced to work in isolation?

11. On the basis of 6–10 above, establish indicators and targets for the sector to achieve improvements in terms of tangible benefits and measurable criteria for success?
    - Are these indicators realistic and challenging?
    - Are timescales established?
    - Is the data to be used transparent and verifiable?
    - Is the sector clearly defined for the purposes of target setting?
    - Is it clear what factors may influence the ability of the sector to deliver these targets?
    - Are costs and benefits identified?
    - Does it also identify action which may be necessary to alleviate any limiting factors?

12. Assess whether the impact of implementing the strategy as a whole is likely to be positive/neutral/negative in terms of the indicators listed in Table D-1 and any other relevant indicators? Are there ways in which the strategy could be refined to make the effect more positive or less negative?

13. Require annual reporting against indicators for improvement? Identify a process by which the strategy can be reviewed and enhanced as lessons are learned?

14. Take a long-term perspective in addition to short-term indicators (at least 10 years)?

Exemplification, Application, and Dissemination

To what extent does the strategy:

15. Relate its assessment of performance and future targets and indicators to practical and actual examples? Is there a sector leader or leaders—organizations or groups of organizations that can demonstrate the strategy as applied to their activities?

16. Include proposals to facilitate and encourage the application of the strategy and achievement of targets by individual organizations?

17. Establish and seek to disseminate and encourage best practice and benchmarking?

18. Raise awareness of sustainable development issues among members and a wider audience?

APPENDIX E

Sample Company Self-Assessment

The following self-assessment form is used by the UK's Sustainability Northwest in their Evolve Notebook approach to sustainability.

Environment

Please describe what your organization does, referring to the guidance and highlighting examples of good practice.

Policy

Guidance

How the organization's leadership supports improvement and involvement by providing appropriate resources and assistance; how environmental

Source: With permission from Sustainability Northwest at www.snw.org.uk/pdf files/Questionnaire.doc.

policy and strategy are integrated into corporate systems, business planning, etc.

Please give examples, such as action taken to:

- Reduce energy and water consumption.
- Minimize the use of primary materials.
- Introduce green transport planning.

1. Our organization has a written **environmental policy** which is signed off by a senior manager and is publicly available.

Yes ☐   No ☐   Under development ☐

2. In what way does our policy commit the organization to adopting **long-term** strategic and operational environmental goals?

Score for response (max. 10)	

Objectives and Targets

Guidance

How the environmental objectives and targets relate to the environmental policy and are used at all levels to review performance.

Please give examples, such as action taken to:

- Establish a baseline to measure change.
- Identify and remedy specific areas for improvement.
- Reduce overall emissions of gases which contribute to poor air quality.

3. Our organization has established objectives and **SMART** (*specific, measurable, achievable, realistic, and timebound*) **targets** covering the organization's environmental performance.

Yes ☐   No ☐   Under development ☐

4. How does our organization ensure that the environmental objectives and targets set contribute to **continual improvement?**

Score for response (max. 10)	

People

Guidance

How the skills, knowledge, and competencies of the workforce have been harnessed to enable the organization to enhance its environmental performance.

Please give examples, such as action taken to:

- Train workforce to undertake environmental audits.
- Involve stakeholders in setting environmental targets.

5. Our workforce is aware of the policy and key staff understand their **role and responsibility** in helping our organization improve its environmental performance.

Yes ☐   No ☐   Under development ☐

6. How does our organization **involve the workforce** in improving its environmental performance?

Score for response (max. 10)	

Results

Guidance

How the organization verifies and validates results, this may include internal or external auditing or external verification and certification.
  Please give examples, such as action taken to:

- Reduce the potential impacts of climate change.
- Highlight and make best use of the results obtained.

7. Our organization has established a **monitoring and review process** to evaluate its environmental performance.

    Yes ☐   No ☐   Under development ☐

8. How does our organization use this review process to **reduce its environmental impacts**?

Score for response (max. 10)	

Communications (Internal and External)

Guidance

How the organization informs and involves all its stakeholders on action taken to identify and then reduce its key environmental impacts and highlights the progress achieved.
  Please give examples, such as action taken to:

- Ensure the use of best practice in the management of waste.
- Move our organization toward best practice for our sector.

9. Our organization regularly communicates **key areas of environmental performance** to stakeholders.

Yes ☐   No ☐   Under development ☐

10. How does our organization use **feedback** from stakeholders to manage and improve its environmental performance?

Score for response (max. 10)	

Social

Please describe what your organization does, referring to the guidance and highlighting examples of good practice.

Policy

Guidance

How the organization integrates social policy and strategy into corporate systems, community relations, employee welfare, etc; how the organization's policies influence the core business behavior to have a positive impact on society.

Please give examples, such as action taken to:

- Encourage stakeholders to be actively involved in local decision making.
- Encourage corporate and employee involvement in the community.

1. Our organization has a written policy making a formal commitment to achieving a **positive social impact.**

Yes ☐   No ☐   Under development ☐

2. How is our policy used to promote active **involvement, dialogue, and engagement** with the community?

Score for response (max. 10)	

Objectives and Targets

Guidance

How the organization benchmarks itself against the best in class across a range of social and ethical issues.

Please give examples, such as action taken to:

- Improve equity and equality of opportunity for people.
- Select indicators which simplify, quantify, and communicate information on social targets.
- Monitor equal opportunities policies and practices.

3. Through stakeholder dialog our organization has established **SMART** (*specific, measurable, achievable, realistic, and timebound*) **targets** on a range of issues which demonstrate its commitment to acting in a socially responsible way.

Yes ☐   No ☐   Under development ☐

4. How is social responsibility **integrated** into our organization's business strategy and working practices?

Score for response (max. 10)	

People

Guidance

How the organization seeks to work with the rich diversity of individuals which make up our society; how the organization has adopted a business strategy which includes and involves people regardless of age, race, creed, color, ethnicity, and sexual orientation.
Please give examples, such as action taken to:

- Improve opportunities for lifelong learning and employability.
- Improve health and healthy life expectancy.
- Reduce the need to travel.

5. Our workforce is aware of the policy and key staff understand their **role and responsibility** in helping our organization to improve its reputation.

Yes ☐   No ☐   Under development ☐

6. How does your organization **encourage staff and give recognition** for taking forward its commitment to social responsibility?

Score for response (max. 10)	

Results

Guidance

Please give examples, such as action taken to:

- Improve access to jobs, basic goods, and services.
- Rectify specific problems identified.

7. Our organization regularly reviews its **standing and reputation** with its stakeholders.

Yes ☐   No ☐   Under development ☐

8. How does our organization **foster relationships** (including those with its workforce, suppliers, and customers) in order to maintain a reputation for high standards of business conduct?

Score for response (max. 10)	

Communications (Internal and External)

Guidance

How social reporting is used to inform stakeholders as to what extent performance corresponds to policy, to learn about their expectations, and to clarify and strengthen the organization's values.

Please give examples, such as action taken to:

- Communicate the broad aims or vision of the organization.
- Make workforce aware of social policy and strategy.

9. Our social policy is **circulated widely** and made available to people both inside and outside of the organization.

Yes ☐   No ☐   Under development ☐

10. How are corporate policy, objectives, and targets **championed** and cascaded to all levels of our organization and to external audiences?

Score for response (max. 10)	

Economic

Please describe what your organization does, referring to the guidance and highlighting examples of good practice.

Policy

Guidance

How policy and strategy are integrated into corporate systems; how ethical working practices are embedded into working practices; how the organization is building a long-term commitment to the region.

Please give examples, such as action taken to:

- Improve profitability by adopting more sustainable ways of working.
- Retain skilled and talented people.
- Improve links between academic research and organizational needs.
- Increase the use of local products and services.
- Increase the use of new and more efficient ways of working.

1. A written plan exists setting out our organization's goals, targets, and plans for its **long-term viability.**

   Yes ☐   No ☐   Under development ☐

2. How does your organization **manage the potential for conflict** in achieving its environmental and social targets within an effective business strategy?

Score for response (max. 10)	

Objectives and Targets

Guidance

How the organization works for sustainable growth by taking a long-term view of the market place and developing strategies and partnerships to strengthen itself and the local/regional economy; how the organization uses various forms of investment and retains the ability to respond to changes at local, regional, national, and global level.

Please give examples, such as action taken to:

- Improve business management.
- Trade fairly with suppliers.
- Trade fairly with producers in the developing world.
- Set payment period targets for suppliers.

3. Our organization has identified its **key processes** which have an economic impact on society.

Yes ☐   No ☐   Under development ☐

4. How does our organization support local, regional or national economic development initiatives **beyond what is needed** for its own growth?

Score for response (max. 10)	

People

Guidance

How the organization's leadership is committed to developing the workforce in order to prepare them for the challenges and opportunities that will occur as part of the organization's long-term planning.

Please give examples, such as action taken to:

- Improve the skills and competence of the workforce.
- Offer a good standard of pay and working conditions for workforce.

5. Our organization has a planned approach to **investing in its people** to enhance its competitiveness.

Yes ☐   No ☐   Under development ☐

6. How does our organization identify the needs and concerns of its economic **stakeholders?**

Score for response (max. 10)	

Results

Guidance

Please give examples, such as action taken to:

- Stimulate innovation and creativity within the workplace.
- Maximize customer satisfaction.

7. Our organization shares knowledge and **best practice** in the interest of the region or local area's economic success.

Yes ☐   No ☐   Under development ☐

8. How does our organization evaluate its business performance in terms of its **impact on society?**

Score for response (max. 10)	

Communications (Internal and External)

Guidance

Please give examples, such as action taken to:

- Remove barriers to employment.
- Improve the profile and image of the Northwest of England.

9. Our organization **publicly reports** its economic contribution to the region or local area.

Yes ☐   No ☐   Under development ☐

10. How does our organization evaluate **awareness of and satisfaction with** its economic contribution to the region or local area?

Score for response (max. 10)	

Action Plans

Please outline what actions your organization will take to progress each of these three areas:

Environment

Social

Economic

Organization Profile

Organization
Address   Telephone

                                           Facsimile

                                           E-mail

                                           Number of employees

                                           Industry lead body

Geographical coverage of sites included in the **Evolve** process Activities under-taken at these locations:

Environmental and/or social issues affecting this sector Additional informa-tion about the organization:

Evolve Team Members:
(please enter **Evolve** Team Leader's details at No. 1)

Name   **Position**   **Telephone number**

Name   **Position**

Signed   **Date**

Index